CREATING THE MODERN AMERICAN NOVEL

Books by Harlan Hatcher

Critical

THE VERSIFICATION OF ROBERT BROWNING
CREATING THE MODERN AMERICAN NOVEL

Novels

TUNNEL HILL
PATTERNS OF WOLFPEN

CREATING
THE MODERN
AMERICAN NOVEL

BY HARLAN HATCHER

NEW YORK
RUSSELL & RUSSELL · INC
1965

To

D. H.

for her objections

CONTENTS

Part Five: The Fruits of the War

Part Six: New Modes for the Thirties

AUTHOR'S NOTE

*A*RICH and living literature really defies neat classifica-
tions. Some kind of ordering is indispensable, however,
if one is to think about or record the accomplishments
of a particular period. Any author worthy of special study is
unique, but he none the less shares certain of his qualities with
his compeers, and together they form a general type. The
grouping in this book is simply a convenience with no thought
whatever of destroying the bright margins that are constantly
overlapping. And no reader will be misled by the apparent
oversimplification. John Dos Passos is a realist, a satirist, a fruit
of the War and several other things. In most cases there is a
vivid center to the work of an author that suggests one affilia-
tion rather than another. The association of these types defines
roughly the trends or movements characteristic of our times.

This book tries to show how the American novel was
lifted from its lowly place in the nation of a generation ago
into a respected position in the literature of the modern world.
It attempts to present the conditions and the atmosphere under
which the novel was created, the people who created it, and
the nature of their work. It endeavors to isolate and if possible
to understand the varied currents that have produced the
stimulating literary enterprise in this century, and the present
state of letters in the Republic. It is conceived as a unit and
the parts are to some degree interdependent.

It is the duty of each generation to treasure the old and
write the new, and to avoid too much ancestor worship in the
kingdom of letters. And it is also the privilege if not the duty
of a generation to appraise itself before the atmosphere in
which it worked has faded and cannot be fully recaptured.
The subject is necessarily controversial, but a measure of the

fun that goes with a study of contemporary literature is the controversy it provokes. And no person in his senses would think of claiming infallibility for his own judgments on a subject at once so extensive and so complex.

H. H.

Part One

THE RISE OF REALISM

Chapter One

PERSPECTIVE

THOSE people among us whose patriotic fervor is more vigorous than their critical principles have pushed the beginnings of American literature back as far as the epistles of Captain John Smith. The more cosmopolitan have been content with Washington Irving as our first man of letters. The cold and inescapable fact of the matter is that none but historians and antiquarians can be excited by any figure before Ralph Waldo Emerson in any *genre*. And with respect to the novel, which has become increasingly the preferred medium of expression, one can hardly go beyond the memory of men now living.

Very little American fiction of the last century has any life left in it. Hawthorne's THE SCARLET LETTER (1850), despite its spare psychological dimensions and a point of view toward a familiar material seldom shared by modern people, still lives because of the perfection of its superb and living art. Melville's MOBY-DICK (1851) must be placed in the present century where in spirit it really belongs and where it was first discovered. After we have mentioned these two memorable novels, after we have acknowledged a mild interest in the pale contemporaneity of the earlier novels of Henry James and William Dean Howells, and after we have declared with the authority of personal experience shared by everyone else that HUCKLE-BERRY FINN (1884) is a classic, we are confronted by the interesting fact that American fiction of scope and distinction began with the close of the last century. In later years, Stephen Crane has come to occupy the same position in relation to the American novel as that enjoyed by Washington Irving in American literature in general.

Until the beginning of this century, there were Englishmen who, ignoring the wise few who had discovered to their profit the works of Emerson, Thoreau, Poe, and Whitman, could still patronize American literature with their "Who reads an American book?" The answer was, of course, "Almost no one." But Americans, still in bondage to their provincial belief that novels were sinful unless written by Englishmen, were reading Scott, Thackeray, Kingsley, George Eliot, and importing Charles Dickens by the ton. The only real balance in trade we could offer was UNCLE TOM'S CABIN for the reformers and James Fenimore Cooper's novels for the English navy. As late as the nineties, Oscar Wilde could depend upon his audience when he gave a character the quip, "What are American dry goods? American novels."

By the end of the third decade of this century, the American novel had emerged as a body of serious literature compelling the attention not only of Englishmen but of Europe as well. After the war English journals, even those which allotted only a brief section to literature, as a matter of course and without condescension, carried reviews and notices of American books. To cite one at random, the English Week-End Review of February 25, 1933, mentioned eight American authors and gave featured reviews to one dramatist, one historian, and two novelists. Frank Swinnerton began his lively survey of modern English letters, THE GEORGIAN SCENE (1934), with a chapter on the American Henry James and ended it with a section on the American T. S. Eliot. Thomas Mann, at the testimonial dinner in his honor in 1934 in New York City, spoke with admiration of the novels of Theodore Dreiser, Sinclair Lewis, Upton Sinclair, John Dos Passos and Ernest Hemingway. John Gunther casually mentioned that he noticed on the table of Andrés Nin in Madrid two books by Theodore Dreiser and several other American novels in Spanish translation. The foreign fame of Sinclair Lewis is a byword, ANTHONY ADVERSE taxed the capacity of most written languages, and one used to see on all Paris book stalls a thin volume entitled, LES GENTILHOMMES PRÉFÈRENT LES BLONDES. In fact, the creation of the American novel as a mature and significant part of world literature might conveniently be dated between the laugh at Wilde's epigram and the general outcry in America in 1930 when Sinclair Lewis was crowned with the laurel by the Nobel Committee at Stockholm.

For better or for worse, it was begotten by the invigorating tonic of the realistic movement applied to the American scene. It should have been quite unnecessary for American authors to wait upon Balzac and Zola to tell them to write about what they actually saw in the life around them. Emerson had told them that in the year of grace 1837, when he said it was time the sluggard intellect of this continent should "look from under its iron lids, and fill the postponed expectations of the world with something better than the exertions of mechanical skill. . . . The millions that around us are rushing into life cannot always be fed on the sere remains of foreign harvests. . . . The literature of the poor, the feelings of the child, the philosophy of the street, the meaning of household life, are the topics of the time." There was the credo, spoken out of no narrow nationalism but from intellectual integrity and a clear perception of the foundation of all art. When the American novel reached adult proportions it was on these principles: that material for literature must be found on your own doorstep, and if a writer illuminates the life he sees in his own street he has interpreted all life in all times. Unfortunately Emerson did not live to see it; his message fell upon fat and busy ears, and he died during the youth of ST. ELMO, TEN NIGHTS IN A BAR ROOM, and BEN HUR.

The principles returned to us with modifications by way of Europe, where the realistic approach to the novel had been used by a distinguished group of writers to produce a modern literature. These men—Flaubert, Balzac, Zola, Tolstoy, Hauptmann, Ibsen—believed that whatever human beings do is material for literature, even though human beings are often cruel and stupid, and do revolting things, and live in every conceivable circumstance from a Gold Coast billionaire to a Georgia nigger levee slave. The artist should write about life as he sees it being lived under his own individual pair of eyes, accepting it as his duty to report it as accurately as possible, withholding no single detail whether beautiful or nauseating whose absence would falsify the picture. And in general, following the spirit of the time, he should be as emotionally detached from the spectacle as possible, as objective, as impartial, and as disinterested as a scientist searching for truth and not striving to prove a pet notion. It was a masculine and full-blooded art determined not to escape into a dream world of purely imaginary beauty, but to face reality and to suppress none of the facts of life merely to give life a character. Under such a discipline it became a new and exciting adventure to explore contemporary life and to reveal those intimate but usually neglected details concerning the Emma Bovarys, the Nanas, and the Carrie Meebers.

Such a catholic taste was revolutionary. It was intended to be so. Queen Victoria would and did disapprove; but she was also disturbed by the morals of Queen Guinevere and the bigamous wife of Enoch Arden, or of anyone whom she could not ask to Balmoral. But writers who knew the world could find no adequate reason for such a nice exclusiveness, or for making such sharp distinctions between life as people live it, and life as recreated and rearranged by imaginative writers.

It would be pointless just now to say that the realism of Émile Zola was no better art than the romanticism of Victor Hugo; or that as a steady fare one form was no more permanently satisfying than the other. The fact remains that a strong draught of unflinching realism with its insistence upon accurate observation of life as it is lived was at that moment indispensable to the well-being of letters. It introduced new and provocative materials and offered a fresh and stimulating point of view from which to order them. The world movement which resulted is ample evidence of its necessity and its power.

Although realism reached America quite late, and after Europe and England had drained the vocabulary of invectives in fruitless opposition to it, it had to fight each step of its way into our literature. One reason for this opposition was the philosophy of naturalism which, in many instances, determined the selection of material for the realistic novel. Naturalism was born of the scientific spirit of the last century, which tried to interpret life as another of the natural phenomena. Using the realistic method, it ordered carefully observed detail to show the helplessness of man, himself a mechanical or chemical accident, in a mechanical world whose cold indifference or outright hostility relentlessly crushes him into dust precisely as it does all other animals. This mechanistic view of life reserved no place for the moral law, and it opened the way to the superman and the survival of the fittest. It was bitterly attacked. The other important reason for the opposition was the low social strata from which the characters were usually taken and the more accurate language in which their lives and their speech were reported. Representatives of the old order tried to impose severe restrictions upon the artists and the ensuing struggle became one of the important elements in the creation of the American novel.

For some curious reason there is a strict convention fastened upon our minds which assumes that no evil exists in the world unless it is created in print. The late Anthony Comstock, following this principle, suppressed the showing in New York of George Bernard Shaw's MRS. WARREN'S PROFESSION, naïvely unaware how ridiculous the gesture was when ten thousand Mrs. Warrens were at that very minute carrying forward the profession itself in the streets outside. The violent hostility to the realistic movement was seldom on the issue of its truth or its faithfulness to the life it sought to portray; more often it arose from the hysterical attempts of good but simple people to deny the existence of anything unpleasantly real by forbidding writers to take any notice of it.

It became necessary therefore for the new literature represented in America by Stephen Crane and his followers to struggle not only with its own artistic problems but even for the elemental right to choose its own themes and viewpoints in the event they did not stand eye to eye with those of the local censors. These writers were abused for their attempt to present in realistic patterns for interested and responsible adults the unromanticized life of ordinary people in the United States. The American public was most reluctant to accept their reports. It liked to believe that life in the city slums and along the Bowery in the golden age of Jay Gould, Jim Fisk, and John D. Rockefeller, Sr., was beautiful and clean and polite in its manners; it was told as an objective truth that this life was more often deformed, enslaved, dirty, and vulgar. This truth was ruinous to long-cherished illusions, but the public thought that the way to save the illusions was not to destroy the evil but to belabor the author with critical and personal blows and to censor the words in which unpleasant things were noticed.

The struggle between the authors and the censors lasted through the first third of the century, beginning in 1900 with the suppression of so true and well-disciplined a story as SISTER CARRIE and ending in the closing days of 1933 with Judge Woolsey's masterpiece of judicial reasoning which admitted to America the long-wandering ULYSSES of James Joyce. During those three decades many of the great foreign classics were attacked and legally forbidden this country, and a long list of American books, such as JURGEN, CYTHEREA, and GOD'S LITTLE ACRE, reached the public only after a tilt with Comstockery in the courts. In nearly all cases the book, the author, and the public eventually won, but the victory was often costly, many unimportant or ephemeral books were boomed into a public notice beyond their merits, and honorable critics had to fight for them to defend the general and indispensable principle of artistic freedom.

This heated controversy was a part of the complete revolution going on in the national life and in minds crawling out from Victorianism into a modern world which realism felt called upon to express. It affected all the arts, but it was most sharply focused in literature. The novel became more than ever before one of the many intricate social forces remaking the world, recognizing and reflecting the changing scene and at the same time becoming a powerful influence in bringing those changes about. Even the conflict in which it was engaged became material for more novels on the subject of the conflict.

The point of view was kept actively before the public by a strong group of critical writers who served the novel well even if they were often less interested in the books than in propaganda for the view of life which they presented. These men, H. L. Mencken, Randolph Bourne, Van Wyck Brooks, Ludwig Lewisohn, John Macy, Floyd Dell, Lewis Mumford, and many others had moved into what we used to speak of as the modern world. They saw clearly that America was expanding from a colony and a province into the first of world powers, that the country was rousing from its sense of isolation and getting rather awkwardly awake, that the old America of the romantic age had died with the frontier and a new one must be born. The country was parceled out for good or ill, the immigrants were here and must stay though we could close the ports to future applicants, the villages were booming into towns, the towns into cities, the independent small farmers were degenerating into insecure wage slaves, Ford was destroying the distance in between, there was the stock market, and we were importing ample quantities of the modernism of Omar, Freud, and George Bernard Shaw. A modern and vigorous literature would be necessary to deal with these matters, it was emerging, and these critics fought for it.

This modernism was primarily a new set of values which contradicted the conventions of an outmoded past symbolized by the two terms which later became quaintly synonymous, Puritanism and Victorianism. The articles of faith represented by these terms were under direct challenge: the sanctity of marriage, the heavenly origin ∴ the moral code, the infallibility of St. Paul, the depravity of Mrs. Warren, the utopian life of an American village, the altruism of big business, the superiority of the male to the female, the inevitability of progress, the good life on a Mid-Western farm—to set down a meager few of the items in debate.

Again it would be pointless to say that the literature created under the stress of constant challenge and struggling for the right to exist was eventually led with victory to distasteful excesses in the exercise of its freedom; or that these excesses were, in their way, as false as the old romances of young love under the mimosa tree against which the rebellion was led. The fact was that freedom to deal with new matter in an honest way was at that moment a prerequisite to continued life in American letters. "You shall know the truth and the truth shall make you free" is a principle which a people ignores at its own peril. No literature can long thrive when it does not remain alert to the life of which it is a part, or when it is artificially restricted in theme and matter by bonds not self-imposed by the integrity of the artist himself. But in America in 1890 these bonds were so tight that they excluded the most significant segments of life witnessed or directly experienced every day by nearly a hundred million people. And young Stephen Crane, who was looking upon the life which drove to suicide the Maggie Johnsons of the Bowery, and young Theodore Dreiser who was reporting for a newspaper in Chicago the life of the Cowperwoods, were expected, if they must write about such things at all, to do it mildly and without offense in the tradition inherited from the Victorians. Charles Dickens was thought of as exemplary.

It was one of those moments familiar in the history of

literature when a vitalizing "revolt" must arise from somewhere. It happened in our time to be realism. The hum and
surge and buoyance of modern life caught up the energetic
spirits, the novel was the chosen medium of expression, realism was the new mode, and in a single generation a respectable body of American fiction was created.

Chapter Two

AMERICA CATCHES STEP

*T*HE last decade of the nineteenth century, important though it was, produced more criticism and heated debate over the merits of realism than memorable fiction in the realistic mode. Not many of the novels survived the extension of honesty and the greater surety of craftsmanship that were developed in the new century. Henry B. Fuller and Harold Frederic each produced one novel that may still be read without leaning too heavily upon an historical interest. Henry B. Fuller (1857-1929) was a typical mixture of academic East, practical Chicago West, and an American longing for the Europe of the romantic imagination of the eighties. By nature he leaned a flaccid spirit toward the contemplation of a completed old-world past. But the quick currents of realistic living in the Chicago of the Exposition era captured him long enough to inspire THE CLIFF-DWELLERS (1893) which Harper's Weekly carried in serial form to a wide audience. By virtue of its attack on vain and fierce women (the "deadly female" being then a fresh topic) behind the competitive mercantile struggle of the men, and because of its vigorous picture of expanding, turbulent Chicago, the book achieved some significance as an early American realistic novel.

Harold Frederic (1856-1898) was not rooted in American soil. He spent most of his brief maturity in London. He too was inspired by the new realism and the critical spirit to produce one novel of continuing significance: THE DAMNATION OF THERON WARE (1896). It was daring in subject material as well as in title. It foreshadowed the more biting strictures on the church and its ministers in the problem novels to be offered by another generation. The still living tissues of the book are its description of the Methodist conference, its indictment of the dull and lifeless existence of a mean New England village, and its portrait of the pastor.

These novels are isolated, sporadic achievements of a decade in ferment with new ideas that were exciting the imagination of younger men and portending greater things. If we except them, and if we leave aside Hamlin Garland for the moment, there are two novelists of indisputable genius— Henry James and Stephen Crane—and two of very great talent—William Dean Howells and Frank Norris—to be mentioned before the appearance of Theodore Dreiser. Of these four men and their part in creating the American novel a few things must be said.

Both Henry James (1843-1916) and William Dean Howells (1837-1920) had written continuously throughout the nineties, and were carrying on their work into the new century. Three of Henry James's finest novels were, in fact, published at the beginning of the era of Theodore Roosevelt: THE WINGS OF THE DOVE (1902), THE AMBASSADORS (1903), and THE GOLDEN BOWL (1904). They show how completely his long exile had cut him off from the expanding and turbulent America of his day. He had a small but loyal following then as now, who willingly accepted his tenuous materials so far removed from common experience, and who delighted in the complicated elaborations of his psychological analyses in the restricted field in which he chose to exercise his genius. Certainly his work was impossible as an art form for dealing with the America of the strenuous age and big business. It was beautifully adapted as an instrument for his studies of idle people of wealth and social position whose drama was usually in the things they tried so hard to keep from speaking straightforwardly about. It was hopelessly unsuited to the job O. Henry found to do in THE FOUR MILLION (1906). It is perfectly clear why Henry James, beloved by many though he is, became an isolated and specialized genius separated from and with little influence in the development of the American novel, except for the suggestion his method offered by way of Joyce, Proust, and others for the stream-of-consciousness technique which flowered here after the War.

There is a corresponding truth about William Dean Howells. At the turn of the century, if not a few decades later, he still had a devoted following who accepted his pictures of American life and bowed to his critical enunciations. But the pace was too fast for his tentative realism and the degree of honesty permitted to an Ohio gentleman adopted by Boston and rising to an editorship and its Olympian authority in New York City. In the new America, Howells was moved to offer THE LANDLORD AT LION'S HEAD (1897), THE KENTONS (1902), THE SON OF ROYAL LANGBRITH (1904), THROUGH THE EYE OF THE NEEDLE (1907). He was nevertheless of much greater importance in the growth of the American novel than Henry James, because he used his high place to swing creative fiction and the reading public into the realistic channel. He refused to follow truth wherever it led, because that might at some point involve adultery, mean marriages and divorce, and vulgar and impolite people. But that was a failure in pursuit and not in principle, and the strict logic of his critical position would have to encompass at some time the materials of MAGGIE, SISTER CARRIE, and SPOON RIVER ANTHOLOGY.

In this sense, then, Howells has a high place of honor in the creation of the American novel, for better or for worse, and it is a part of his memorial that he properly praised Stephen Crane when all others cried the boy down and said nasty things about his forthright books. Furthermore he recognized and gave encouragement to the brave new novels coming out of the Middle West where for more than a generation the great American writers have been born and goaded into expression. It is also to his credit that in the column and a half given to E. W. Howe's THE STORY OF A COUNTRY TOWN in the Century Magazine (1884) he declared that realism was "the only literary movement of our time that has vitality in it," and said of the book which could find no publisher, "It is not in the presentation of individuals, however, but in the realization of a whole order of things, that the strength of the book lies; and what I most admire in it is the apparently unconscious fearlessness with which all the facts of the case, good, bad, and indifferent, are recognized." To say those things in 1884 would, in the light of future events, justify any man's claim to fame. And as for his own accomplishment, the fact remains that in spite of his defects it took thirty-eight years to displace Silas Lapham in favor of George F. Babbitt as exhibit A of the American man of business.

From the perspective of time there is even more to be said for Frank Norris (1870-1902), who died at the age of thirty-two, but with a brilliant accomplishment already behind him and a fine promise still ahead. His career was so brief that it cannot justly be compared with that of William Dean Howells, but there can be no question about his unusual talent and the genius of his conceptions. Already he is firmly planted in the books that deal with his period. His reputation rests upon three novels which show with complete clarity the turn our fiction was taking, and which also influenced it in the new direction.

MCTEAGUE (1899), with its relentless probing into the stolid, brutish mind of the unlicensed dentist and the narrow, miserly soul of Trina, his wife, is, even on this side of Freud, still a living and moving book. In its realistic point of view, in its choice of material from the working class, in its honest pursuit of truth through the gradual degeneration of Mc-Teague into drunkenness, desperation, and murder, to the sordid finish in the blazing desert when McTeague is fatally handcuffed to the corpse of his Nemesis, it was and is a novel of importance for those who would understand what has happened in literature during the twentieth century. Its elements of permanency are further witnessed by the successful revival of the story as a cinema, and by the fact that after all the years with their astounding changes in our national habits, it seemed more faithful to life than the popular modern drama about a submerged dentist in ONE SUNDAY AFTERNOON.

The American public has been more partial, however, to the incomplete EPIC OF THE WHEAT because its matter is less sordid and the story has greater sweep and action on a grander scale. THE OCTOPUS (1901) and THE PIT (1903), both coming after SISTER CARRIE, are live and readable novels in our time, with a go still in them. They tried to come to grips with the turbulent life of the great West where more than a hundred thousand miles of railroad, built in forty years, had bound together the new states beyond the Mississippi and joined them to Chicago, and where thousands of farmers had settled on fresh land for growing wheat. Caught between the monopoly of the railroads upon which they were absolutely dependent, and the parasitic speculators in the Wheat Pit in Chicago who ruled the price of their grain, the farmers were in a serious plight. It was the most representative of native material for a great fiction, the very stuff out of which the nation was being formed or deformed. It is part of Frank Norris's hold on fame that he saw the need and met it to the best of his powers. He attempted, as he himself declared, to give the people not a lie but the truth. And both books are very satisfactory as truth.

THE OCTOPUS, with its characteristic title symbolizing the grasping railroad and the death of its agent with poetic justice in an avalanche of wheat, is truth about the tumultuous West and the desperate struggle between producers and distributors for the spoils of the land. Frank Norris got into this book not only the spirit of the robber barons, the tough frontiersmen, the lawless drifter and fortune hunter, the educated men from eastern colleges, and violent transmutation of fortune, but also some of the romance of empire-building, of panting locomotives on the Western plains, and of the lingering beauty of golden prairies and the excitement of young love. It was a

satisfactory design and Norris filled it in with gusto and a
youthful sharpness of perception which included both objective reality and the more subtle overtones of beauty too often
omitted by later and more scientific realists.

THE PIT is just as good and no better than THE OCTOPUS.
The first chapter is a little masterpiece of early realism as it
presents the two attractive and sensitive Dearborn girls from
Barrington, Massachusetts, waiting on a cold evening in the
vestibule of the Auditorium Theatre in Chicago for their rich
hostess, who has invited them to her box for the Italian opera
and is late because the bridge was turned. Then in strong
contrast it pictures the romantic self-giving and exaltation
of Laura under the effect of the music while the business-
deadened ears of Chicago's first citizens hear nothing but the
talk of the Helmick failure which continuously punctures the
stage illusion with audible whispers about "bears" and "margins" and "one hundred and six carloads." Norris was at
his best in such symbolic scenes, and in his fast moving pictures of the activity in the Pit and the workings of the minds
of big speculators. He saw their activity in terms of jungle
warfare where the combatants asked for and gave no quarter,
where the nice young man of the drawing room becomes a
hard-faced fighter for the profits. It is an exact parallel to the
view of life fabled forth by Jack London in THE CALL OF THE
WILD (1903) and has the feeling for human frailty before a
greater power outside of itself so graphically presented in THE
SEA-WOLF (1904). Wheat is too big for Curtis Jadwin, capitalist
and speculator, and Samuel Gretry, broker, of Chicago, Illinois.

Frank Norris caught the spirit of Chicago with a poetic
vitality which few writers have equaled. His description of
that brawny city climbing out of the swamp into a metropolis
is a first draft for Carl Sandburg's famous poem a decade
later. Space into free verse this passage from THE PIT and you
have a free-verse poem on the city which was to be the scene
of so many American novels.

"It was Empire, the resistless subjugation of all this central world of the lakes and the prairies. Here, midmost in the land, beat the Heart of the Nation, whence inevitably must come its immeasurable power, its infinite, infinite, inexhaustible vitality. Here, of all her cities, throbbed the true life—the true power and spirit of America; gigantic, crude with the crudity of youth, disdaining rivalry; sane and healthy and vigorous; brutal in its ambition, arrogant in the new-found knowledge of its giant strength, prodigal of its wealth, infinite in its desires. In its capacity boundless, in its courage indomitable; subduing the wilderness in a single generation, defying calamity, and through the flame and the débris of a commonwealth in ashes, rising suddenly renewed, formidable, and Titanic."

Frank Norris's attainment was an inspiration to a younger group of men who carried on and developed both his method and his material. His importance has been somewhat unjustly in the shadow of the great critical praise heaped in our day upon the work of Stephen Crane. Stephen Crane (1871-1900) had an authentic genius which it would be unpardonable not to praise and rejoice for. But, whatever its promise, it remained in the few years allotted to him excessively narrow in range and consisted in an austerely objective approach to his matter and an impressionistic style that was new and welcome. It was his method and his style that first caught the eye of literary men like Joseph Conrad at the beginning of our era of experimentation with technique in fiction and brought about the wide recognition of his peculiar genius.

The great and immediate success of THE RED BADGE OF COURAGE (1895) rested largely upon the concentrated if imagined realism of the picture of one of the thousands of boys who left their peaceful farms and marched, trembling with fear, into enemy muskets to save the Union or to save Southern Civilization. The book is artistic in plan and execution, it eschews the romantic attitude toward the Civil War so dear to the Mary Johnstons, and its psychology of fear and its picture of the sense of helplessness and meaninglessness of the activity of a common soldier being maneuvered by the Great at headquarters could go unrevised into contemporary war books. Even its style and its selection of detail are definitely post-World War, as when Crane describes the dead soldier leaning against a tree with his sodden eyes staring out like those of a dead fish, the ants crawling over the death-swollen lips while the hero, Henry Fleming, creeps away backwards in nervous terror. Erich Remarque might have penned it. How important such writing was to the creation of the American novel can best be understood by reading along with THE RED BADGE OF COURAGE the description of Pickett's charge at Gettysburg from the pen of Mary Johnston in her best seller, CEASE FIRING (1912), where there is much about Woden, the Valkyries, old Aztec gods, and heroism while the five thousand brave soldiers are understood to shrink to four, then three, then two on their way to immortality. Stephen Crane's style, once so fresh and impressionistic, has been copied by dozens of hands in the present century. One element in it may be seen full blown in Waldo Frank's CITY BLOCK, and another in Joseph Conrad's THE NIGGER OF THE NARCISSUS.

Stephen Crane was also important for his choice of materials. He knew his New York slums at first hand, and he quite rightly saw no reason why he should not report its life as honestly as possible. That resolution is a vital part of the story of the rise of the American novel. MAGGIE, A GIRL OF THE STREETS (1896), which was privately printed by Crane in 1893 because no publisher would then risk it, is the story of a girl from the Bowery in the day when that district was mean and famous. She has a brother, Jimmie Johnson, who later steps straight into the O'Neill plays, and when he gently replies to Maggie, "Ah, what de hell! Shut up or I'll smack yer mout', see?" we might be listening to the Hairy Ape himself in his first scene. It was new in Crane's day to report with no expressed interest in reform and with touches of irony how Maggie tried to keep her character by working at five dollars a week in a collar factory; how she was seduced by bartender

Pete and cast off by him for another female more perfect in her technique; how she was bullied and turned out by a drunken mother without protest from brother Jimmie; and how she was borne relentlessly across town, alone among hurrying and unresponsive men, to a final peace in suicide in the river.

If we add to this material with its distinction of style the third novel, GEORGE'S MOTHER (1896), which continues the study of the slums and shows the heartbreak of a mother who sees her son drift into companionship with gangsters, we may understand why Stephen Crane has been conceded priority in influence upon fiction in our day, and why his critical reputation is greater than that of Frank Norris, whose understanding of the real forces at work in American life and their appropriateness for the novel was so much more penetrating than Crane's. But taken together they offered a solid foundation for building an American fiction.

Chapter Three

REALISM AND THE PUBLIC TASTE: 1900-1921

THE first decade of the twentieth century was filled with a burst of energy in the making of novels. There were three parallel lines of activity. One pushed forward the new industrial process of making, advertising, and selling in job lots certain bound volumes which were becoming known as "best sellers." Another followed the lead of the modern drama and wrote about the problems and the topics of the times. A third carried on the work begun by Crane, Howells, and Norris with a series of novels of steadily growing power and importance to the new America.

In the popular entertainment group were the familiar names of Paul Leicester Ford, Edward Noyes Westcott, F. Marion Crawford, Mary Johnston, Booth Tarkington, James Lane Allen, Maurice Thompson, Harold MacGrath, Ralph Connor and a score of others who maintained their standing for years among the authors in greatest demand. Winston Churchill with his popular problem novels was at the head of the second group. In the third list of those who were trying to create a novel capable of expressing American life in terms of honesty and reality the most distinguished were Robert Herrick, Ellen Glasgow, and Edith Wharton.

A few of the books by the authors in the third list enjoyed a wide reading, but the great popular favor was reserved for the novels in the first two groups. These novels offer interesting material for reflection on the character of American fiction at the turn of the century, and the measure of the task before it if it was to become an important body of international literature. Historical romance held the public eye for several years after the war with Spain, and the America which suppressed and damned SISTER CARRIE bought Ford's JANICE MEREDITH (1899) and Churchill's RICHARD CARVEL (1898) by the thousands. Mary Johnston's TO HAVE AND TO HOLD (1899) led the list of best sellers through 1900 until it yielded first place in September to Allen's THE REIGN OF LAW, and second place in November to THE MASTER CHRISTIAN by Marie Corelli. From 1901 to 1911, the strenuous decade of Theodore Roosevelt, the books in the front of public interest were:

1901—Thompson's ALICE OF OLD VINCENNES, Churchill's THE CRISIS.

1902—Parker's THE RIGHT OF WAY, Major's DOROTHY VERNON, Wister's THE VIRGINIAN.

1903—Hegan's LOVEY MARY, Ward's LADY ROSE'S DAUGHTER.

1904—Fox's THE LITTLE SHEPHERD OF KINGDOM COME, Churchill's THE CROSSING.

1905—Dixon's THE CLANSMAN, Hichen's THE GARDEN OF ALLAH.

1906—Nicholson's THE HOUSE OF A THOUSAND CANDLES, Wister's LADY BALTIMORE, Churchill's CONISTON.

1907—Connor's THE DOCTOR, Nicholson's THE PORT OF MISSING MEN, Little's THE LADY OF THE DECORATION.

1908—Burnett's THE SHUTTLE, Churchill's MR. CREWE'S CAREER.

1909—Fox's THE TRAIL OF THE LONESOME PINE, Anonymous, THE INNER SHRINE.

1910—Rinehart's WHEN A MAN MARRIES, Churchill's A MODERN CHRONICLE, Barclay's THE ROSARY.

1911—Abbott's MOLLY MAKE-BELIEVE, Wright's THE WINNING OF BARBARA WORTH.

These novels are representative of several score of prominent titles which held popular attention during the decade. Remembering that this was the muck-rake period, it becomes evident that the era preferred escape literature. It is also clear that most of these books seem of little importance in the sweep of literary expression. As social documents, as evidence of the quickening stream of American life and attempts to catch and express it through the medium of the novel, some of them are still interesting. It would be futile to belittle them from the perspective of the present day. The fact that few of them can now be read except by historians bears witness to the change in literary technique and the shift in interests which the passing decades have brought about. They were books of the day and they perished when their entertainment value lapsed or when the problems which provoked them lost their currency.

From the point of view of the growth of American fiction, however, these problem novels have considerable historical interest. The problems with which they dealt were seldom those universal concerns of all men independent of time and place. Few artists and only a small public were interested in careful representations of life based upon well-rounded and accurate observation of the permanent qualities of mankind set in the unique social patterns of the American democracy. They were more concerned with dramatizing specific abuses and questions of interest at the moment in a society whose fundamental rightness was above debate, as the drama under Pinero, Fitch, Thomas, and Moody was doing.

It was the era of "the strenuous life," of nature cults, of imperialism, of "he-men" and the open spaces, of the exposure of the high-handed banditry of big business and of state and municipal politics, of dramatic reforms, of the emergence of women, of the reconsideration of religion and the church. And each issue had its discussion in fiction.

It is still quaintly entertaining and not without value to set down some of the questions which inspired heated controversy in the novels of those days. Here are a representative few. Have married people the moral right to escape each other by divorce? Or should a man in high position whose marriage is a failure, and who is madly in love with another woman,

count all well lost for love (THE ONE WOMAN, etc.)? Has a
doctor or a nurse the moral right to relieve a helpless cripple,
invalid, imbecile, insane or suffering person, whose death is
certain, by putting him painlessly out of the misery of his life
(THE FRUIT OF THE TREE, etc.)? Should a highly trained and
well-educated man save an invalid or a slum child from death
at the sacrifice of his own life which presumably is more valuable to society? (A dozen short stories lasting throughout the
war.) How should society receive a man who has served his
sentence in prison or has been acquitted of crime through the
skill of a clever lawyer and now returns to his citizenship
(THE ANCIENT LAW, THE RIGHT OF WAY, etc.)? Can the church
receive "tainted" money given it by a wealthy parishioner who
made it by renting brothels and mean houses in the slums
(V. V.'s EYES, THE INSIDE OF THE CUP, etc.)?

Others maintained definite theses: That the original Ku
Klux Klan was a necessary and helpful instrument in the reconstruction period (THE CLANSMAN). That an architect should
be stronger than the temptations put before him by selfish and
dishonest contractors (THE COMMON LOT). That the fine old
Southern ideal of feminine self-sacrifice is no virtue and vic-
timizes its followers (Ellen Glasgow's novels). That American
citizens accept success as its own criterion with no regard for
its methods (THE MEMOIRS OF AN AMERICAN CITIZEN). That
politics in the commonwealths of this Republic is corrupt, that
popular government is no better than any other form except
as the virtue and the wisdom of the people make it so, and
that good men should do something honest about it (CONISTON,
MR. CREWE'S CAREER).

These novels had their greatest vogue in the decade before
the World War. They lost the center of interest when Sherwood Anderson, Sinclair Lewis and the post-War group took
the stage. But the form did not die, by any means. It has been
carried on with conspicuous success by a few writers, notably
by Charles G. Norris, younger brother of Frank Norris.
Chicago-born in 1881, he has been writing fiction on contro-

versial and timely themes since 1915. Choosing for his novels abrupt titles like SALT (1917), BRASS (1921), BREAD (1923), PIG IRON (1925), SEED (1930), he has discussed education, marriage, women in industry, the effect of business and the business mind on American life, and the problems of eugenics and birth control.

The difficulty with the strenuous decade's thesis novels as literature was that the thesis dominated all other elements. Only occasionally and in the hands of a gifted artist did a novel such as ETHAN FROME (1911) submerge the sermon, the problem, and the propaganda in living character so graphically wrought that essential truth and permanent interest resulted. More often the sense of life was warped and falsified to bear out the thesis, and the novel became in substance a magazine article or a newspaper editorial.

This is pointedly true in the work of David Graham Phillips (1867-1911). He had a brilliant career as a newspaper man. He turned to fiction at the beginning of the century, and during the last decade of his life he headed the list of the muckrakers both in vigor and in quantity. He wrote on the average two novels each year for ten years. He exploited all the themes of interest to the era of Roosevelt, and he presented thinly veiled a number of portraits of living people. He pictured the newspaper world in THE GREAT GOD SUCCESS (1901). He exposed the omnipresent political rottenness of the decade in THE PLUM TREE (1905) and several other novels. He attacked the fraudulent manipulation of the life insurance companies in LIGHT-FINGERED GENTRY (1907). He joined the forces released by Ibsen and Strindberg and rebuked the rapidly emerging new woman as vicious and parasitic in a half dozen novels before he was murdered by a man who considered himself victimized as a character in one of the books. This activity was all very interesting and occasionally exciting, and it did help to pave the way for the reception of the work of Theodore Dreiser and Sherwood Anderson in the second decade. But it had little to do with the final and significant body of enduring letters.

While these entertainment and thesis novels were engaging public favor, the novelists in the third group were slowly advancing their art. From the first they could count on a small but understanding audience. Some of their books were quite well received, even rivaling for a time the accepted type of best seller. Popular success came to Ellen Glasgow's THE VOICE OF THE PEOPLE (1900) and THE DELIVERANCE (1904), to Gertrude Atherton's THE CONQUEROR (1902), Frank Norris's THE PIT (1903), Jack London's THE SEA-WOLF (1904), Edith Wharton's THE HOUSE OF MIRTH (1905), Upton Sinclair's THE JUNGLE (1906), Jack London's THE IRON HEEL (1907), Robert Herrick's TOGETHER (1908), and to William Allen White's A CERTAIN RICH MAN (1909), and Jack London's MARTIN EDEN (1909).

Jack London (1876-1916) poured himself out into nineteen novels and a score of miscellaneous books in sixteen years, and thus dissipated his powers. His personal career was more amazing than any of his books. It furnished material for several stories of an autobiographical nature, one of which retains some of its original interest and importance. That is MARTIN EDEN. It is based upon Jack London's experience as poverty-ridden youth, newspaper boy on the Oakland, California, waterfront, helper in a saloon, member of a tough gang, dreamer of superman exploits, Socialist orator and labor sympathizer, and his astounding feat of preparing in three months the work normally allotted to two years in order to pass the entrance examinations at the University of California, only to find when he got there that the rewards were unsatisfactory. The book is one of the many good autobiographical novels of personal achievement in the face of great odds written in the present century, of which Abraham Cahan's THE RISE OF DAVID LEVINSKY (1917) is another worthy example.

The keen interest in Socialism of the 1900 variety so frequently referred to and explained in MARTIN EDEN was more fully developed and the difficulties it faced were presented in

THE IRON HEEL, a novel that appeared in the same year with Hutchins Hapgood's slightly fictionized biography of a Chicago labor leader in THE SPIRIT OF LABOR (1907). They anticipated the proletarian fiction produced by a newer generation in the thirties. As a piece of writing THE IRON HEEL is no better than the later attempts to fictionize the problem of labor struggling under the iron heel of its master. In spite of his immense popularity in America and abroad, Jack London's work is of minor importance in the development of our modern fiction.

Robert Herrick (Massachusetts, 1868), whose distinguished career as professor and author has extended throughout the present century, was among the first of our American writers to attempt to express through the medium of the novel the significance of the life of which he was a part. His best novels are THE GOSPEL OF FREEDOM (1898), in which he dealt with the importance of personal dignity and integrity in a society which made worldly success its criterion of value; THE COMMON LOT (1904) and THE MEMOIRS OF AN AMERICAN CITIZEN (1905) in which he followed more powerfully the same general theme by picturing the scheming and ruthless business man rising to success and the position of a hero at the sacrifice of every virtue which the author holds sacred; TOGETHER (1908), in which he studied the problems of married life in America; WASTE (1924) in which he reasserted his importance in fiction by surveying the life of a generation up to and including the breakdown and disillusion of the post-War period. His work was closely related to the problem novels of the period, but he was too good an artist to permit it to be weighed down by temporary concerns. He strongly disapproved of the things by which his contemporaries in the market-place set great store, he protested against the complacent attitude of the generation which brought about the World War, he satirized the parasitic position of women, and in general his novels show the drift of advanced thinking during the period. It is a part of the merit of his work that its first purpose was to recreate human life in the form of the novel rather than to argue a point of view, and that one must deduce the theses by observing the life led by his characters. They have lost some of their immediacy with the passage of time, but their historical interest is unrivaled.

Ellen Glasgow, whose later and more important work is discussed in a succeeding chapter, laid the basis for her career in the first decade of this century with a series of books in the manner of the historical romance, but distinguished by their purpose, their scholarship, and their art. THE VOICE OF THE PEOPLE (1900), first of the group to be written but third in the completed sequence, was an excellent novel to come from the pen of a young woman in her mid-twenties. It profited by the current vogue for historical novels, but it was not dependent upon it. It was a painstaking study of the post–Civil War Virginia of the eighties. And it was a serious and modern attempt to understand the Virginia of her own day by recreating the conditions which were responsible for it. THE BATTLE-GROUND (1902) went behind and into the Civil War to picture the old way of Southern life and the forces which overwhelmed and crushed it. She returned to the theme once more in THE ROMANCE OF A PLAIN MAN (1909) to fill in the years between, embracing the sad days of the Reconstruction.

Against this solid background of historical understanding she also produced her noteworthy story THE DELIVERANCE (1904), which, in a way, foreshadowed BARREN GROUND (1925). It studied the subtle social differentiations in Virginia, based upon family heritage and not upon wealth. It centered around the plantation which was lost by the Blakes of good family to the Fletchers of vulgar origin. These earlier novels were very definitely feeling their way toward the modern spirit which was, a decade or so later, to place Ellen Glasgow in the first rank of the American post-War novelists.

Edith Wharton also founded her career and made her great reputation in the decade before the World War. She too began *à la mode* with THE VALLEY OF DECISION (1902), a lengthy historical novel set in the Italy of the eighteenth century, but she quickly turned in the spirit and the manner of Henry James to a series of studies of the fashionable New York life which she knew intimately. She published THE HOUSE OF MIRTH in 1905; THE FRUIT OF THE TREE in 1907; THE REEF in 1912, a story strikingly suggestive in situation and in method of the later Henry James of THE GOLDEN BOWL; and THE CUSTOM OF THE COUNTRY in 1913. There is a little of the problem novel about them, but the realistic portrayal of society and the psychological analyses of the characters distinguish them above other novels in that *genre*. Two of them—THE HOUSE OF MIRTH and THE CUSTOM OF THE COUNTRY—are of especial interest because they are so nearly the real thing, and because they indicate both the strength and the shortcomings of the developing American novel. If they now seem less significant and a little dead, it is partly because the characters of Undine Spragg and Lily Bart are not fully released from the "problems" in the two novels, and partly because they are taken from a highly specialized group of people who were quite out of touch with the millions down in the thick of American life. To the twentieth-century realistic writer, it was more interesting and mort important to know what was happening to these submerged millions who gave life to the nation than to learn whether Undine Spragg of Apex City was introduced to the inner circle of the Driscolls and the Van Degens of New York City, whether she used white ink on pigeon-blood note paper, or whether her vulgar mother succeeded in pushing herself and her daughter from the Stentorian across Central Park into the "Olympian portals" of Fifth Avenue. As a matter of fact, the measure of success she achieved was bitter and disappointing to her. But the surviving interest in THE CUSTOM OF THE COUNTRY springs from the author's exhibition of the impoverished values for which such people were toiling and stewing away their lives, and of the code under which they were exploiting the country and their less aggressive fellow citizens for the empty ambition of dining with bores.

This enormous gap separating the world of Edith Wharton from that of the great and growing industrial democracy
portrayed in JENNIE GERHARDT (1911) is even more emphatic
in THE HOUSE OF MIRTH, where the air is stifling and the people
are embalmed animosities. With a stimulating touch of restrained malice and satire, Edith Wharton pictures the soulless
and utterly futile set of people surrounding Lily Bart. It requires a degree of historical imagination on the part of those
who came later to understand why a girl of twenty-nine with
the intelligence and the sensitive mind of Lily Bart should flit
on the edge of disaster for the sacred privilege of sailing to
Nice on a yacht with a set of ruthless bandits with social
pretentions, or of being permitted to lose money (which she
didn't have) at a game of bridge (which she never liked)
with a group of vultures (whom she loathed) at Bellomont
(where she was bored). She is the intelligent but helpless
female of the pre-War days whose character is not strong
enough to meet her rather simple problems, who feels herself
on the rubbish heap for want of adequate outlet for her
talents, whose only prospect is marriage to wealth so that she
may continue an idle existence in the den of social cruelties
where a girl is, incongruously enough, "ruined" because she
takes tea with a gentleman in his apartment, and appears in a
private entertainment in a gown that suggests to the gentlemen present her "outline."

In the enterprising America of Theodore Roosevelt, what
should Lily Bart do with herself? Actually, she visits the
happy poor-class home of the once outcast Nettie Struther,
she sees Nettie's baby by the magnanimous young man who
"knew all" and yet loved her enough to make this renewal
possible; then she thinks of the opportunities she and Lawrence Selden have had for understanding in which they failed;
she deposits the paltry legacy with which her aunt had cut her
off, and takes an overdose of chloral.

This story of Lily Bart was representative of one small
element in the America of its day. It was an important achieve-

ment, even though it fell short of greatness. It indicated how rapidly the new fiction was maturing under the discipline of its struggle to bring together life and letters in the early years of the new century. And the success which came to many of these books bore witness to the fact that the tempo of American life was changing, and that the intellectual bondage was relaxing enough to permit authors to do an honest work on the new or neglected aspects of the contemporary scene.

During the second decade of this century the new realism won some degree of tolerance and increasing attention; but it still had strong competition. JENNIE GERHARDT (1911) was neglected in favor of THE ROSARY and MOLLY MAKE-BELIEVE. THE FINANCIER (1912) had to compete with THE MELTING OF MOLLY and THE HARVESTER. THE TITAN (1914) could not hope to rival THE EYES OF THE WORLD and POLLYANNA, which were ironically the best sellers of the year.

In 1915, although THE "GENIUS" was suppressed, there was a curious portent in Ernest Poole's THE HARBOR. For several months it was enormously popular. Its success seems all the more symptomatic when it is remembered that, while the first part deals with the growth to maturity of an intelligent boy, and with his education in Paris in the days when glamour was still there, the last and best part was a graphic picture revealing the conditions behind a desperate strike of the stokers and dock hands, and the way it was broken by the hostility of the newspapers and the ignorant Negroes brought in by the employers.

From 1915 to 1920 there appeared a group of novelists who were determined to write realistically about any phase of American life of interest to them. They were overcome at first by strong foreign competition. H. G. Wells's MR. BRITLING SEES IT THROUGH was unrivaled in 1916 and a part of 1917. Sherwood Anderson's WINDY MC PHERSON'S SON (1916) was a few years too early for the public taste. In 1917, Joseph Herge-sheimer's THE THREE BLACK PENNYS and Ernest Poole's HIS FAMILY were popular but they were subordinate to John Galsworthy's BEYOND and H. G. Wells's THE SOUL OF A BISHOP. In 1918, America read war books and neglected Willa Cather's MY ÁNTONIA. In 1919 James Branch Cabell's JURGEN was suppressed, Sherwood Anderson's WINESBURG, OHIO was fought over, THE EDUCATION OF HENRY ADAMS was acclaimed, and the general public read Blasco Ibáñez's THE FOUR HORSEMEN OF THE APOCALYPSE. Such a list might be greatly extended, but it would lead to the same observation: that the "new" literature and the wider reading public were finally converging. In fact, they collided with a violent explosion in the autumn of 1920 with the publication of Sinclair Lewis's MAIN STREET. Since then the public has often been recalcitrant and has voiced its protests, but none the less it has bought and read and recognized the "new" novelists. And a new generation of readers, who could see eye to eye with the contemporary novelists, arrived to support them.

Both were eager for a more adequate representation of the American spectacle in fiction. They were aware of the inadequacy of Hegan's MRS. WIGGS OF THE CABBAGE PATCH, or Nicholson's THE LITTLE BROWN JUG AT KILDARE to represent the America that was seeing Chicago boom into a Western metropolis oozing its millions through the stench of Halsted and the revolting squalor of the South Shore toward Gary, Indiana; that was permitting the Standard Oil trust to corrupt the politicians and dominate the law in strategic commonwealths; that was handing over to selfish men in Chicago and Pittsburgh and Philadelphia the public utilities for personal exploitation; that was seeing the Swedes conquer the Northwest and thrive into prosperity under its bitter climate; that was witnessing the rise of the millionaires, the descent into poverty of the industrial workers in the cities and towns, and the vulgar and prosperous middle class between them; that was seeing the motorization of American life, the ghastly and unplanned expansion of thousands of American towns to house the new migration from the farms, the flocking of women into industry, the rapid rise of the divorce rate, and a score of other changes which were remaking the modern world.

It was impossible to prevent such new and challenging materials from finding their way into the hands of the novelists who understood a little of what was happening to the republic. And by the accident of time, the realistic manner had become the accepted pattern for presenting directly and graphically the significance of American life as seen by its literary men.

Chapter Four

THEODORE DREISER

DURING the first decade of the twentieth century, Theodore Dreiser began to attract an ever-increasing amount of attention as the chief spokesman for the realistic novel. The crucial controversies provoked by the suppression of SISTER CARRIE in America and its publication and acclaim in England soon made of the author a rallying point for the moderns. His literary importance grew in spite of the fact that he was not producing novels between 1900 and 1910. He was, paradoxically enough, editing magazines in which he could not have published his own fiction. But he was persistent in his fight for the elementary freedom to report and to interpret life as he had lived it and as he had seen others live it in the cities and towns of America. He was rewarded with misunderstanding and abuse, but the drift of the times was on his side. The controversy is now dead, Theodore Dreiser has a solid place in American and world literature, and the passing years seem to sharpen the outlines of his importance among his contemporaries in the realistic novel. He is, therefore, interesting as a major figure in American fiction; but he is also interesting because he represents the very elements in American life which the novelists had neglected; and because he exhibits in the development of his career the formative influences at work upon our modern novelists, the materials which have inspired them, and the conditions under which they have worked.

Theodore Dreiser had a birth, a social background and a preliminary training as nearly perfect for his work as the rich and educated man-about-town background of John Galsworthy was for THE FORSYTE SAGA. Had some farsighted person deliberately set about to fashion a man for the important job of novelist to the America in transition from the post–Civil War into the modern age, he could hardly have brought more adequate experience into the confines of one man's life. It was a task for which the Shermans, Brownells, Jameses, Mores, and such gifted men were astoundingly unsuited. The America of Indiana mill towns and the Chicago Loop had little in common with Harvard culture prior to the establishment there of the school of business.

But it was the rich stuff for literature, once it had been filtered through an understanding heart which could survive the hard experiences of living it without being done in by that very experience. Theodore Dreiser lived it and survived.

One is permitted to be specific without intruding upon his private life. He has left a record of his life with a candor and completeness which no one else would have dreamed of setting down about him, even if he were in possession of the facts. He is one of the great autobiographers, and his story is frankly told in A TRAVELLER AT FORTY (1913), A BOOK ABOUT MYSELF (1922), DAWN (1931), and portions of TWELVE MEN (1919), HEY RUB-A-DUB-DUB (1920), and A GALLERY OF WOMEN (1929).

He was born in Terre Haute, Indiana, 1871. The date is significant: he would reach maturity in the nineties when realism was becoming the way of looking at life and the mode of expression. There were thirteen children because Mrs. Dreiser, who was susceptible to the world of spirits, felt that the death of the first three was a visitation upon her for her reluctance to continue her pregnancies. Theodore Dreiser was the twelfth. The order is important because the lives of the older children and their relations to the family and the world affected the character of Theodore Dreiser and through him that of the American novel. He was sensitive (more acutely so than he actually states in DAWN) and every detail of the family struggle against poverty, scandal, and social humiliation cut him. The scars are plainly visible behind the reticence and the mature philosophy which make light of them in the otherwise frank autobiographies.

His father was German born, an expert in the selection and manufacture of wool, but without the necessary ruthlessness or the will to power, or the business sagacity to turn his uncommon ability into prosperity for himself and his family. He had power and success within his grasp, but for lack of some one slight element in his chemistry, as Theodore Dreiser sees it, and, perhaps, because of a dirty deal from the hand of chance when his uninsured mill burned down, the father was a failure and the gifted family struggled in want instead of enjoying the comfort and social acceptance which were so nearly theirs. And as a consequence, Theodore Dreiser lived with his ability on the wrong side of the railroad tracks, deprived in his youth of the education, the social setting, and the companionship which he craved and which came as a matter of station to other young men in the town less naturally endowed than he. The effect is preserved in the fundamental texture of every single one of his novels. It is as natively American as an Iowa silo and expresses the experiences of millions in our democracy.

The narrow and offensive religiosity in which his father sought escape from his failure is also molded into the very structure of Theodore Dreiser's novels. We have unforgettable pictures of this man from the son who saw in him an irritating mixture of a tender and loving old man who tried hard to keep the hot spirits of his children confined to the demure and priggish code acceptable to the priest, and an incompetent and foolish crank unfit for human intercourse because of his blind fanatical acceptance of all the child-minded superstitions of his religion. The gap between the conduct normal to the growing body of a boy and a girl and the preachments of the moralists was too great to escape the eye of Theodore Dreiser. And that honest and often bitter rebellion against the inadequacy of his education in the various Catholic schools to which he and his brothers and sisters were sent, against the priests for filling his head with useless fairy stories while scientific truth was ignored, and against his father because he was so preoccupied with his religion that he had no understanding of normal human beings and as a result intensified the family unhappiness—these are topics which command central attention in the novels.

The mother, who died at the close of Theodore Dreiser's youth, inspired a poignantly tender affection in the family. She had a tolerant understanding of her wayward children which was the exact opposite to the hard censorship of their father. The children reciprocated with a sentimental devotion. Theodore Dreiser portrays his mother as a dreamy, lovable woman, too wise to be concerned with condemning the world for being the way it is, sympathizing with her adolescent children and their problems, shielding them from the violence of their straight-laced father, struggling to keep the family together against bitter adversity, seeking cleanness and respectability in poverty despite the venomous tongues of her neighbors, always even-tempered and optimistic, hoping that next year things would be better. Her disposition and character, and their effect upon the spirit of the family, and especially upon Theodore Dreiser, became one of the most significant formative influences in his life. The results are embedded in the novels, and particularized in the portrait of Mrs. Gerhardt. The mothers of the novels are always wise and full of understanding in contrast to the sharp tongued ignorance and bigotry of the fathers.

Inasmuch as Theodore Dreiser was the youngest but one in this large and struggling family, he was affected by the older children and their attempted adjustments to life. His brother Paul, much older than he, a successful song-writer and comedian who helped the family and lived the easy, unmoral life that used to be expected of an actor, prospered outside the code of his father. He was to the eyes of the younger boy the one authentic success in the family, and when

Theodore finally went to New York, Paul was there to show him the city in transition and say to him, "Sometime you ought to write about these things, Thee. They're the limit for extravagance and show. The people out West don't know yet what's going on, but the rich are getting control. They'll own the country pretty soon. A writer like you could make 'em see that. You ought to show up some of these things so they'd know."

There was also the brother who paid visits to the family as it was gaining respectable standing in a new community (of which there were several), was haughty with his brothers and sisters, exploited the credit of Paul, put on airs in the town, and ended each sojourn by getting drunk and being thrown into the jail. This was humiliating to Theodore. So was the gossip about his beautiful and healthy sisters who were excessively admired by men and who went out with them under circumstances which angered their father and excited the tongues of the neighbors. These things were burned deep into the mind of the novelist, and they reappear fashioned into literature as the understanding portrayal of Carrie Meeber, Jennie Gerhardt and her brother Bass, Aileen Butler, Eugene Witla, Clyde Griffiths and Roberta Alden. And it took only a little experience in the world of men and outside the dogma of his diocese to see clearly that their deeds would have been quite differently regarded had these young people enjoyed the $20,000 a year income which their father just missed providing them.

Expose to these experiences and conditions an observing boy whose uncommon ability is immediately recognized by his teachers; give him enough education in high school and a year in Indiana University to sharpen his understanding and prepare him for self-education in the world of men; and then release him into the struggle for a living without benefit of influential friends or other favors to rise to the level of his own ability and genius. It is excellent training if he has the good fortune to come through, and he will know what the world is like when viewed realistically. Theodore Dreiser carried newspapers in Chicago, delivered groceries, nearly killed himself bending over an onion row in the heat of the sun, washed dishes in a filthy eating house, located cars in a Chicago yard until he was laid out with grippe, labored in a hardware store and in one that sold stoves, tried to sell and rent real estate for an incompetent old man who became the Asa Griffiths of AN AMERICAN TRAGEDY, drove a wagon for a laundry, distributed Christmas packages for a Chicago newspaper, collected payments for predatory furniture dealers who sold cheap goods at high prices to the poor on the installment plan, and finally, with desperate perseverance, got a foothold as reporter for a Chicago paper, and began the career which took him to St. Louis, to an Ohio country town, through Toledo and Cleveland to Pittsburgh at the time Carnegie was clubbing down the workers at Homestead and the industrial barons were flaunting their profits by erecting mansions in Schenley Park; and at the last to New York City. Theodore Dreiser saw more of the basic America in five years than Stuart Pratt Sherman saw in a lifetime.

These experiences had meaning for Theodore Dreiser. The world unfortunately was not run on the treasured principles of the Sunday morning sermons which had assured the boy that the meek shall inherit the earth, that it is more blessed to give than to receive, and that you should give your extra coat to your needy brother. Rather, he saw, as every honest man sees, the inadequacy of polite conventions to cope with the fires within, the irrelevancy of dogma to life, the heavy hands upon the poor, the ease of life and the suspension of the rules for the well placed, the ruthless exploitations carried on by the favored with the silent connivance of the church which enjoyed their support, and of the press which, under a pose of freedom, suppressed embarrassing news and wrote hypocritical editorials which were denied by the facts on the front pages.

By nature he was, in his earlier years at least, sentimental, and he liked to read the romances of Ouida and Mrs. Harrison. He was full of dreams. He escaped the dark oppression of the storeroom full of rusty stoves by flights of imagination wherein the dreary railroad yards became beautiful with the colored lights on the switches "winking and glowing like flowers." But he believed that true life never lacks romance when honestly set down, and that realism is compounded of romance and drama, as any one with half an eye can see for himself. As he has phrased it in A GALLERY OF WOMEN, "There are strange, trying, gloomy, even rancid effects on every hand. What about these? And what is it that I personally am trying to do? A smooth countess with a white book in a long green lap? A lady absorbed by a Persian bowl filled with orchids? Not at all!" He had tramped through Halsted. Instead of Whitman's vision of a glorious race of men and women making a beautiful new world out of the untouched West, he saw the lives of those whose laundry he gathered up or whose weekly installments he collected; the powerful Cowperwoods building their Gold Coast mansions, fighting their way to the enormous graft of the public utilities, and following no law except that of a tiger in an African jungle; and the miserable women leering at passers-by from the doorways of dingy basements. When his first opportunity came for writing special features for the paper, he wrote honestly from accurate observation of these things which he had seen and experienced.

Some years later, after Theodore Dreiser had become more mature, had labored on various newspapers, had pried into all corners of life, and had become more interested in the meaning of his own existence, he came upon certain books which helped him to understanding. He has recorded and analyzed this experience in a BOOK ABOUT MYSELF. Huxley, Tyndall, and Spencer, all nineteenth-century minds who were trying to understand the world and human life in objective, scientific terms, shattered the last few illusions left to him by his newspaper career. The remarkable and only important thing about the experience was that the point of view of these men and the conclusions which they had reached were borne out by his own life and observation. He was suddenly and finally emancipated from an older ideology which did not fit the facts as he had observed them. He had found a new organizing principle which enabled him to accept the meaningless welter of experience without trying to impose upon it values which did not fit. And when he had added to his education a careful reading of Balzac and Zola who had found a way of presenting a realistic record of life through the medium of the novel, he was ready for his own work.

Theodore Dreiser has written six novels and they all survive. They are SISTER CARRIE (1900), JENNIE GERHARDT (1911), THE FINANCIER (1912), THE TITAN (1914), THE "GENIUS" (1915), AN AMERICAN TRAGEDY (1925).

SISTER CARRIE is important not only because it is a great American novel, but because it is a symbol of the freedom of letters which Emerson had prophesied. It caused a tremendous stir—in the spirit of Frank Norris when he recommended it for publication, in the household of the publisher after his wife had read it in outrage, in the office where it was suppressed, in the basement where it was for years buried but not dead, and finally in the wide world. Fortunately for us the English were without the pusillanimity which was hampering our letters. They not only published but properly praised the book, and while America was organizing the United States Steel Corporation and reading WHEN KNIGHTHOOD WAS IN FLOWER but refusing recognition to SISTER CARRIE, Theodore Watts-Dunton was pointing out its solid merit and documentary value, its faithfulness and rich interest, and observing that "between its covers no single note of unreality is struck. It is untrammeled by any single concession to convention or tradition, literary or social. . . . Throughout its pages one feels pulsing the sturdy, restless energy of a young people." And he indicated his critical vision by placing it on a shelf beside NANA. Arnold Bennett found it "eye-openingly good," and other sober critics placed it beside Maupassant's BEL AMI.

America could not be expected to continue its resistance in opposition to such English praise, and the book was finally released in 1907. It has been offered in several editions since, and the story of its trials is told by the author in the Modern Library edition (1932). One looks back with incomprehension to the day when this book caused such a flutter among those who think that purity is so frail a virtue that it withers under the faintest breath of temptation. Yet the facts are there, and the critical attack was so severe that years afterwards Henry Mencken was at his boob-baiting best in defending the author and Stuart Sherman was at his sentimental Puritan best in belaboring him, while neither was at too much pains to understand him.

The fact that a book of this character could cause such a commotion is ample proof of the need for it in pre-War America. With large tolerance and sympathy, and with a solemnity almost biblical, Theodore Dreiser pictures one of the thousands of American girls from poor, inadequate, often squalid, homes in small western towns and villages, going into Chicago to find work and buy her own bread to ease the burden at home. He knows Carrie Meeber because he has lived under the same roof with her, has seen her live this story, and has experienced many of her problems in his own person. Authenticity is written large across it. He follows her through the heartbreaking search for a job, through the devitalizing and degrading life in a sordid factory and a joyless boarding house, and the natural longing for companionship and recreation. He lets us feel the relentless approach of disaster because the income doesn't balance the outgo for bare subsistence, and the impersonal fashion in which she is stricken from the payroll when she is absent from work because she is sick. Why should she struggle on against certain defeat when young Mr. Drouet, the salesman whom she met on the train, is eager to give her a beautiful coat, a clean room, and social freedom.

That part of the story was not so new. It was in Victorian novels, in a slightly different form, the defenseless young milk-

maid inevitably falling victim to the nearest young lordling on
the first moonlit evening of the spring. But these novels as-
sumed complete individual responsibility for one's acts, and
demanded that sin be punished on the part of the girl not
later than on the last page, and earlier if expedient. But a close
and detached scrutiny of the way of the world as Theodore
Dreiser had observed it did not confirm the easy generalization
that righteousness brings rewards, and the tents of robbers
never prosper. North Chicago and the West Seventies of New
York were, until the depression, well equipped with apartments designed for the Caroline Meebers, as every sociologist
knows. Theodore Dreiser knew this as well as other men.
The trouble was, however, that on the last page of SISTER
CARRIE, the heroine, far from desolation in a New York gutter
as becomes a woman of unconventional behavior, is sitting in
her comfortable apartment, the toast of the town, a successful
actress.

One concession is made to poetic justice: the second man
disintegrates under the impact of his experiences in eloping
with Carrie from Chicago to New York, losing his position,
hunting work without success, relaxing his grip, and step by
step going down and out. But one does not exult as he does
when Iago is carried away to his doom or when Rasputin is
murdered. Hurstwood is not a villain. You pity him and his
helplessness in a world which proved too much for his powers
when he tried to seize one of its prizes.

The book seems restrained to us now. Any modern reader
coming to it by chance for the first time would wonder what
the outcry was all about. The language is tame but appropriate, the intimacies of sex are rigorously suppressed, and its
selection of detail is nearer George Eliot than Ernest Hemingway. It pleases us with its honesty and the natural manner in
which it unfolds. If it now leaves its audience undisturbed,
it is because the right of an author to his point of view was
confirmed by the struggle over this book.

We have already seen how the public mind had changed

in these matters in the first decade of the twentieth century. By 1911 it had altered so completely that the publication of JENNIE GERHARDT was accepted without controversy although it should have been more shocking to readers with 1900 attitudes than its predecessor. For Jennie is an unmarried mother, and even more frankly and faithfully a mistress than Carrie; and she compels a more affectionate sympathy because of her rare personal attractiveness. She is portrayed with an engaging tenderness, as though the author were saying, "See what inscrutable fate may do to the life of one lovely girl when it is concerned enough to move her helplessly about in unconventional patterns." An irresistible destiny broods over her from the moment she enters the old Neil House in Columbus, Ohio, to scrub the steps of the central stairway, until she faces her blank future after the death of Lester Kane, who deserted her to inherit his million and a half. She is the toy of Destiny, and its gradual unfolding disciplines the materials of this novel into a moving work of art. In tone and pace it is similar to SISTER CARRIE. In several chapters it is, in style and content, representative of some of the best writing Theodore Dreiser has done, and the best of these are his eloquent passages on the beauty and wonder of sex and motherhood even under the misfortunes which make Jennie's child illegitimate before the law.

Theodore Dreiser knew Jennie Gerhardt as intimately as he knew Caroline Meeber. He knew that she was a splendid girl, and that the evil which befell her was more a consequence of her station in life than a flaw in her character. The beautiful daughter of an impoverished charwoman unblessed with a charwoman mind had no defense against Senator Brander and the wealthy Lester Kane. She was in the position of the maid in the tower when Sir Lancelot rode by. But she could and did have character and nobility of soul within the sphere into which the fates had thrust her. No sacramented wife could have been more spiritually faithful than Jennie,

or could have held more loyal regard for her daughter, her
father, or the man she lived with.

Much of the conviction which the novel carries has its
source in actual life, as related in detail in DAWN. With slight
and unimportant modifications, the early part of the story is a
record of the Dreiser family. The Lutheran Gerhardt with his
hard condemnation of his daughter, driving her into the street,
is the Catholic Dreiser pictured in the autobiography. The
kindly, sympathetic, hard-working Mrs. Gerhardt is drawn
from life. So is Jennie's brother, and so is Jennie herself as
she accepts the generous and timely gift from the senator and
later and somewhat accidentally and helplessly becomes the
mother of his child. But Theodore Dreiser does not belong
to the impoverished group of autobiographical writers who
construct novels by detailing family secrets. He is autobiographical in the sense that the pity, the humanity, and the
understanding in his books are the precious fruit of having
lived spiritually with his materials.

Although SISTER CARRIE enjoys the distinction of being a
landmark in the creation of the American novel because of its
priority, JENNIE GERHARDT is an equally good book. It lacks
the masterful delineation of the collapse of Hurstwood beside
whom Lester Kane is without dimensions, but it has Jennie
and her family and the irresistible baby girl, and it has more
soul than the first novel. Its appeal to truth is so strong that it
could be put faithfully on the screen more than a score of
years after its publication, with Sylvia Sidney giving a first-
rate interpretation especially of the Jennie of the first half
of the story.

Theodore Dreiser had given up his editorship of the
Butterick publications for his personal writing. He now turned
from the materials of SISTER CARRIE and JENNIE GERHARDT to
plan "a trilogy of desire" which would exhibit one of the most
native of all our social phenomena—the rise to wealth and
power of the "rugged individualists" between the Civil and
the World Wars by following, in the exploiting of the public

domain, the superman's code: *I satisfy myself.* Only two of the novels have been published.

The subject-matter of THE FINANCIER and THE TITAN was congenial to the author. By a curious but entirely human inconsistency it embodied those values of wealth, power, ruthlessness, fight, display, and sensual indulgence which Theodore Dreiser both envied and condemned. One portion of himself, hurt by his own lack of self-assertion, by the deprivations, the ostracism, and the humiliation he had suffered as a boy, was too conscious of ability of some sort, too hungry for life and companionship, and too ambitious to rise from the morass not to genuflect before the successful Cowperwoods. The other part of his character which has grown steadily through the years in its passion for justice and mercy and has commanded admiration throughout the world was outraged by the system which permitted Schenley Park to rest on the broken backs of the slaves in the mills below Mt. Washington, shot them down when they resisted, and muzzled the press which might have reported it. This side of Theodore Dreiser and the reluctance of modern authors to write directly of the things they admire, must be held in mind while one reads the story of Frank Algernon Cowperwood, utility magnate of Philadelphia, Chicago, and New York. For the author has not written explicitly in the reforming spirit; he has entered into the character and the motives of Cowperwood and the corrupt system of which he was a part, and he has presented both with conviction. For the novel it is the better method.

Theodore Dreiser came to the composition of THE FINANCIER and THE TITAN under the compulsion of observed fact. His motive for creation is not to be confused with that which lay behind many of the "naturalistic" novels of the period. Much of the early naturalistic fiction, as written, for example, by the young Frank Norris and Jack London, was fashioned to illustrate a thesis derived from Darwin and others to the effect that under the veneer of cultivation man carries a brute in his breast and that only the ruthless endure. The young authors invented the iron man devoid of sentiment or pity, believing, if he thought at all, that might makes right, six feet tall and with enormous fists, bristling with muscle and brutish energy, and trampling the corpses of the weaklings. This type of superman bruises his way through many of the earlier and now successfully dead novels like VANDOVER AND THE BRUTE.

Theodore Dreiser did not write THE FINANCIER and THE TITAN because he thought it would be entertaining to construct exhibits to illustrate an idea he had caught from Nietzsche that one should be *hard,* or from Spencer that the appropriateness of conduct is to be measured by its aid toward self-preservation, or from Huxley that men succeed by virtue of their jungle heritage exercised without compunction. Instead of inventing a story about a blond beast sailing the seven seas, he collected with painstaking accuracy the record of the traction magnate, Charles T. Yerkes of Philadelphia and Chicago, and unraveled the methods of intrigue, bribery, and machination by which he and his tribe seized and held their power in democratic and free American cities.

THE FINANCIER and THE TITAN are the results of this research, touched into life by passing through the creative spirit of the author. They are not so alive as AN AMERICAN TRAGEDY because the background is too great and the details of sharp business deals are too bulky to be fully dominated by the human characters who manipulate them. The methods of the stock market, the formation of pools to fleece the uninformed, the whole sorry Wall Street mess, the powerful ring of politicians in control of the public funds and in league with the financiers—it is these matters which compel attention in this unfinished trilogy.

In THE FINANCIER, Theodore Dreiser presents Cowperwood and his career in Philadelphia down to the panic of 1873. The reader is immediately taken in by the atmosphere of authenticity on the first page, documented as it is with the population of the city, methods of transportation, the salary of H. W. Cowperwood, the kind of house he occupied, the street he lived in, and what he looked like. The boy Frank quickly emerges and begins to offer unmistakable evidence of his genius for finance by a very grown-up deal in castile soap which profits him almost one hundred per cent. Unimpeded by Christian ethics, he rises rapidly and concentrates all his energy on money-making. We follow him as he climbs from a post with a grain and commission house into a place of responsibility with a bank and a brokerage firm, then into the note-brokerage business for himself in time to take full advantage of the financial uncertainties of the Civil War. He branches out into street-railway securities and forces his way into the ring of politicians and the fat graft they are taking from the city by using its money at a nominal interest or at none. Cowperwood, aged thirty-four and worth in excess of two and a half millions, has all of his plans laid to become the richest man in America when the Chicago fire of 1871 produces a panic which practically cleans him out. But he goes down largely because the city treasurer is without courage or audacity, and superman Cowperwood is made vulnerable by the weakness of squid Stener. One of the best passages in the novel is the part which contrasts the two men in the moment of crisis. The weakness of Stener lands them both in jail on a technicality because the politicians, who have for years played the game by the same rules, want to be rid of their powerful and shrewd rival.

Cowperwood is important enough to avoid the extreme unpleasantness of prison life. He has visitors, carries on his business in a small way, and is pardoned after thirteen months, just in time to grab a fortune by selling short in the panic of 1873. He immediately removes to Chicago in time to gather in another fortune by manipulating the public utilities of that city. How this was accomplished is the story of THE TITAN.

He became partner to an old Chicago broker who knew his way about, outwitted the Chicago utility magnate by securing, with generous bribes, franchises for gas in the suburbs, and finally sold out to his startled rivals at his own price.

With that deal closed, he began his long and corrupt fight to control the street railways of Chicago. The story of that struggle and how its ramifications touched banks, newspapers, councilmen, legislators, mayors, governors, and how Cowperwood was finally defeated in his drive for a fifty-year franchise, forms the substance of the novel.

Theodore Dreiser was among the first to see the importance of the epic and the possibilities for a great fiction in the life story of these titans among us who held the country in their fists from the Civil War through the 1920 boom period.

These business activities are paralleled by the domestic affairs and the private intrigues of the superman of business. Cowperwood grew tired of his prudish wife and had a secret affair with the devoted and passionate Aileen Butler, beautiful daughter of a wealthy contractor and politician. He maintained a fashionable house of assignation for her in the approved manner, but they were seen, reported, and Mr. Butler had them shadowed, also in the familiar mode. The disclosure came at the time of the panic of 1871 and motivated Mr. Butler to deny the aid to Cowperwood which would have saved him from prison.

In THE TITAN, Cowperwood is divorced and married to Aileen. But the scandal excludes them from Chicago society. Cowperwood soon becomes promiscuous again and there is a long procession of mistresses, including wives of artists and bankers, actresses, stenographers, and finally the young daughter of a "Mrs. Warren" of Louisville and New York. As in THE FINANCIER, the anger against him incited by these philanderings helps to effect his final defeat, although the facts are left to speak for themselves and the author points no moral. Rather, when he steps forth to comment, it is in this vein: "How shall we explain these subtleties of temperament and desire? Life has to deal with them at every turn. They will not down. . . . We see much punishment in the form of jails, diseases, failures, and wrecks; but we also see that the old tendency is not visibly lessened. Is there no law outside of the subtle will and power of the individual to achieve? If not, it is surely high time that we knew it—one and all. We might then agree to do as we do; but there would be no silly illusion as to divine regulation."

He does indicate the bent of his own mind by binding THE FINANCIER together with a symbolic prologue and epilogue drawn from biology after the fashion of the naturalists who believe in appetitive motivation of conduct and the survival of the strong. The first is the celebrated episode of the armored lobster slowly devouring the vulnerable squid placed in its tank in a downtown window, teaching the young boy that in this world creatures prey upon one another and the victory is not to the feeble. The epilogue, less famous but more exact in its analogy, describes the black grouper whom an all-wise Providence has endowed with an uncanny knack of deceit by changing its color from black to white, from earthy brown to watery green, and destroying its unsuspecting victims by virtue of its simulation. All those who remember the October days of 1929 have had occasion to appreciate the analogy. Whether we like the figure is beside the point. The author refused to permit a wishful humanism, which would make men good by the act of desiring it, to blind his appraisal of the ruthless exploiters. And as a matter of fact, the Cowperwoods were the lobsters to the squids of the municipalities in the 1870's, precisely as the Insulls, the Harrimans, and the "Ohio gang" were the black groupers of the 1920's. It is not helpful criticism to patronize the novelist by giving him a label and discovering that philosophers and scientists have also observed human conduct. And it is equally irrelevant to berate him for not using the novel as a direct instrument for reform.

THE "GENIUS" (1915 and 1923) and AN AMERICAN TRAGEDY (1925) are both long and intricately detailed novels, each running to only a little less than four hundred thousand words. Whereas the first two novels were concerned with poor girls and their unconventional careers, and the next two dealt with the superman of business, these are studies of two Ameri-

can weaklings who are crushed under by the same forces which
Carrie uses and Cowperwood dominates. Both Eugene Witla
and Clyde Griffiths are victims of social maladjustment and
their own weakness of character. And society is not without
responsibility for a share in creating this weakness and its
consequence. Theodore Dreiser does not say that in straight
words; he shows it by letting the facts speak their own conviction in their own way.

THE "GENIUS" is a careful study of the character of Eugene
Witla and its effect upon his career. In certain details at least
it is quite frankly autobiographical. Eugene's experiences on a
Chicago newspaper, his social relations, his intellectual awakening after reading Spencer's FIRST PRINCIPLES, his migration
to New York City, his attacks of ill health, his marriage: all
these things have been declared personal experiences in the
published autobiographies; and the letter which Ruby sends
to Eugene is reprinted with slight variations in A BOOK ABOUT
MYSELF from "Alice" to "Theo." These observations are unimportant except as they tend to confirm the impression of truth
made by this book which had to fight like SISTER CARRIE for
its right to be heard.

Eugene Witla is a talented boy living in a small Illinois
town in the 1880's. His retiring manner, his pride, sensitivity,
and artistic moods set him apart from other boys. He develops
an ability to draw and paint, goes to Chicago, makes good
there, and sets out for New York, leaving behind him some
emotional ties and obligations—in particular with Angela
Blue, an inhibited girl five years older than he for whom he
has a curious attachment and to whom he is engaged. In New
York he mingles with the art crowd, does good, strong work,
has a measure of success and great promise, several engage-
ments with women, and finally, from a sense of duty, marries
Angela and brings her to New York. She does not fit in,
either then or later, and that makes for unhappiness. They
have a journey to Paris, then a struggle with poverty and ill
health, and a slow and miserable ascent to prosperity with

Eugene's amours adding complications. He begins to make his way to the top in the publishing business, commands a salary of $25,000, lives well, moves in clever society, and is a respected and envied success. But as he nears forty he goes crazy over a nineteen-year-old society girl, Suzanne Dale, and wrecks his home and career by the blind and blundering manner in which he pursues her. Angela dies in childbirth, Suzanne is carried away by her mother, and Eugene, bereft of his position, goes in for Christian Science and finally for his daughter and his art. The story of his pursuit of Suzanne fills the last third of the book and is in itself a novel with swift action, violent passions, and a plot.

THE "GENIUS" is full of an astonishing variety of living people, from the workmen in a carpenter shop to the wealthy Colfax. The triumph of the book is its portrayal with equal understanding and justice of the two unhappy people, Eugene and Angela: Angela with her admirable virtues of devotion and practical management, her unfortunate failure to understand the complicated subtleties of sex and its part in Eugene's temperament, and her attempts to bind him with too sharp a tongue; Eugene with his unstable emotions, his promiscuities, his cruelties and weaknesses, and yet with his tenderness, charm, a passion for creation, and like Shelley an unfulfilled longing for the ideal in the beauty of a young woman. There are many great passages on art, the thrill of successful accomplishment and recognition, the irritations of failure and low energy; and on the heart-tearing antipathies of these two personalities bound together in marriage. The quarrel scenes are good, and they bear out the analogy of the protozoa which remain unmoved by the presence of certain bacteria but instantly and instinctively let fly a dart for the victim when one specific genus comes near.

Superman Cowperwood got away with his conquests, but indecisive Witla pays a heavy price for his folly, his weakness, and his will to sin. But Theodore Dreiser is more concerned with the mystifying fact that, in the face of the known penalties which may crush and destroy them for their misdeeds, there are always people like Eugene Witla who by a perverse fatality go straight ahead and take the plunge. Nothing seems to deter them—neither warning, nor exhortation, nor the fate of others. For some reason the prisons are always full from generation to generation and the tabloids are never without front-page sensations. Theodore Dreiser wonders why that is, and has come to the conclusion that a subtle disturbance in their constitution becomes a "chemic compulsion" which drives them outside of the conventional mold. The fact is incontrovertible, and the explanation as plausible perhaps as any.

These four novels had come one after another on a wave of great creative energy from 1911 to 1915. He devoted the next decade to less demanding composition while the critics divided into camps and fought over him. Then in 1925, having gathered together all his mature powers, he published AN AMERICAN TRAGEDY. By any standard it is the greatest and most powerful novel yet written by any American, and it stands beside BUDDENBROOKS, THE FORSYTE SAGA, and OF HUMAN BONDAGE as among the best in world fiction in our time.

It tells the story of no superman and no genius but of an inconspicuous, weak, ignorant American boy, Clyde Griffiths, who represents thousands lost and unfriended in an indifferent republic. He aspires to those values which are held before American schoolboys when they are urged to go to college because it will mean a social fraternity and so many dollars more in wages each week. He wants to share in the ease and luxury of the life flaunted before him and be the companion of the lovely and cultivated girls of the smart set so charmingly at leisure in their motor cars and their country clubs. But unfortunately he had no choice of station when he was born, and when he came to consciousness he was the humiliated son of a fanatical religionist preaching on a street corner. He was in poverty and ignorance, but he revolted blindly from the life of his parents. He begins the long pilgrimage to defeat from a job in a drug store, to being a bellhop in a Kansas City hotel where he glimpses one corner of life, gets involved in an accident and runs away to a job in the Union League Club of Chicago, meets his uncle who owns a factory in Lycurgus, New York, and goes there to take a job. He has dreams of being received into the circle of his uncle, which overpowers him with its luxury, its cultivation and its charm. But those doors do not open to him. He labors in undershirt and trousers at the shrinking rack, and gradually rises to become a department head with authority over twenty-five working girls, all of the mating age but shut away in this factory to earn their bread.

The disappointments, the bitter loneliness, the sex hunger and the longing for companionship drive him and Roberta Alden, one of the girls, into a clandestine affair, since there is no provision for a decent social life for these underprivileged youth, and no guidance or understanding. There are only harsh and unwise prohibitions. Their training is so inadequate, their social and sex ignorance so abysmal, that they are soon in desperate straits because of Roberta's pregnancy.

But Clyde has found a partial acceptance in the fine society for which he longs, and has fallen madly in love with the beautiful Sondra Finchley. The promise of having so exquisite a girl for himself, so superior to the uncultivated Roberta, enthralls him, and when he learns that he is trapped by paternity, his weak soul is thrown into a panic. Torn by a sense of loyalty to Roberta, bewildered by his ignorance and powerlessness, and at the same time determined not to lose the fascinating Sondra, Clyde wanders about in a daze of planning and scheming which finally leads him to attempt the murder of Roberta by upsetting the boat. His nerve fails at the climax, but accident accomplishes the end and the girl is drowned. Clyde is arrested, tried in the usual atmosphere of sensationalism, and condemned to die in the electric chair. The story of his crime, the masterly presentation of the conflict within him, and the whole atmosphere of pity and terror which surrounds him are unsurpassed in the American novel.

The best of Theodore Dreiser is in this book. It is an epic of one important aspect of American life, its crass materialism, its indifference to all that is not glitter and show, its irresponsibility for the youth, its condemnations instead of understanding, its thirst for punishment instead of prevention, its hypocrisy, its ruthless savagery, and the ferocity of its mobs and courts of prosecution. There is less naturalistic detachment and more of the fire and the brooding pity for men who live with such impoverished ideals. It is indictment without malice, informed with the same spirit which enables him to accept with compassion instead of anger the treatment he himself received in the Harlan district. The fact that the novel was based on an actual occurrence, that many of the characters were drawn from the life, and that it appeared at the time the Leopold-Loeb crime held the suspense of the nation, testifies to its nativity and the appropriateness of its title.

It was an international success. In the opinion of H. R. Lenormond, speaking for his countrymen in the *Saturday Review* for October 27, 1934, the acclaim of AN AMERICAN TRAGEDY was "the result of the creative power of the novelist, which has given life to characters who take their place in the portrait gallery of fiction with those of Balzac, Flaubert, and Dostoievsky. Those French readers who respond to the atmosphere and the artistry of a novel, to its ideological extensions, enter into the drama of fatality in *An American Tragedy* as into that of a Greek tragedy. Puritanism and religious fanaticism, projected as the instruments of individual destruction, and as forces of dissolution which menace a people, are tragic elements to which we in France respond strongly. The emotional impact that was produced by *The Scarlet Letter* was enough to make predictable the success of *An American Tragedy*."

As to the style of Theodore Dreiser, it has become a fashionable commonplace to say that it is crude. And too much has been made of the obvious point that his sentences are without the polish of Walter Pater. His style often is unpolished, but he often writes beautifully. There is a rugged strength about it which seems appropriate to the matter and the mood. If one cares for his work, one accepts his style and wonders seriously whether a different or more finished cadence would not rob it of its striking power. When an American novelist writes more movingly and with greater strength in a more distinguished prose style, the controversy might take on a meaning.

The source of the objection to the work of Theodore Dreiser was the kind of life he pictured and the detached and skeptical attitude toward sinners and their punishment. The Puritans were against him because they wished to have their literature affirm the moral law that sin is always punished and righteousness rewarded. But Theodore Dreiser believed, along with the author of JOB, that a careful scrutiny of life as one sees it lived fails to place this rule beyond controversy. Some men do suffer for their misdeeds, and no writer has pictured the disastrous consequences of evil more movingly than Theodore Dreiser. Hurstwood wasted away in a flop house because his character collapsed through larceny and personal immorality. Frank Cowperwood went to prison for his turpitude in seducing Aileen Butler and embezzling $60,000 from the city treasury. With prompt severity the state punished Clyde Griffiths for his weak-kneed murder of Roberta. But the sad experiences of these characters are not due to an immutable moral law which exacts revenge. While they are suffering their deserts, others equally culpable are at liberty. This is the disturbing element in the Dreiser novels. Cowperwood loses his fortune and goes to prison because Butler, the contractor and politician, and some of the party leaders find it highly expedient to send him there. He was no whit different from the other business men who were not molested; he was the sacrifice. And when it is again expedient to release him, the governor signs the pardon. These characters suffer, but it is a chance that overtakes them, and it falls only upon the few. The effect therefore is to challenge and not assert the moral law. "Wherefore do the wicked live, become old, yea, are mighty in power?" The punishment which a few undergo is set by those no better than their victims, and the great power which forms and dissolves the subtle chemistry of transitory man fails to take any notice of either the judges or the judged.

The controversies which raged after Stuart P. Sherman published ON CONTEMPORARY LITERATURE in 1917 have died. Only an occasional echo is now heard. And as the years have passed and the position of Theodore Dreiser in the creation of the modern American novel has become clearly established, less importance is attached to these philosophical considerations. His work lives, and he is a major figure because he has created a gallery of living people who represent the age of which he was and is a part, and because he has portrayed them with honesty and compassion.

Chapter Five

WILLA CATHER AND THE SHIFTING MOODS

*T*HEODORE DREISER, like Sinclair Lewis, Sherwood Anderson, and a few others, has been so sure of himself and of his point of view that he has not been swerved by the variety of doctrines and changes of mood which have made up the complex spectacle of our national life. Other gifted writers have not been so rigid. Some have been quite sensitive to the unstable winds of a restless age in revolt, and their work reflects the diverse pressures to which it has been exposed. Zona Gale (1874) is an illustration. When it was the fashion to see only the Christian sweetness of rural souls panting with benevolence, she offered FRIENDSHIP VILLAGE (1908). But, alert to the changes affecting the land, she corrected that sentimental portrait during the years when novelists were taking on more honesty in observation. BIRTH (1918) leaves few illusions as to the power of a small town to misshape the little lives of Marshall Pitt, the traveling man and newspaper owner of Burage, Wisconsin, and of his sorry village wife. MISS LULU BETT (1920) completed the exposure. It came on the crest of the debunking wave which lifted MAIN STREET into its fame. As a play, it received the Pulitzer award for drama in 1921, curiously enough in the same year that the Sherman-Garland-Lovett-committee selection of MAIN STREET was nullified by the Columbia authorities in favor of THE AGE OF INNOCENCE. Zona Gale to her credit as a novelist, had shifted with her times and she continues to be *au courant*.

Booth Tarkington (1869), also a Pulitzer-crowned novelist (THE MAGNIFICENT AMBERSONS, 1918, and ALICE ADAMS, 1921), and one who was enormously popular while the American novel was being created, was always in the current. His work followed the curve of fashion from the day of costumes and rosemary (MONSIEUR BEAUCAIRE, 1900), through the turmoil of industrial change and social unrest (THE TURMOIL, 1915), into the more stringent realism of the early twenties, tapering off toward romance again as the realistic tide began to ebb with the 1930's.

Willa Cather is the strongest of these novelists who have been in the movements, developing with their times rather than influencing them or dominating them. Her work is firm and finely wrought in one of the most satisfactory prose styles for pure clarity and precision in contemporary use; it is at the opposite pole from Sherwood Anderson's quivering and passionate sentences. Her novels have grown steadily in popular favor, and the publication of SHADOWS ON THE ROCK in the summer of 1931 was an occasion for universal homage. She had comforted the hearts of millions who revered her because she had written a realism which could be read in schools and women's clubs where Theodore Dreiser and Sherwood Anderson would have caused a panic. That is, she was a fine novelist who did not attack too strongly or disturb the minds of the nice people too deeply. She is an important figure in the creation of the American novel.

It is idle to try to classify her neatly as a realist, or a "novelist of character," or as one who went "beyond naturalism," as a satirist or a romanticist. She is all of these things. She is Willa Cather, mobile, capable, sometimes great, always clear-cut, and most of the time interesting, a social commentator whose pen is never sharp enough to hurt anybody, and whose vision is frequently inspiring. In her court the human race is acquitted of the most serious charges against it and given a character. It is very grateful for it, being in sore need.

She is one of the few distinguished contemporary novelists who could write of Mid-Western life in a realistic mode without scorning its shabby inadequacies. The reason is perfectly

clear and most important to an understanding of the development of our fiction. She was not hurt by her own Western
environment. Neither was Dorothy Canfield. Most of our
writers were. Consider the wounds inflicted on Theodore
Dreiser, the humiliations forced upon Sherwood Anderson,
the barrenness of Minnesota to Sinclair Lewis, the struggle
with poverty and oppression which Floyd Dell waged; extend
the list and observe the effect upon their writings in the period
under the dominance of realism. While they were struggling
desperately in the pit along with many millions of our citizens
and fighting toward an understanding of the conflict and a
fuller life, Willa Cather had the good fortune to be able to
ride her own pony among the alien settlers in Nebraska,
watching them make bread and churn butter after their native
customs, chatting with children and housewives, and then at
her pleasure riding home in happy excitement as the prairie
grass waved under the evening wind. She was a well-placed
spectator and not one of the victims of the poverty and grinding toil which was the portion of the Shimerdas. One does not
normally build up a satirical or even a bitter emotional response to life under such tutelage. It is good to have among us
an author of such distinction who has been able honestly to
preserve some of the illusions of human nobility.

A few points about her life are necessary to an understanding of her work. Born in Virginia in 1875 she went to
Nebraska in the 1880's when she was eight years old. It is the
right age for transplanting a sensitive, impressionable child,
and the contrast between the northern corner of Virginia and
the southern edge of central Nebraska is sufficiently bold. It
stimulated her. She has left her own reports of the intense
excitement aroused in her by the open prairie and the lives
of the immigrant pioneers in that neighborhood. Her impressions were sharp, her emotions were easily enlisted, and she
had the Wordsworthian trait of living in the memory of experiences already complete. Ten years of this intense absorption of the life about her supplied her with most of the ma-

terials out of which she built the novels. Unlike Theodore
Dreiser, Sherwood Anderson, or Sinclair Lewis, she has returned again and again through the years to renew the scenes
of her early life and to capture anew the feel of the mesas in
vacation journeys to the Southwest. She has cultivated a natural love for the people and the places of which she writes
instead of protest and rebellion.

From this somewhat romantic childhood she went to the
university. Her generation of women was the first in all history to escape with public approval and support from woman's
hallowed place in the kitchen and the bedroom to the great
world of affairs. Their lives ran in a new but conventionalized
pattern from the universities to the newspaper offices to the
writing of novels or plays or both: Susan Glaspell from Drake
University to the Des Moines Daily News, Edna Ferber without benefit of college to the Milwaukee Journal and Chicago
Tribune, Zona Gale from the University of Wisconsin to the
New York World, Fannie Hurst from Washington University to the St. Louis newspapers. There were a few who eschewed the newspaper period for some other interlude:
Dorothy Canfield from Ohio State University to a Ph. D.
degree and a New England farm; Elizabeth Madox Roberts
from the University of Chicago to loneliness in New York;
Gertrude Stein from Radcliffe and Johns Hopkins to Paris;
Ruth Suckow from Grinnell and the University of Denver to
school-teaching and apiculture. Willa Cather went from the
University of Nebraska to the Pittsburgh Daily Leader, to the
English department of the Allegheny High School, to Mc-
Clure's Magazine in 1906, and then after 1912 she freed herself from distractions and began to create her novels. It was a
good training to follow her Nebraska girlhood and bring out
from it the moments of significance. Beginning with ALEXAN-
DER's BRIDGE in 1912 at the very moment when the creative
spirit was seizing America to produce a new poetry, drama
and fiction, she published in twenty years ten novels, all save
the first and the last in some way concerned with the West

she had known: O PIONEERS! (1913), THE SONG OF THE LARK (1915), MY ÁNTONIA (1918), ONE OF OURS (1922), A LOST LADY (1923), THE PROFESSOR'S HOUSE (1925), MY MORTAL ENEMY (1926), DEATH COMES FOR THE ARCHBISHOP (1927), SHADOWS ON THE ROCK (1931).

ALEXANDER'S BRIDGE was derivative but promising. It tried to study the problem of middle-aged Bartley Alexander, a bridge-building engineer, about whom the managing editor of McClure's could know very little. It also called in part upon a London background outside of the author's experience. She attempted a symbolism in which the flaw in the bridge represents the weakness in the character of Alexander caught between the old duality of abandon and restraint as the way to the good life. Willa Cather was no more satisfied with it than were her few readers. But among her audience was one both interested and able to offer advice, Sarah Orne Jewett.

Sarah Orne Jewett took the risk of telling Willa Cather to be herself, to develop her own bent and not to follow after her literary models, to write of the things she really knew and tell the truth about them. She was grateful for the advice, and what is more, she was so free from conceit as to act upon it, and so generous in spirit as to do public honor to her mistress. In her second novel she went back to the windy Nebraska table-land and its Swedish pioneers for more native materials, and she wrote it "truthfully and simply" for Sarah Orne Jewett, to whom it was dedicated. It was quietly issued in midsummer, 1913, without attracting public attention away from V. V.'s EYES and THE HEART OF THE HILLS. Cautiously, after its manner, the Nation ventured to say, "The familiar matter of 'rural tragedy' is here. Whether its detail is dwelt upon too ruthlessly is a question which readers will decide according to temperament and individual taste." The truth was incontrovertible, but the readers were few.

The novel stated the theme which was to occupy Willa Cather for six years: how vision and strength of character in gifted Western girls of pioneering immigrant families triumphed over severe hardships and won success. In o pioneers! she was Alexandra Bergson of a strongly hostile section of Nebraska. Her father dies at the opening of the novel and leaves the farm, as well as his wife and three sons, in the capable hands of Alexandra of the beautiful hair. It is a wild and a bitter land which these foreign tailors and joiners and shipbuilders have challenged. They are little and without strength before the vastness of the prairies. The malicious spirit of the grassland destroys their cattle with blizzards, their hogs with cholera, their horses with snake bites and broken legs in prairie-dog holes, and often cuts off the people themselves in the prime of their years. Many surrender and return to the soft ways of the cities. But Alexandra persuades her brothers not to sell but to buy more land against confidence in the future. The author foreshadows the rewards to come from this faith by a sentimentalism wherein the great spirit of the unfriendly soil bends a little before Alexandra's love and yearning and her indomitable will. The rewarding fruit of this vision is the transformation of the wild land into the prosperous countryside with telephone wires, white roads, gayly painted farm houses, red barns with gilded weather-cocks, still windmills, and mile-long furrows in the squares of corn. And to Alexandra's material success which is beginning to appear barren in itself there is added in the last chapter the emotional fulfillment of which she has dreamed with Carl Lindstrum.

A theme of minor interest is the fatalistic acceptance of the tragedy in which Frank Shabata shoots his beautiful wife Marie and Alexandra's beloved youngest brother, Emil, when he finds them dreaming in each other's arms in the tall grass like two enchanted children. Marie was simply too beautiful for this world, and helplessly and innocently she brought destruction upon herself and others because of an excess of loveliness. Emil and Marie could not escape their destiny; and "being what he was, she felt, Frank could not have acted otherwise." The idea is repeated in the song of the lark:

"There was certainly no kindly Providence that directed one's life. . . . One's life was at the mercy of blind chance." That was the philosophy which goaded the watchers in the books of Theodore Dreiser.

The book is important only in the perspective of its author's career. It is a story of the open spaces, as so much of Willa Cather's writing is. Through it one sees the observing girl on horseback among the picturesque foreign groups, visiting the mentally unbalanced Russian, attending weddings and funerals among the Bohemians and the Czechs; and from its simple pages there emerges a sharp sense of the land of badger holes, of lagoons and red grass, of golden coreopsis in clear water, the whirr of wild ducks' wings, the smell of hay fields, the lark songs in the vast silence and blue depths of sky.

In THE SONG OF THE LARK Alexandra Bergson becomes Thea Kronborg, and she concentrates the full force of her character in the struggle to conquer and subdue the equally difficult and hostile world of art. Her career, which begins in the home of a poor Swedish minister in Colorado and rises at last to operatic success, is unfolded in minute detail, swelling the novel to considerably more than twice the length of O PIONEERS! Everything is closely documented after the technique of modern realism, and the same attention is given to the stark incidents of the fine old drunken musician Wunsch chopping down the Kohlers' dove cote as to Thea's struggle toward success. It is the longest and most ambitious of Willa Cather's works, and it achieved the astounding miracle of pleasing both Henry Mencken and Stuart Sherman.

As the author explains at the end of the book, she is concerned with the forces which have beaten upon the soul of a girl with an artistic gift and the manner in which she brought her powers to fruition in art through a long and severe discipline. It was Alexandra Bergson's fate always "to be surrounded by little men." Thea Kronborg was more fortunate. But while Wunsch and Ray Kennedy and Dr. Archie and Harsanyi and Fred Ottenburg were able to aid her to self-knowledge, it was her own potentialities which exalted her, and these she had to cherish from within herself. They lifted her as rapidly as her unfolding instincts could permit out of the commonplace, petty, in some respects revolting environment of Moonstone, Colorado. And the date of the book being 1915, there is no satire on the dingy life, but an emotional response to the sand dunes and the prickly-pear blossoms and the afternoon sun on the grape leaves.

It is in this book that Willa Cather first indulged her fancy for the land of the Cliff-Dwellers to which she often returned in the later novels. The use she makes of it is noteworthy. After two years in Chicago, not without their drabness, Thea reached something resembling a crisis. It corresponds to the period in Alexandra's life when the drought was driving the unimaginative from the Nebraska table-lands, and she went down to the river farms to clarify her purposes. The restorative which Thea finds is in kind and in effect the same. She visits the dead cities among the cliffs of Panther Canyon, where under the spell of the ruins and the silent testimony of a forgotten race she fortifies her vision of the power and importance of art. It is symbolized for her by the timid lives of the swallows confined by the echoing cliffs and never daring "to rise out of the shadow of the canyon walls"; by the rude pottery of the Indian women designed to hold water in the dry rocks, which suggests to Thea the thought that art is simply "an effort to make a sheath, a mold in which to imprison for a moment the shining, elusive element which is life," and her voice has the same function as the pottery. Toward the end of her days in this country, there appears the symbol of the eagle who came sailing for a moment into the gulf between the canyon walls and then went soaring out again and up until his plumage became golden in the light; he signified to her the continuous, undying desire for achievement in art. Like him she should soar from the timid and commonplace lives of swallows and prosaic people in Colorado desert villages to the "disciplined en-

deavor" which dignified her life and made supportable her
sorrows.

Alexandra became a successful farmer and business
woman at the sacrifice of her personal emotional life whose
barrenness often depressed her. Thea paid the same price for
her career. In MY ÁNTONIA, Ántonia Shimerda, the third of
these foreign girls, became the symbol of emotional fulfillment in motherhood on a Western farm. The thesis was
arresting, appearing as it did in 1918 at the very moment
when farm and village life was coming under the critical eyes
of the novelists intent upon exposing its pollution. Without
satire or bitterness, and with only a little sentimentalism,
Willa Cather pictured a strong character developing under
severe difficulties which would crush a less heroic soul, surviving the most primitive hardships in a sod hut, toiling like
an ox in the field with the men, enduring want, cut off from
ordinary pleasures, withstanding betrayal and the cheap life
as a hired girl in a village, and emerging at last from such
desperate conditions to a triumphant serenity as mother to
a healthy group of shy, awkward but happy and laughing
boys who are content with their life on the farm.

Ántonia is the kind of mother to the race of whom Walt
Whitman dreamed. She belongs to another breed and another
age from Carol Kennicott, of MAIN STREET. These two heroines
measure the extremes in the disrupted modern age. When
comparing them, one should remember that Carol went to
college and was educated for a metropolitan culture which
embraced the plays of Schnitzler and made Main Street a
prison to her, whereas Ántonia's nature and experience led
naturally to the farm. She is one of the few heroines in
modern fiction untouched by the longing for escape and social
advancement. It is this self-reliant spirit of Ántonia, serene
through long contact with the soil, which gives the novel its
dignity and makes it unique in this period in the creation of
the American novel.

For the country was rapidly moving toward the 1920's

and into a mood quite different from this romantic spirit among realistic details of immigrant life in the Nebraska of the 1880's. Willa Cather was affected by it, and after a four-year interval of transition she joined the procession and published ONE OF OURS (1922). It was a clear indication that no serious artist could long remain blind to the suppressions of American life. One might in a week's journey come upon an isolated Ántonia, but the unhappy Claude Wheelers were to be found on every farm. The fact that in ONE OF OURS Willa Cather chose to study an American family instead of a foreign one may be only incidental, but at any rate the hero is devoid of the strength of character and the will by which the three non-American heroines "live out their potentialities." The heroism of the people had according to Willa Cather passed with the development of the frontier. The fine promise of a noble race of men on the prairie was not realized. The author of the three novels of virtue triumphant now wrote three more on the theme of the frustration and defeat of American characters. In each case the subject of the study is sensitive and gifted, but unable to dominate the adverse pressures of his environment. They are as diverse as a Nebraska farm boy, a cultivated woman of social position and wealth, and a college professor, but they are all crushed by the shallow views and the vulgarity of the life into which they are thrust.

Claude Wheeler, the farm boy in ONE OF OURS, is tormented with glimpses of a fuller life of cultivation and refinement. The grinding toil grows more unbearable and sharpens his longing for escape. But he is quite unable to escape from the blind conventions of his clod-visioned father, who forces him to leave the university after a brief awakening. He is caught in the joyless, cramping religious bigotry of ignorant Americans. All potential greatness is squeezed out of him by the brute struggle for animal existence and by lack of recognition and cultural surroundings. The frigid and cramped soul who shut the door against him on their wedding night is only the final contrast with the noble heroines of the earlier novels. The author, however, seems incompletely aware of the ironic pathos of Claude's futile death in the glorious War of 1914-1918.

It was not a remarkable novel but it received the Pulitzer award of the year 1923, and Willa Cather became popular. She continued the theme of the day in a study of the disintegration of Mrs. Marian Forrester in A LOST LADY. It is a brief, closely knit psychological study of what seems to be the tragedy of a woman who cannot retain her fastidiousness and refinement when deprived of the background of wealth and ease. Captain Forrester has the old nobility of character which survives all hardship and reverses. His pretty wife is quickly vulgarized by the crude younger generation. The absence of the stalwart virtues in Mrs. Forrester's character leaves the title open to serious objection. But she is broken by comparative poverty and boredom in a small village, and she is lost as the symbol of beauty and feminine exquisiteness to the disillusioned boy, Neil Herbert, who had adored the image. To see it degraded by the lust of a vulgarian like Ivy Peters was tragedy. Willa Cather weaves into the story a sense of loveliness passed away, and poses Marian Forrester as the lost generation between the pioneers who once were great and their sons and grandsons whose age is vulgar and stultifying.

And for the third time she returned to that theme in 1925, in the very height of its fashion, in THE PROFESSOR'S HOUSE. Professor St. Peter finds the passing years are growing more barren of satisfaction instead of expanding with his years and powers. They have brought frustration and suppression of soul. Willa Cather saw the way the modern world was splitting the souls of men, and the two houses symbolize the disunion. One house is up to date with cheap devices, and its atmosphere is as shallow as the professor's stupid wife and silly daughters. The other is old-fashioned and inconvenient, but rich in the memory of good living. The professor's life is confronted with the same contradiction. One side of it is trapped in the new house and stifled by the sterile social concerns of the faculty wives. The other struggles to exist in its artist dream of Spanish adventurers, and the romance of Tom Outland. Even that long short story attempts to reinforce the duality by setting the adventures of this unusual boy in the cliff cities of the old Southwest and his idealized death over against the gaudy pleasures of his fiancée. Something precious has gone out of the world, and out of Professor St. Peter's life. Even a casual suicide is denied him. He must resign himself to the life without joy which is the reward a dull and mechanized age has reserved for its creators.

Willa Cather was once more at dead end. She was not born to chronicle the life of an ordinary man at hard grips with the conditions which oppressed and threatened his life. Her contribution to the subject in these novels was not robust but delicate and fragile and on the side lines. Not one of them was completely satisfying, and only A LOST LADY was closely knit and artistically constructed. Although her great popularity was established in those years, her readers began to look back to THE SONG OF THE LARK and particularly to MY ÁNTONIA as the best of her work. Clearly to the disinterested eye, her strength was not in the defeatist or satirical mood of the modern temper. It was in a not too sentimental brooding over the past, and in the illusion that there were giants in those days. From the moment she penned the first section of O PIONEERS! she was by nature and by the quality of her talent pointed toward the escape from an unflinching realism which she could not fully and honestly confront into the imaginary world of heroic Archbishops. It is quite evident that the early 1920's were a homeless interlude between the pioneering days in Nebraska and the rocks of old Quebec.

DEATH COMES FOR THE ARCHBISHOP was the novel of transition. In the magic land of the Southwest, among placid Indians and adobe houses, and all the physical exoticism of that country which has justly fascinated Willa Cather, two gentle and courageous men of heroic proportions once lived lives of peace and refinement among the most primitive conditions. They were sustained at all times by a belief in their church which lent dignity to prosaic hardships. Interwoven as it is with the author's passion for the country itself, expressed in dozens of memorable pages, it breathes a great faith which inspires with its beauty even those who cannot share it. By calling upon this faded past and creating within it the symbols of the Catholic faith and worship, Willa Cather evokes and sustains an atmosphere of poetry which softens all conflict and transforms such intrinsically desperate scenes as that of Magdalena and her brutal husband, and the savagery of some of the Indian episodes.

It was a beautiful book of its *genre,* and coming as it did near the end of the wild post-War era, it filled a nervous public with a sense of release through romance into a glorious past. The public liked it. It was coincidental with, if not one of the causes of, the shift from realism to romance which began to be felt in the year 1927. For that was also the year of the Lindbergh miracle performed at the very moment when John Erskine's GALAHAD was heading the list of best sellers.

Four years elapsed without exhausting the popularity of DEATH COMES FOR THE ARCHBISHOP, years which saw the proud nation toppled from its confidence of 1927 into the despair of 1931. When the new novel came in the dark days of that summer, it was SHADOWS ON THE ROCK, at the farthest possible remove from the contemporary scene and A LOST LADY. We were among a group of cultivated French pioneers of old Quebec in the far-away seventeenth century. They were trying to lead the good life in their isolated wilderness by keeping alive on the rock the sacred shadow of France which symbolized for them and the author the beauty of living. She wrote at some length in the Saturday Review (October 17, 1931) of the fascination exercised over her by Quebec and the mood which prompted SHADOWS ON THE ROCK. Even without that illuminating confirmation, it would be clear that she was trying with all the delicacy of her art to imprison a shadow. And it is the same shadow she pursued through the mesa lands with Father Latour and Father Vaillant. It is very beautiful and completely static. Her audience was divided and the reason is clear. The diverse elements in her work fulfilled their long-standing threat to split in twain. The preceding books had both narrative and the poetic style. This one had the poetic style.

Willa Cather has written more about her artistic aim and her creed than most of her contemporaries. These statements are always valuable even when they bear, as they usually do, so little relation to the effect of that art on a reader. She has clearly enough striven for selection and simplicity. She has in each book created a poetic symbol which beautifully holds the central theme, always the triumph of the heroes of the Old West ennobled by their vision and their struggles, the cheapness of soul of their sons in an age vulgarized by things, or the nostalgic recreation of a vanished past. She has, according to her aim, achieved a classic precision and clarity in her sentences, though not always in the total art form. But paradoxically enough, in her writing about her writing she has emphasized her desire to cultivate a prose which might lose itself in the materials, whereas in effect the style is so carefully wrought that it frequently becomes the chief source of artistic pleasure. Likewise with her belief that the scene should be unobtrusive and the play of emotions supreme. In every one of her books the magic is more often in the scene itself than in the people, and it is not often that the brilliant surface is stirred by high passion or warmed by the glow of rich as opposed to static living. And in contrast with most of her contemporaries there is in her novels little of the great upheavals of sex. In a bewildered age whose uncertainties and preoccupation with fundamental problems of economics and government suggest nothing to challenge her fine pen, she has become the most talented of our escapists.

Chapter Six

THE "YOUNG GENERATION"

*A*FTER the year 1915—to take an arbitrary date but a significant one because it marked the sensational appearance of SPOON RIVER ANTHOLOGY, the great popular success of Ernest Poole's realistic novel, THE HARBOR, and the conclusion of Theodore Dreiser's middle period in THE "GENIUS" —after 1915 it was impossible for any serious author in America to remain unaffected by the discipline of realism. The movement was at last fully triumphant and ready to maintain for a dozen years its undisputed dictatorship in the republic of letters. Every kind of writing became, in one aspect at least, a flowering of realism. It was no longer a question of the desirability of realism as a method or as an approach to literary materials, nor of the right of an author to choose those materials from any stratum of American life which happened to please him; it was rather a question of the end or purpose to which the inevitable method should be applied. It developed simultaneously in several directions. In the work of Sinclair Lewis, for example, it went satirical and became an instrument for social protest. In the work of Sherwood Anderson it was primarily interested in sex and the subconscious. In James Branch Cabell it was concerned with the more enduring types of human folly mirrored against an imaginary background. In Joseph Hergesheimer it cropped out in several different interests from the sailing days of old Salem to the sex problems of the middle-aged moderns. In the war generation it was used to debunk the romantic lure of war and military heroism. It is now used to recreate the past, especially of the Civil War and the Old South, and to

72

record the desperate sufferings of the workers in depressed America. After 1915, therefore, we may take realism triumphant as one of the facts and confront the difficult problem of seeing the various manifestations and ramifications driving their different wedges through the complicated welter of published books since the War.

One of the most engaging of the diverse interests of the period came sharply to a focus in the year 1920 with the dramatic creation of the official "young generation" and its problems by Floyd Dell in MOON-CALF, and F. Scott Fitzgerald in THIS SIDE OF PARADISE. These two books shared the spotlight of the year with MISS LULU BETT and MAIN STREET, and with the Pulitzer prize novel, titled with coincidental irony, THE AGE OF INNOCENCE. The unrest, the sense of impending change which everyone had been feeling as an unsettled and mysterious power in the air since the War, were suddenly crystallized and given expression. What had been vague and bewildering was now clarified and in the open, and the novels were soon streaming from the press to define it.

The post-War mood was so new, so unexpected, so full of shock and surprise that it bore up with it and into expression a great many novelists of limited talent who gave breadth if not depth to the movement. Some of them—Percy Marks with THE PLASTIC AGE, "Warner Fabian" with FLAMING YOUTH —without being novelists, used the popular narrative form to carry critiques and exposures of the new generation which might have been done with more propriety as essays for the upper-middle-class quality magazines. Floyd Dell and F. Scott Fitzgerald lifted the discussion close to the plane of literary distinction. They gave pace and color to the fashion. They popularized it among thousands of readers who had never read the novels of Theodore Dreiser, James Branch Cabell, or Willa Cather. But a few novelists of large dimensions make it possible to accept others of a genius individual but less rare who picture facets of the contemporary scene neglected by greater writers. Floyd Dell and F. Scott Fitzgerald are not great in the total sweep of humane letters, but they are both vivid figures, they represent the generation between Theodore Dreiser and Ernest Hemingway, and they are significant in the creation of the American novel which has interpreted for us the age in which we live.

The work of Floyd Dell and F. Scott Fitzgerald came like a cold shudder on the spines of those idealistic souls who lived through the War to believe implicitly in the power of Volstead to do what no power on earth could do before him and save our youth from alcohol; who thought their sons and daughters were disciplined and demure when unchaperoned at a midnight dance, and who were sure that, now the War was over and everything was safe at last from further change, the young people could once more become pure like their grandparents, only, of course, more cultivated and more prosperous in the new land of greater plenty. But the things that shocked the old brought the thrills of forbidden sweets to the new generation. The college youth had sessions about it, and young married neighbor women gathered on the back steps of the big new apartment houses springing up in the towns with their F. Scott Fitzgerald and their Floyd Dell in their laps and whispered about freedom and felt awfully sophisticated. It was one of those periods when literature and sociology become hopelessly conjoined.

The two young novelists had little in common except contemporaneity and success as authors. For although the first novel of each was published in 1920, the authors were a decade apart in age. Floyd Dell was born in 1887, F. Scott Fitzgerald in 1896. But Fitzgerald left Princeton for a brief war experience and then, after a few months in an advertising office, plunged immediately into the job of writing THIS SIDE OF PARADISE. Floyd Dell, on the other hand, tried numerous factory jobs in the Middle West, worked on a newspaper in Davenport, Iowa, read socialistic literature, went to Chicago, where as the twenty-three-year-old literary editor of the Chicago Evening Post he led the critical vanguard in the attack on the outmoded, then moved on to Greenwich Village, opposed the War at considerable peril to himself, and finally turned to autobiographical fiction after the peace had brought to a close one phase of an intense and colorful career. These two authors, therefore, represent the upper and nether age limits of the young generation who created the "problem" that had the world so badly worried at the beginning of the twenties. And they each dealt with quite different aspects of the modern scene.

Floyd Dell was the zealous reformer and individualist. He was a gifted poet and a dreamer. He was irked by the narrow life of his own poor boyhood struggling to keep afloat above indigence in the cramped towns of Illinois and Iowa. A free and joyous life was impossible in these towns and they were therefore repulsive to Floyd Dell. The factory life had quickly shown him its dreary, devitalizing, underpaid monotony. The newspaper life had left few illusions as to the way a town was run by the well-to-do. The social theories of Engels, Marx, and other writers had led him to believe that an economic system of greater justice was possible, and he was energetic enough to try to bring about change. In these activities he was so vigorous that he was widely known as a "radical" and an editor of the Masses before he was known as a novelist. This reforming, radical period reached its climax in the inspiring fight which he and the editors of the Liberator so stalwartly put up in 1918 for personal integrity and the right of free speech in the hysterical War days. It was one of those brave gestures which renew man's faith in the courage and nobility of men. And they conquered by their audacity and their valor.

F. Scott Fitzgerald followed a very different career. He was sent to the Newman School in New Jersey, and then to Princeton where he worked hard at writing a musical comedy for the Triangle Club in which he later appeared as a chorus girl. While Floyd Dell, Max Eastman, Art Young, and the others were defending themselves against the charge of "conspiring to promote insubordination and mutiny in the military and naval forces of the United States, and to obstruct recruiting and enlistment to the injury of the service," F. Scott Fitzgerald was a lieutenant in the army writing a novel on his free Saturday afternoons. He was in no sense a spirited crusader for an idea. The different temperaments of the two men are representative of the two sides to the character of the young generation—Floyd Dell presenting its positive lust for action and revolt in his eager young lovers, for whom all the Gods were by no means dead; F. Scott Fitzgerald picturing its restless mood of futility and disillusion symbolized by jazz and gin, with candles burning at both ends and snuffed at last in cocktails.

Floyd Dell's passion for freedom against all tyrannies made him the champion of the young generation in its drive against the rigidity of the moral code, and its spokesman for revolt against the tight social conventions which tried to restrict and bind it. The revolt was thrilling. It brought under scrutiny the whole body of traditional attitudes toward morals and social conduct. The young rebels proposed to try them out and to discard everything that hampered the free development and expression of the individual. They charged full force upon the restrictions which had surrounded the lives of American youth with fears, superstitions, and taboos. The academic scholars overemphasize the place in this revolt of an ordered and reasoned philosophy of naturalism built up out of the scientific researches of the past century. Few of these people knew anything about such abstruse matters. Rather, they had felt the spirit of revolt in the air, as it were, and had accepted the new orthodoxy about man's base origin and inglorious destiny; the loss of authority on the part of the church and the Bible; and the general relaxation of all restraints that came with the War. All those attitudes which we now call "modern" were making rapid entrance into the texture of American life and the old vied with the young in the quest for emancipation.

Greenwich Village (and its equivalent in a dozen large cities) became the symbol of escape, the dream Mecca where life was joyous and love was free. Young college men and women fled their Western villages for the absolution of a hall bedroom and a stool in the Village Café. A great deal of the young generation's defiance was the excess of youthful spirits in an excited and excitable age. At heart it was a genuine unrest and a search for a wider freedom than the stultifying atmosphere of pre-War American life permitted. The fact that only a few of the rebels achieved anything permanent, that only a small number knew how to utilize their freedom towards ends that were really more satisfying than those they fled, is only further proof that the soul is competent to vision heights which it can never fully gain. But it did produce an interesting literature.

Floyd Dell became the focus of this phase of the young generation: its dreams, its poetic emotions, its high spirits, and its longing for a richer life. Even MOON-CALF, a "study of a boy living between the years 1887 and 1908 was," the author said, "to my surprise, [interpreted as] a comment upon 'post-War' youth." Floyd Dell had worked at it off and on for several years trying to make it capture the dream life of Felix Fay and his romantic ecstasy in imaginary love scenes with Rose-Ann, as well as the story of his poverty-ridden life and family in and about Quincy—the Vickley of MOON-CALF. Floyd Dell has the rare felicity of being able to remember and re-create the experiences of childhood and by a flawless selection of significant detail to bring out a "clear emotional pattern." The very nature of his materials in MOON-CALF permitted him to work in the realistic manner and at the same time introduce the poetry as well as the humiliations to which youth is subject. The book was so autobiographical that when he wrote his excellent HOMECOMING (required reading, along with Malcolm Cowley's EXILE'S RETURN, for all who would understand the movement) he incorporated into it pages and paragraphs from MOON-CALF without change. The appearance of MOON-

CALF was properly timed. "It profited by a sudden and rather hysterical fury of popular resentment against business, regimentation and conventional life." But with the charm and sly wit so characteristic of Floyd Dell, he disavowed the intention ascribed to him by the reviewers of writing an exposé of the Middle West, and he told Sinclair Lewis that he did *not* approve of Felix Fay, and that he "thought it would serve 'Felix Fay' and Carol Kennicott right if they had to marry one another and live on a desert island the rest of their lives."

For good or ill, then, Floyd Dell was the spokesman for the young lovers without money in the search for happiness in the machine age. The novels which followed MOON-CALF more nearly justified the honor. THE BRIARY-BUSH (1921), followed Felix Fay alias Floyd Dell to Chicago and told of the temporary triumph of love in marriage and the joys of apartment hunting, and pictured the Bohemian group in Chicago before the War. In the characters of the frustrated Clive, the drunken Eddie, and the drifting, futile, talking esthetes, Don and Roger, he portrayed as a minor theme the kind of people who were central in the F. Scott Fitzgerald novels. In Floyd Dell's books they remain on the periphery or in the background as foils to the more assured and life-loving characters.

The novels came along through the twenties, amplifying with unequal power the themes defined in the first two. JANET MARCH (1923) moved directly into Greenwich Village in search of the ideal of joy, companionship, freedom, self-giving love, picnic excursions to the beach by moonlight or to the woods, and a carefree, irresponsible existence in an attic studio. Floyd Dell has written beautifully about it all in HOMECOMING in a fine chapter entitled *Greenwich Village*. In fact, the autobiography is done so capably that, in a sense, it supersedes the novels.

The interest in the feminine side of the revolt was continued in THIS MAD IDEAL (1925). The author did not neglect the drab and tragic aspects of life while emphasizing the spirited quest for freedom. There followed RUNAWAY (1925),

AN OLD MAN'S FOLLY (1926), AN UNMARRIED FATHER (1927), SOUVENIR (1929), and LOVE WITHOUT MONEY (1931). By 1930, the day of the "young generation" was done, and the revolt of runaway youth to the mad ideal was over. Floyd Dell in DIANA STAIR (1932) turned back to the 1840's for a study of a courageous young girl who revolted against the social and economic slavery of women in the New England mills, and built one of his best novels to date around her struggles. In 1933 he offered his autobiography, serving final notice that the Greenwich Village adventure was history and presenting his log of the exciting journey. THE GOLDEN SPIKE (1934), contained those qualities now so well associated with the name of the author, and treated his favorite theme of love, money, and the struggle for adjustment in the modern world.

In the meantime, the other discoverer of the young generation was exploiting with continued success the shocking collapse of the old moralities and the bored sophistication of the newly free. F. Scott Fitzgerald's people have none of the childlike innocence of the Felix Fays and the Rose-Anns. They are hard and cold. They are flippant and blasé. They are the "problem children" of the ministers and the sociologists. They are self-centered individualists. They know what they want and take it. They know all about sex and they talk it constantly to avoid dreadful inhibitions disastrous to their personalities. They kiss not one man but dozens with abandoned casualness and confess it in mixed company, adding observations on the qualities involved in satisfactory sex. They are not the eager young Janet Marches with a zest for living and in love without money. They are well-to-do and frustrated in love with too much money.

Amory Blaine in THIS SIDE OF PARADISE was pampered by his foolish, shallow mother. His journey through Princeton made him neither a scholar nor a gentleman. It left him, on the contrary, inept, disillusioned with life and religion, at a dead end beyond the reach of his intellect. The book abounded in metaphors and aphorisms which seemed to the readers of

1920 to summarize the "modern attitude." Two passages from the end of the novel have inseparably attached themselves to the period. "There was no God in his heart, he knew; his ideas were still in riot; there was ever the pain of memory; the regret for his lost youth. . . . Here was a new generation, shouting the old cries, learning the old creeds, through a revery of long days and nights . . . a new generation dedicated more than the last to the fear of poverty and the worship of success; grown up to find all Gods dead, all wars fought, all faiths in man shaken. . . ."

It is difficult to read the novel now, and after the revolution in conventions since the War one is amazed to recall the stir it made in 1920. Its historical interest is, therefore, considerable. It was a serious document in a comparatively conservative day, it challenged the beneficial influence on youth of the universities in the moment of their greatest popularity and expansion, and it was regarded as a "disconcertingly realistic investigation of a sensitive mind growing up in our own present-day civilization." It was also ultra-modern in technique, utilizing the impressionistic style then in its first flower through the success of James Joyce's PORTRAIT OF THE ARTIST AS A YOUNG MAN.

In THE BEAUTIFUL AND DAMNED (1922) the despairing mood which the first novel defined had grown sharper and more brittle. The type became known as the "highball," the "cocktail" the "jazz age" of fiction. The "moderns" had become "advanced." They had the stimulation of gin, of arrogance, of defiance, of Puritan-baiting, of being different from the herd and shocking to the uninitiated. Yet all the fury and rebellion led only to barren lives wasted in excess—Anthony Patch, a millionaire's grandson, who did not finally inherit the millions and was wrecked in bitterness; the hard, cold, modern, uninhibited female, Gloria Gilbert, his wife, likewise damned by the fast, shallow pace and the loss of her beauty. It was a tawdry and a sorry conclusion to come to after the freedom and the gayety they were seeking. But the end was not yet, and in one more novel, THE GREAT GATSBY (1925), the author attempted to carry the vogue into the highest pitch of the post-War abandon. It is his best piece of work, and it has some qualities that survive the period. Its pace and drive, its proportion and firmness of structure, its vividness of character-drawing, its feeling for rhythm, its mastery of the material furnished by the Long Island smart set of the mid-twenties and seen through the eyes of an alert young man who narrates the story in the first person, combine to give this novel an uncommon distinction.

But even the "young generation" seemed to offer only a limited quantity of material and the vein ran out on both Floyd Dell and F. Scott Fitzgerald without enlarging their stature much beyond the limits set by their first novels. There was a news value in their work. When it ceased to be news the novels were stale because they lacked the permanent searching of the soul which makes one generation read another's novels. Gertrude Stein expansively declared in THE AUTOBIOGRAPHY that F. Scott Fitzgerald would be read when his contemporaries are forgotten. But it is safe to say that she has not tried rereading him. F. Scott Fitzgerald is not misled, however, and he shows his sanity by accusing Gertrude Stein of saying such things merely to annoy him.

F. Scott Fitzgerald did not return to the novel form until 1934, when he published in Scribner's Magazine TENDER IS THE NIGHT, most surprisingly advertised as a *romance*. Since he had said in 1932 that "the 1920's are as dead as Dickens' doornail," it was also surprising to meet in this "romance" set in part on the Riviera the further degeneration of the same maladjusted lot with whom he had dealt in the twenties, with a hero wanting to give "a really *bad* party . . . where there are brawls and seductions and people going home with their feelings hurt, and women passed out in the *cabinet toilette.*"

There was some good writing in TENDER IS THE NIGHT; there was also much pathological material and considerable repetition of matters already disposed of in the day of FLAPPERS

AND PHILOSOPHERS and TALES OF THE JAZZ AGE. If F. Scott
Fitzgerald has failed to add to his importance in this return
to the novel form, at least the fact remains that he helped
to dramatize the "young generation" and to fix it in place in
the unfolding American novel.

Floyd Dell and F. Scott Fitzgerald were supported in
their attempts to fictionize post-War American life by a remarkable group of talented younger men who came early
into expression. There was Stephen Vincent Benét, for example, who did one notable novel on the early youth, prep-
school and college life of a poetic boy, and his first adjustments
to maturity. It was titled THE BEGINNING OF WISDOM and it
appeared in 1921 when the author was twenty-three. It revealed those qualities of sensitive perception that were to turn
the genius of the young writer to poetry rather than to prose
fiction.

There was also Cyril Hume. He is nearly four years
younger than F. Scott Fitzgerald, being New York born in
1900. Fresh from Yale and the New York World, he wrote
boldly, sensitively and well in WIFE OF THE CENTAUR (1923)
about the new college generation that was vocalizing its sex
life and surprising itself and its parents with the discovery.
It received a wide reading and the plaudits of the critics. He
followed it with CRUEL FELLOWSHIP (1925), a novel of sex for
the sex age, and THE GOLDEN DANCER (1926), a romantic relaxation from the previous themes. MY SISTER, MY BRIDE (1932)
belongs with the ultimate extensions of cruelty. It is a very
good example of the gradual intensification of the comparatively simple behavior of the early twenties. It is minutely
psychological in its study of the tangled and tragic love triangle of a middle-aged artist, his son, and a wondering,
romance-struck young neighbor girl. There is a brutal fight
between father and son, and a tormentingly beautiful suicide
of the once idealistic girl. Cyril Hume has a firm command
over his narrative and his characters, and he is the master of
a style that is always supple and often distinguished for its

beauty and precision. His work shows the effect of the "young generation" upon the slightly younger who reinforced them.

Nor was this creative impulse limited to the men. The young women took it up. They showed a talent for swift narrative and ironic comment upon the wild period, its sins and its foibles, and a hard, unsentimental understanding of the modern fast set that descended upon the offices and the fresh new country clubs of the nation. You may choose your own examples. Katharine Brush, Connecticut born in 1902, is quite representative of the spirit of the group. She was of the favored generation of women who could find jobs in the twenties. She preferred the practical excitement of life in a newspaper office to the academic removal of Wellesley. She completed her preparation for writing by marrying, living in Ohio for several years, and then settling in New York City.

GLITTER (1926), was a novel with a college setting. LITTLE SINS (1927) centered about Atlantic City life during the era of "Miss America" beauty pageants. YOUNG MAN OF MANHATTAN (1930) brought to life the character and the occupational experiences of a New York sports writer. RED-HEADED WOMAN (1931) presented the colorful rise of a calculating young and beautiful office girl who had her living to make and made it. And DON'T EVER LEAVE ME (1935) pictures the bored, gossipy, feline country-club crowd, young and old, as it existed in Northboro in 1932, just before repeal. It is a wry comedy of manners, a skillful report of the smart slang of the moment, an inimitable feminine analysis of the women in the dressing rooms and on the dance floor, a report on their cosmetics, finger nails, gowns, and color schemes, and a more serious portrayal of Mrs. Billy Cunningham, widowed by the War, and of her seventeen-year-old son, the product of the satiated and extravagant twenties, lost in the bewildered thirties. These novels are not great by literary standards, but they are a striking part of the flamboyant surface of life, arrested and recorded with irony and gusto by a sharp and facile pen. They represent the type of expression that has dramatized the external appearance of the age for the thousands who did not read THE GREAT GATSBY.

The activity of the times was so feverish indeed that there seemed to be no limit to the number of writers who could create entertaining novels about the new day and report what they had seen, heard, or experienced, give it the flavor of a fast-moving newspaper report, and color it with indignation, satire, gayety, or a hard aloofness. Two other representative figures who must be singled out from among a large number of capable and popular novelists on this fringed edge of the literary boom were Ben Hecht and Carl Van Vechten. Future generations may, perhaps, be unfamiliar with any of these names. That possibility need not disconcert us. Nor does the mention of the talent in this chapter imply any disrespect for literary standards. There are writers who probe into permanent matters which survive their setting in time. There are writers who vivify the times for the times. Ben Hecht and Carl Van Vechten vivified the times.

Ben Hecht, the younger of the two (born in New York in 1895) was the first to express himself in the novel. The more personal story of Ben Hecht should be read in Harry Hansen's splendid recreation of the Chicago group in his MIDWEST PORTRAITS. In rapid succession, and while hard at work on a Chicago newspaper, Ben Hecht began issuing his sensational volumes. ERIK DORN (1921) was one of the early characterizations of the hard-boiled and cynical hero, a journalist divested of all illusions, who sees life as a crazy and meaningless spectacle, whose mind, opinions and sex life are rather brilliantly explored in "sophisticated" style. FANTAZIUS MALLARE (1922) was a fantasy sufficiently objectionable to cause its suppression at the request of the federal government. Its sequel, THE KINGDOM OF EVIL (1924), showed how Fantazius in a Faust-like bargain went down to the kingdom in search of freedom and found a bondage in a destructive sensuality, kindred in spirit to that of ERIK DORN and THE BEAUTIFUL AND DAMNED. GARGOYLES (1922), was a malicious attack on hypoc-

risy as practiced by George Cornelius Basine and his ilk from
the sabbath May morning when he issued with a friend from
Madam Minnie's house of ill fame to the day when he was
chairman of the vice committee, a United States senator, and
war worker. It is full of penetrating satire on people, the
newspapers' dishonesties, utility magnates, and the frailty of
women. THE FLORENTINE DAGGER (1923) was a detective story.
HUMPTY DUMPTY (1924) was a study of the ultra-modern
novelist, Kent Savaron, who concentrates in his single person
all the superiorities of the young generation and their bitter
emancipation from all moralities and ordinary human emotions. COUNT BRUGA and BROKEN NECKS (1926), and A JEW IN
LOVE (1931) continued in the same vein, but with less popularity because this vogue was distinctly on the wane. Since 1928
Ben Hecht has had considerable success in the drama, both on
the stage and on the screen.

Ben Hecht was a very self-conscious young cynic, bred by
the dehumanized life that passed through Chicago's streets
across the desks of a metropolitan newspaper. He evidently
enjoyed the game of baiting the yokels and the soft souls who
thought life was nice and lovely and all. He showed them.
He wrote in a sharp style. It was chiefly a series of simple
declarative sentences. The sentences are short. They march
in a goose-stepping procession. Each repeats the rhythm of its
predecessor. They move at a fast pace. They are monotonous.
They pound away like the tapping of a hammer. They are
often clever. They are sometimes brilliant and gay. They are
sentences of the jazz age. They sound its shallower cadence.

Carl Van Vechten was thirteen years older than Ben
Hecht (Cedar Rapids, Iowa, 1880), but he did not begin to
divert the readers of novels until 1922, and after a brilliant
career as a critic of music and musicians. He had not waited
on the "young generation" to become clever and adequate
and full of enthusiasms. When he turned to the novel he had
only to be natural and present his report on the appearance
of the times. He knew well and intimately the "arty" folk

of the new era and he knew something of society. In THE BLIND BOW-BOY (1923), and again in FIRECRACKERS (1925), he exploited them in the spirit of the times, all very clever and gay.

Like so many other writers of the day who had been born in the Middle West, Carl Van Vechten looked back from the center of culture to the backward village of his birth. The contrast was overpowering. The native of Cedar Rapids, Iowa, studied the natives of "Maple Valley, Iowa," in THE TATTOOED COUNTESS (1924), and found them equally if not more stupid and socially insufferable than their neighbors some three hundred miles to the north in Sauk Center, Minnesota.

Carl Van Vechten was among the first and the most popular of the novelists who presented the colorful life of the Negroes in Harlem. He was interested in their life and enjoyed their confidence. In NIGGER HEAVEN (1926), at the peak of the interest in the Harlem phenomenon, he gave a brilliant picture of the more exotic and sensational aspects of the new Negro city. The book enjoyed a great popularity, and was for many a sociological document on an exciting phase of modern American life.

In SPIDER BOY (1928), he presented a satirical portrait of Hollywood and its equally exotic life and customs. It was one of many novels and plays poking fun at the extravagant, haphazard manner in which the manufacturers of the cinema produced their dramas. It was the day of feverish transition from the silent to the talking picture which the play ONCE IN A LIFETIME lampooned. PARTIES (1930), the year of Joseph Hergesheimer's THE PARTY DRESS, brought the cocktail-consuming, thrill-seeking young set of the 1920's down to date, just at the instant when time and the beginning of the long depression were sweeping them away in favor of a more conservative, still younger generation, and more searching and more important problems in a life suddenly grown serious.

Chapter Seven

POST-WAR REASSERTIONS

*T*HE quickened tempo of American life immediately following the War not only brought into prominence the Dell-Fitzgerald-Hecht-Van Vechten group
of younger writers, but it also reanimated certain authors with
reputations well established before 1910. They may be represented by four distinguished women.

Gertrude Atherton (California, 1857) had made a name
for herself as early as 1900 with her SENATOR NORTH, a book
that was a sensation in its day, more because it touched the
taboo of miscegenation than because it presented corrupt politicians. THE CONQUEROR (1902) was a popular contribution to
the historical romances then enjoying such an unprecedented
vogue. It too had a suggestion of forbidden themes, for it
indicated that Alexander Hamilton, the love child, was the
superior of Washington and Jefferson. She alternated through
the years before the War an interest in the social history of
old California with novels on problems of the day, such as
JULIA FRANCE AND HER TIMES (1912) on the rising question of
feminism, and PERCH OF THE DEVIL (1914) on the problem of
marriage and divorce. Her views were considered "advanced."
In fact, she was thought of in the earlier days as a somewhat
dangerous writer, and it was a matter worthy of remark that
the world continued to survive the publication of her nearly
two score novels.

Her post-War popularity was based on BLACK OXEN, which
leaped to the top of best-selling novels in June, 1923, displac-
ing Sinclair Lewis's BABBITT. It held first interest through 1923,
and until June, 1924, when it yielded to Edna Ferber's SO BIG.

It was a piquant novel in the midst of the sex vogue based on the experiments in rejuvenation by glandular surgery which were then exciting the world.

The triumph of BLACK OXEN seemed temporarily to satisfy Gertrude Atherton's interest in up-to-date topics. She retired once more into the past to the contemplation of ancient Greece, which she treated in several novels. She returned briefly to the contemporary scene in 1931 with THE SOPHISTICATES. She has never been counted among the greatest of American novelists. Her popularity was based largely upon the timeliness of her themes and the provocative attack she made upon them. These facts are recorded not because they are vital to the rare flower of genuine literary accomplishment, but because they represent an important phase of the infinitely diverse energy that was released in modern times through the medium of the novel.

A second figure who returned to prominence in the twenties was Anne Douglas Sedgwick (New Jersey, 1873). She is really more European than American. She went to England to live when she was only nine, she spent several of her first adult years in Paris, she is married to an Englishman and lives in Oxfordshire, and for a score of years before 1930 she had not been in America. She has chosen foreign rather than American materials for her novels, although ADRIENNE TONER (1922) had an American heroine.

Anne Douglas Sedgwick had published seven novels dealing with English life before FRANKLIN WINSLOW KANE (1910) and TANTE (1911) brought her a considerable and well-deserved reputation. Her career was interrupted by the War. Like Edith Wharton, Dorothy Canfield, and Gertrude Stein, she devoted herself to work in a hospital in France to the neglect of her writing. With the return to peace, however, she again took up the novel form in a modern spirit and in 1924 produced the international success, THE LITTLE FRENCH GIRL. It beautifully utilized the contrasts between English and French temperaments which the War period made so vivid.

It was followed by the excellent if less popular THE OLD
COUNTESS (1927), DARK HESTER (1929), and PHILIPPA (1930).

Anne Douglas Sedgwick is a careful artist. She often
probes deeply and sympathetically into the delicate springs of
character, and through character to the less basic questions of
national attitudes toward the moralities and the sex conventions. Her people are genteel, their problems are those of personal adjustment to human relationships, and she writes of
them with conviction and considerable artistry.

Edith Wharton, as we have already seen, enjoyed a long
and successful career beginning with THE VALLEY OF DECISION
(1902) and concluding with THE CUSTOM OF THE COUNTRY
(1913), a rather clearly defined "period" under the artistic
discipline of Henry James. The brief return to the more
austere and objective realism of ETHAN FROME in SUMMER
(1917) was only another indication of the power of the new
mode and the ability of Edith Wharton to create within it.
SUMMER is short and firmly wrought without Jamesian invo-
lutions. It relates the sad story of Charity Royall who had been
brought "down from the Mountain" to the village of North
Dormer by the local lawyer and reared in his home. And it
tells how she fell in love with Lucius Harney, the summer
visitor who brought romance to her restricted life, how she
was seduced and deserted by him, and how the essentially
kind lawyer, her guardian, married her. It emphasizes the
malice and the dreary isolation of the small New England
town from which Charity Royall longed in vain to escape.
"How I hate everything! . . . We all live in the same place,
and when it's a place like North Dormer it's enough to make
people hate each other just to have to walk down the same
street every day." Such passages are signposts on the road to
Main Street.

SUMMER is arresting as a transitional novel in the career
of Edith Wharton. Her literary work was interrupted by the
entrance of America into the War, and by her own arduous
services in the cause. After the sacrificial interlude, she re-

turned with notable success to the creation of a second "period" beginning with THE AGE OF INNOCENCE (1920), which received the Pulitzer prize of 1921, and received the award against the advice of the advisory committee. The book announced that the most distinguished woman of letters of her generation had felt the strong current of the new day, and that she could remain abreast of it in spirit without losing her established bearings or the delicate odor of Victorian lavender which had set her apart in a drawing room beyond the crucial and demanding scenes of modern turmoil. She had remained the cultivated and decorous lady, fastidious in taste, restrained in irony and in wit. She had preserved her cool detachment from the specimens under her edged scalpel, and under the assault of modernism she had not relaxed her firm grasp on her own materials and her individual methods in creating her art.

Edith Wharton's art was conscious and painstaking. She has discussed it at length from time to time in various essays, and in her book, THE WRITING OF FICTION. It is an art appropriate to a novelist with her ideology of the importance of the refined social and personal code in the struggle for the good life. That life is removed and selective. It is not the fate-driven soul set upon by the complex welter of blind but perverse forces in the naturalistic world and done in at last by obscure combinations of circumstance. Such a view of life demands an art more muscular and less discriminating, and it leads, in Edith Wharton's opinion, to "the blank wall of 'naturalism.'" In Edith Wharton's world the hostilities are clear and positive. There is no question about their origin, their purpose, or their powers. If you are worsted by them you know precisely what struck you and why. In so compact and comparatively simple a world, therefore, the first principle of art is a rigorous selection of significant material turned to creative use. "Transmutation," she wrote in the Saturday Review, "is the first principle of art, and copying can never be a substitute for creative vision." She has, within her sphere, an unerring eye for details appropriate for "transmutation." If this process sometimes robs her novels of a robust sense of life, it compensates by giving them a grace and a finish which have been satisfying in an age when neither quality has been in the highest favor. At its worst it is still competent, as in THE GLIMPSES OF THE MOON (1922), where creative power and conviction are relaxed. At its perfection in clarity, selectivity, and restraint at work on materials nearer to the throb of life, it produced in ETHAN FROME (1911) one of the few undisputed classics of the twentieth century.

The subject matter to which this art has been applied has been unique with Edith Wharton. In a period which has, quite justly and inevitably, been almost exclusively concerned with the American masses in the machine age, and with the revolution in ways of life and attitudes toward morality and the social conventions, Edith Wharton has remained aloof. With few exceptions, and those not in her best manner, she has cultivated, not the revolution of the 1920's, but that which attended upon the gilded age. The subject was as native to her as that of Greenwich Village youth was to Floyd Dell. While Theodore Dreiser was struggling in the fury of the American market place, while Sherwood Anderson was manufacturing paint in a northern Ohio town, and while Sinclair Lewis was observing the social code of the Mrs. Bogarts of Sauk Center, Edith Newbold Jones Wharton of New York City, London, Paris, Provençe, Newport, and Lenox, well born in 1862, and living in the tight respectability of the older social register, was observing with regret in a mood suggesting nostalgia for a better day the decay of the fine old respectabilities before the assault of the more newly rich vulgarians. She wrote of what she knew but she happened to know a different stratum of American life of which few were permitted more than the glimpses in the social columns. In America, people with her cultivation and background were seldom talented or inclined to authorship. Edith Wharton conducted readers behind the sacrosanct scenes.

She was not always reverent toward the spectacle of the exclusive. She was sharp-eyed, and she had a pen barbed with a fine irony which never failed to delight the intelligent circle of her readers. And since her interest was not in the vague down-town offices to which her shadowy males retreated to manipulate the luxuries, but in the women in and on the edge of the exclusive social set, her keen-edged gifts of expression were uncommonly appropriate. She could release against these idle wives, fiancées, daughters, and their "poor" relations, the woman's malice just this side of spite, which is so becoming to a woman novelist who analyzes other women. She exposed the esoteric spirit of the clan. It had barricaded itself behind its set of little rules, and had bound its members together until the delinquency of one, like the sin of Achan at Jericho, involved the entire tribal solidarity. You must obey the rules and observe each detail of the prescribed etiquette. If your individual happiness or the personal needs of your own soul should come into conflict with "the thing to do," there must be no instant of indecision. The clan must go on. In most cases the regimentation was strong enough to sweep the individual into the groove. If the individual should rebel against the discipline—one was of course really awfully sorry that a girl like her should go "vulgar."

Edith Wharton saw both the merits and the silliness in this life. She presented both, analyzing the people, their motives, the values involved in a decision, and exposing the destructive powers of the codes when confronted by an exceptional person. She also understood the importance of a discipline to preserve the desirable amenities in a cultivated society. Without overemphasis, with more minute analysis than sweep of plot or action, she has built up her novels around this segment of American life.

THE AGE OF INNOCENCE, the title itself suggesting the refined irony characteristic of the author, brought into concentration all her powers and applied them to her favorite subject. The powerful clan is represented by the Archer-Welland circle. The individualist who refuses the discipline, marries a Pole and leaves him to seek a divorce when proceedings meant disgrace and ostracism, is personified by Countess Olenska, and she is made to feel the pitiless revenge of the clan. The tribe illustrates its power by bringing Newland Archer and May Welland into a disagreeable marriage. It demonstrates its effective control of its members by holding Newland Archer firmly to the yoke when he contemplates escape into freedom with Countess Olenska. With the news that May is to bear him a child, he accepts the sentence and joins the respectable men in the offices down town. To point even more vividly the continuity of the code, there is an epilogue in which Newland's son re-enacts the emotional crisis of his father, and the father refrains from visiting Ellen in order to preserve the beautiful memory of that spirited and self-sacrificing young woman.

The novels since THE AGE OF INNOCENCE have maintained a standard of excellence without adding to the fame or the accomplishment of the author. It was difficult to be convinced of the importance of THE GLIMPSES OF THE MOON (1922), a story of two young honeymooners with little money but with wealthy friends who generously offered them villas without charge in which the couple lived while they tried to work out a more adult basis for their lives than the one upon which their marriage was founded. A SON AT THE FRONT (1923) was one of those books about the nobility of sacrifice in the War which tried to preserve into a disillusioned age the sentimentalism which the war generation itself so successfully debunked. THE MOTHER'S RECOMPENSE (1925) combined the old plots of THE SECOND MRS. TANQUERAY and LADY WINDERMERE'S FAN to tell the story of a mother who returned to America only to find that her daughter was in love with the man who had been, a decade earlier, her own lover. To protect her daughter's happiness, and to preserve some of her own, she retains her secret and retreats to Europe.

TWILIGHT SLEEP (1927) and THE CHILDREN (1928) brought

her studies of the moneyed sets into the contemporary era of PARTIES and THE PARTY DRESS, to show the effect upon the older virtues of the new, fast-stepping, and vulgar crowd who were breaking down the last of the barricades, and to show the débris of wrecked, innocent lives left behind the easy and rapid divorces of a generation who gave its selfish, individual desires priority over parental and social responsibility.

In HUDSON RIVER BRACKETED (1929) and THE GODS ARRIVE (1932) she told the story of Vance Weston of Illinois in his quest for escape from the stultifying atmosphere of contemporary American life. His adventure led him from the Middle West to a village on the Hudson which had retained a mellow atmosphere, to a marriage and a try at authorship, to a promiscuous affair with a married woman, and to a sense of futility. The dissatisfactions are continued in the second novel through a disillusioning elopement abroad with the married woman, a cheap success in his art, and finally a new grasp on life and a vision of honorable happiness in eventual marriage to the woman of the affairs.

This is as near as Edith Wharton has come toward joining the procession of realism and modernity. Even in these two novels which approach the turbulent life of today we are still concerned in the Edith Wharton manner with people in a newer house of mirth and with the customs of the country. She has been at her best in a witty, ironic, but ladylike debunking of pretense and in exposing the suffocating traditions and the respectable conventions behind which the moral fiber proceeded to decadence. If her work has seldom shown a lift of spirit, the fault lies in part in the nature of the life she has lived and pictured. In the process of creating the American novel she has an honored and unique place. She is an artist.

Ellen Glasgow was a fourth among the older writers who returned to the front of American fiction in the 1920's, and in the opinion of many she was more effective than the others in the reassertion of her talent in the new and changing era. She had built her earlier career on a solid foundation and it richly deserved the recognition it received. She was, as we have seen, among the first realists at the turn of the century. And in the period of historical romances in which she gained her first success her books recreating the past of old Virginia were distinguished for their honesty and their scholarship as well as for their humanity and their art. Her work in the second decade was not by any means in complete shadow, for it included the successful challenge to the chivalric ideal in VIRGINIA (1913) and in LIFE AND GABRIELLA (1916); but it was distinctly not a part of the contagious currents which were beginning to run with such strength with the War years. The overwhelming success of the Cather-Lewis-Gale vogue at the beginning of the 1920's shouldered to one side her new novels, THE BUILDERS (1919), ONE MAN IN HIS TIME (1922), and THE SHADOWY THIRD (1923).

There was, however, a rare genius behind the pen of Ellen Glasgow which could not be long in eclipse. In the year 1925 she published BARREN GROUND, a strong novel in the vanguard of the modern spirit and done with conclusive skill. Since that time it has required a mental effort to remember that the author of the contemporary successes, THE ROMANTIC COMEDIANS (1926), THEY STOOPED TO FOLLY (1929), THE SHELTERED LIFE (1932), was not one of the new women geniuses tossed up by the twenties, but the author of THE VOICE OF THE PEOPLE and THE BATTLE-GROUND in the first days of this century.

Ellen Glasgow also peered without illusion behind the forbidden scenes, and told what she saw. The act required bravery, for the probing was begun at a time when it was treason to the fair state of old Virginia and to her citizens with genealogies to utter any forthright truth about the real nature of life in the houses behind the pine groves. And Ellen Glasgow, indisputably a native daughter of Richmond (1874), and a Phi Beta Kappa from Virginia's own state university founded by Thomas Jefferson, had a persistent perversity for speaking the truth unsoftened by the velvet of the old Southern courtesy. In fact, she was in avowed rebellion against the romantic gentility of the South, sentimentalized with mimosa trees and crêpe myrtle and magnolias and moonlight, and the finest women ever untouched by a Southern gentleman. She was too intelligent, too hard of fiber to pass these affectations by with no challenge. And she had seen the tragic results which this failure to confront the facts of life had brought to its women victims. In her way, she was a feminist, a champion of spirited, flesh-and-blood women as opposed to the languorous belles in stiff brocade. In one of those sharp flashes so common to her pen she has put it all in an epigram (1925): "What the South needs now is—blood and irony." Ellen Glasgow has both.

These qualities were superbly adapted to one of the requirements in danger of neglect in the creation of the American novel—the exploitation of the ample and untouched materials of the life of the Virginia upper classes grown anemic behind the First-Family codes. James Branch Cabell had the gifts, as he well knows and says, but he chose to bear them elsewhere, leaving to Ellen Glasgow this virgin field. She had defined it and proved her parts before the contagion of the new era brought with it the tonic of a freer and more vivid statement of her consistent point of view. Her work became sensational in a lethargic South where the favorite question of the interviewer had become, according to James Branch Cabell, "What are the prospects for a Southern literature?" As though any section in whose midst resided and worked two such geniuses should entertain that question.

The very titles of Ellen Glasgow's later books start the sacred walls to topple. They suggest the subjects which she has chosen to treat and give a clew to the choice spirit to be found behind them: THE ROMANTIC COMEDIANS, THEY STOOPED TO FOLLY, THE SHELTERED LIFE. And the sentimentalities which she has charged are especially vulnerable to the gay thrusts of an epigrammatic pen.

She restrained these qualities while she wrote BARREN

GROUND (1925), but it was merely for the sake of attacking her favorite theme with a different strategy. Instead of presenting the defeated creatures with her protest against the scheme of life which frustrated them, she created a positive character—the woman who did. She was Dorinda Oakley, of a respectable station a little higher than poor white, a little lower than the gentry—a kind of Alexandra Bergson, whom she resembles. She is eager to embrace life, but her lover lets her down. But instead of pining away in faded sadness, she exhibits courage and assertion against adversity. The barren ground of her father's broom-sedge acres is conquered by her will and her energy, and the hired man she marries takes his place as *her* helpmeet. The grimness of the material is relieved by the poetic feeling and human sympathy behind the realism.

In the next two novels she released her reserves of irony and wit and they sparkled at their gayest. It does not task the mind to foresee with what relish Ellen Glasgow in THE ROMANTIC COMEDIANS would debunk for the 1920's the old Southern customs when once she had built up a situation in which a sixty-five-year-old widower judge, who has genteelly and becomingly worshiped at his departed wife's grave, suddenly abandons his grief and marries Annabell, aged twenty-three. With equal felicity she penned the satirical picture of the changing mores and their effect upon characters in slightly different periods of time in THEY STOOPED TO FOLLY. The words "stooped" and "folly" were mockingly subversive understatements for misdeeds which in an earlier day were considered the tragedy of ruined womanhood.

THE SHELTERED LIFE, less effective as a work of art, is more serious in theme and treatment and summarizes the central drive of Ellen Glasgow's novels. She has always objected to the results of the sheltered life, and to the chivalric idea which caused them. The chivalric concept of behavior may do for a Walter Scott novel, but when it is used in modern times as an effective male instrument for exploitation, the women are stultified. Their lives are not filled up by a brief honeymoon of passion and a casual possessiveness on the part of the groom thenceforward. If they accept the code and enter the shelter they lead bloodless, easy-going, pathetically inadequate, and barren lives. Ellen Glasgow pried into the facts of life which no Southern woman is presumed even to suspect, and she discovered a Southern gentleman in a visit to the house of an attractive Negress. THE SHELTERED LIFE is a social document built around the symbol of a once genteel house in a decaying neighborhood surrounded by factories and pervaded by an evil smell. The lives it portrays are in the same state of decay behind the façade of social pretense until the final tragedy drags everything into the open.

Although Ellen Glasgow has remained in Richmond, Virginia, removed from the discontented Mid-West and the newspaper world which bred the younger generation of American women novelists, she is not provincial. Above the smell of the Virginia creepers, the charm of the gardens, and the out of doors, there is always evident a civilized and a cosmopolitan mind in quest of the permanent and the similar which transcends "sectionalism." The American novel was enriched by her work.

Chapter Eight

NEWER ARRIVALS

*T*HE basic discipline of realism permitted many ramifications in the creation of the American novel. Its diversity reached from the naturalism of Theodore Dreiser through the more humanized realism of Willa Cather and Ellen Glasgow to the definite admission of sentiment in the novels of Dorothy Canfield. The point of view makes considerable difference in the selection of the detail. Literature is a house of many mansions and a too rigorous walling in or walling out is harmful to its welfare.

Dorothy Canfield has been for many years on the periphery of modern literature. Her place in the less central zone is due in part to the absence of that something more (and how much it is) which lifts a novel from competency into distinction, and in part to the fact that she has consistently cultivated a set of values too humane to be fashionable in a hard, modern age full of scorn and restlessness.

Her career had just begun—with THE SQUIRREL-CAGE (1912), a novel laid in the Middle West and dealing with the empty social demands which cage the soul within their limitations; and with THE BENT TWIG (1915), a study of the power of good breeding, cultivated background, and personal integrity to resist the demoralizing influences which a modern girl must face—when her writing was interrupted by the War. For Dorothy Canfield has always led an active and publicly useful life, and she gave herself without reserve to relief work in France. After the War she returned to her Vermont home in the Green Mountains and resumed her career as a novelist with THE BRIMMING CUP (1921), splendidly titled, which opens with the tender and tremulous scene of two lovers in the Campagne about to accept the hazards of life together. The theme of sensitive people adjusting themselves to life and marriage has been central in most of her novels since THE BRIMMING CUP: ROUGH HEWN (1922), THE HOME-MAKER (1924), HER SON'S WIFE (1926), a book of power and feeling in which the charity and the sanity of a mother with the silver-cord attachment for her son who married beneath him finally triumph over selfish possessiveness; THE DEEPENING STREAM (1930), developing the theme, suggested by the title, of a gradual deepening through the years of the life of a woman with resources of character; BONFIRE (1933), a study of Vermont village folk, whom Dorothy Canfield knows intimately, and the impact they make on one another's lives, some of them ruined by the woman villain from whose character the title is doubtless derived.

Dorothy Canfield, almost unique in her day, has written with a human sympathy unembittered by the shortcomings of human nature, and unwarped into a mode by measuring the people in her novels against the exaggerated merits of a sophisticated culture said to be prevalent in preferred sections of the metropolis. She has been sensitive to more things overlooked or scorned by the disillusioned than any of her contemporaries. It is a part of her honor that she steadfastly maintained her viewpoint through the storms of fashion, and made the age remember that there were human depths in the soul uncatalogued in Freud. Within them were to be found dignity, cultured but simple living, and some elemental kindness of heart.

She came from an easier background than many of our realists. She and a few others of her generation were able to transmute their New England heritage from the religious Puritanism of their fathers into a reliance on a culture at once fastidious and unselfconscious. She had the stimulation of cultivated surroundings, travel, and economic security. She grew up in university circles and attained distinction in the

scholarship of the academic world. There was no reason why
she should choose sordid or drab materials, and her spirit was
not satirical. She too could be realistic and yet permit the strain
of sentiment in her novels.

This is not to suggest that there is no edge to her work.
On the contrary she has been vigorous in her attack on elements tending to limit the full capacities of the individual soul.
She has chosen to strike from another sector. She deliberately
attempted one of the most difficult feats in the history of
literature: to write directly about and in championship of the
virtues of cultivated, intelligent people and their manner of
meeting the actual problems of living. Only the very greatest
artists have succeeded in this, and that rarely, without becoming somehow sentimental or silly or both. On the other hand,
thousands of ordinary, trained reporters can do you a fair job
of writing about the sins of rudimentary folk in Georgia and
receive the encomiums: elemental, powerful, bitter, savage.
The vocabulary of invective is more highly developed than
that of praise.

Dorothy Canfield has found, studied, and created with
convincing vividness the kind of human beings you meet at
a dinner with your friends who have two children and no
maid. It is remarkable how a little sympathetic understanding,
avoiding the treacherous pitfall of sentimentality, can produce
in her novels a glow and a lift of spirit which compensate
for more shortcomings than critics have yet accused Dorothy
Canfield of. Her gifts are as effective in her medium as those
of Edith Wharton and Ellen Glasgow in theirs. Although the
tide favored a more stringent realism, she went on doing her
work in terms adapted to a wide audience, sustained by an
honesty quite as real in its way as Sherwood Anderson's. She
studies human beings in marriage, understanding the stress
and strain which it brings, but believing also that imagination
and sympathy and confidence can usually resolve the difficulties with emotional enrichment. She believes in a self-reliant
and discriminating womanhood, rich in activity and capable

of its own salvation. She finds in motherhood a poetry which is not soft but alive and virile and not blind to or defeated by trying moments or lapses from the nobility of an ideal. And she is certain that people have richer lives in the world of home and children where love is cherished as a privilege than among the young selfish individualists experimenting with temporary lovers, contraceptives, and the pursuit of physical sensation. This world of delicate spiritual values by which people must finally live, whatever their intellectual tenets, is always present in her work either directly or by reference. Nor are these merely thesis novels. The characters are firmly created, and they live.

Her work holds up well and retains brightness with the passing of the vogues. In a day when so many American writers have measured themselves in their first novel and then proceeded to shrink within the limits, Dorothy Canfield has gone on enlarging her work. It is not a brilliant art; she has often been too eager for the theme and too lax in structure. At her best she weds the sense with the form and only occasionally is one reminded of lapses in stylistic distinction. She enjoys the position singular among her contemporaries, of seeing the times, after the jolt of the depression, finally catching up with the vision of a simple life, which she had been living with dignity and joy long before the migrations set in for the New England farm houses. If she was not in the main current of the post-War period, she represented a strong counter stream deepening with the 1930's.

A realism of a firmer texture and great power has been wrought by Ruth Suckow (Iowa, 1892). In some respects she is the most important of the younger women novelists. Her work has an enduring strength for which one looks in vain in novels of the type of THE PERENNIAL BACHELOR, THIS YEAR OF GRACE, and LAMB IN HIS BOSOM, which have attracted wider attention because of their more immediate charm for the less exacting. It is quiet and unspectacular, but it is built into the

earth, solid with the inconspicuous contours of the flat, resisting Iowa plains of which she writes.

Ruth Suckow has lived her life in the land and among
the people of whom she writes. Her father was a Congregational minister, and he moved about a great deal. The parish
house is a good focal center from which to study the lives of
average people, and to glimpse the quality of soul beneath the
surface. From a very early age she was trying to get commonplace people created in words and her first concern was to
satisfy herself rather than any magazine formula to easy popularity. Certain stories in IOWA INTERIORS (1926) are classic in
their success in realizing the "interiors" of the lives they study.

She has been helping to create the American novel since
1924 when her first book, aptly titled COUNTRY PEOPLE, appeared. In a period not lacking in new talent and stamped
with the genius of several great writers, Ruth Suckow's uncommon parts shone in their own strong, individual right. She
at once became a distinct figure with an artistry, already highly
developed by her work in the short story, and with rich
native materials observed with the eye and felt with the
heart. And the feeling was under a strict artistic discipline
which permitted it to glow just warmly enough to fuse and
to humanize the record of the rigid lives which interested
her.

Ruth Suckow is at her best in the stark selectivity of
COUNTRY PEOPLE. In a little more than fifty thousand words
she created the entire Kaetterhenry family, and presented
their characters, their values, and their life cycle from birth
through years of hard labor and careful saving for the ultimate happiness of retiring to idleness in the village, to decay
caused by overfeeding and lack of exercise, and a final trip
to the Mayo hospital for an operation before death carries
them off. The style is subdued almost to flatness, and yet it
lives in the mind with startling vividness because of the careful observation behind the writing, the exact detail necessary
to illuminate rather than to extend, and the general economy

of effort. Any passage chosen at random would serve as an illustration, as this one dealing with the retired German farmer.

"Most of them had a kind of seedy look. They walked heavily, without spring. They didn't know what to do with themselves.

"People said, 'Have you noticed how old Mr. Kaetterhenry's getting to look? He don't seem like the same man he did when they first moved into town. I wonder if he can be well.' He wasn't very well. He had headaches, trouble with his stomach, once a dizzy spell. He was eating the same heavy meals that he had eaten when he was working hard on the farm, coffee and meat three times a day."

Ruth Suckow is the mistress of such materials in an art form none the less finished because of its severity and apparent artlessness. She has continued to exploit Iowa and its people in the series of novels which followed COUNTRY PEOPLE. THE ODYSSEY OF A NICE GIRL (1925) presented an unforgettable picture of a nice Iowa girl of just enough talent to make her pathetic in her haphazard struggle with her life and ambitions. The opening scenes, with their deceptive art of selection and characterization of the girl and her family making a visit to the home of a relative, are memorable among contemporary novels on the same theme. The nice girl, not strong or gifted enough to compel her destiny, never has a chance against the good, narrow life of the farm and village, against the well-intentioned interference of her family, against all the little battering forces which wrap around her life and thwart it into a barren pocket. Her brief escape to the elocution school in Boston only heightens the pathos of the inevitable. It is a novel to be set squarely beside MY ÁNTONIA as its necessary complement.

THE BONNEY FAMILY (1928), made up of an Iowa minister, his aged parents, his wife who dies, his several individualized children, including the daughter Sarah, who takes over the management of the house, covers a score of the years of their lives hedged in by the same inevitable elements strongly humanized which abounded in THE ODYSSEY OF A NICE GIRL. It is one of her best books. It shows again her unusual ability to strike immediately into living dimensions an undistinguished family of commonplace, middle-class Americans, and to bring into life the kindly, jerky-voiced Reverend Bonney, his tired wife sitting out her summer vacation on their own lawn while she darns and listens to the family reading of the Congregational Herald, the son wanting to argue about everything, the sister Sarah snorting and laughing aloud over Dickens, the cat asleep on the church steps. It is a photograph of the things such people do, and deadly in its accuracy.

CORA (1929) dealt with immigrant German folk, their resistance to Americanization, and the growth and formation of the character of a daughter in the new surroundings. THE KRAMER GIRLS (1930) studied the lives of three sisters and the influence upon each of the sisterly affections of the other two.

These books were all pretty much of a piece. The first three had defined the method and the people and had apparently indicated the limits to which Ruth Suckow would carry her art. In CORA and THE KRAMER GIRLS she was competent without enlarging her scope. Then in the autumn of 1934 THE FOLKS was published. Except for perfection of art form, it justified the expectation of her earlier admirers. It told the same general story about the same commonplace Americans whom Ruth Suckow understands with uncanny penetration. On an exceedingly ample canvas she portrayed the dull but kindly Ferguson family as they faced the problems common to millions in the periods of rapid change immediately following the War. Echoes of THE ODYSSEY OF A NICE GIRL and of THE BONNEY FAMILY are plainly heard in the relentless analysis of Carl, the "good boy," who drifted into a sorry marriage to a prim little neighbor girl who was handy and all bound up in her inhibitions; in the pilgrimage of the pathological Margaret in a pathetic search for freedom and happiness which are not to be had; in kindly old Mrs. Ferguson and her farmer-banker husband who are good, unimaginative parents ignorant of what it is all about.

And yet, with all its echoes of earlier and successful novels, THE FOLKS was distinctive because it brought to the familiar materials a deeper understanding of the appalling dullness possible to life in America, and a perspective sharpened by the harsh experiences of the five years of the depression. It lost some of its potential force by overextending the detail, and by the method of building the form in long episodic panels requiring new expository sections at successive stages of the narration which weaken the cumulative effect of the drama. In its best sections it conveys a sense of flesh-and-blood people living out their lives before you. In fact, no one now writing in America can catch with equal accuracy the intimate details of ordinary family life and the exact vocabulary in use in everyday speech. And, apparently without being fully conscious of the ultimate effect of her work, Ruth Suckow in THE FOLKS penned a terrific satire on middle-class life in this republic.

Ruth Suckow has joined no side in the controversy between Main Street and Friendship Village. While she has been at pains to avoid sentiment, she has been equally careful to be true. With resolute honesty and with calm control she has spied out the barren corners in the lives of her Iowa farm and village folk—German and American—and illuminated their few amenities. She has rigorously excluded author's comment and trusted to the accuracy of the representation to state its own meanings. And she is not afraid of sobriety nor the homeliness of commonplace detail because she has always elevated it with humanity and given an authentic ring to the apparent flatness of her surfaces. Such work is independent of the vicissitudes which so quickly overtake novels with less substance but with a more immediately engaging surface brilliance.

Part Two

SATIRE AND SOCIAL PROTEST

Chapter Nine

SINCLAIR LEWIS

D URING the first two decades of this century Theodore
Dreiser was the greatest single force in the rise of
the American novel and by all odds its most important liberator. Then came Sinclair Lewis, not to rival but to
supplement and to popularize. Theodore Dreiser was neither
a reformer nor a satirist, and he never wrote a caricature.
Sinclair Lewis was a satirist and by implication therefore a
reformer, and he did not hesitate to advance his thesis with
caricature. Theodore Dreiser said: Here is the way men live
in this incomprehensible world; it is a strange and pitiable
spectacle. Sinclair Lewis said: Look at these stupid fools living
in bondage to smugness and mass pressures when they might
have gay and amusing lives; they're dumb and they're scared.
The possibility for satirical treatment of life in American
towns and villages seemed to be especially preserved against
the emergence of the valuable genius of Sinclair Lewis. The
time was so ripe for his work, and it was so inevitably the
next and necessary step in creating the American novel, that
the time made the man at least as much as the man made
the time.

The America which had fought against Theodore
Dreiser's novels had been opening its eyes through the ten
years before MAIN STREET. The reasons were so intricate and
often so subtly interacting that they have been only partially
disentangled. But the effects of whatever causes were perfectly clear. The certainties were no longer reliable, and the
most superstitious churchman of the Bible belt had his awful
moments of misgiving when he saw the young generation

openly violating his code with apparent impunity. In the great cultural centers of the world—Vienna and Paris, Berlin and London, New York and Chicago—a new generation had brought in startling changes in ways of living and modes of thought about the mores of the nineteenth century. Whether it was the sparkling and annihilating wit of George Bernard Shaw, or the scientific attitude which tried all experiments objectively and held no dogma above the test of experience, or whether it was the general restlessness of the War period suggesting that life was poorly adjusted to give satisfaction to living men, the fact remains that novelists in our time attempted to look life straight in the eye and accept the report of their examination. They were very bold and brave with the fortitude that comes from being certain of the uncertainties, and the terrible lions feared by the Victorians proved on closer inspection to be tame cats with velvet paws. Older readers may be asked merely to recall the spectacle still vivid in their minds to supply illustrations. The generation which so complacently accepts its freedom to dance until dawn at a road house fifty miles from home, to wear scant one-piece bathing suits and tennis shorts, and which has made no researches into the social customs that included chaperons, may read with profit and illumination the first half of Vera Brittain's TESTAMENT OF YOUTH.

These social changes were for a long time limited to the advanced groups in metropolitan centers. They cultivated Freud and talked sex and avoided frustrations and inhibitions; they bobbed their hair and shortened their skirts and painted their lips and went in boldly for cigarettes, cocktails, culture, and D. H. Lawrence. But in those thousands of small towns which stretch with a weary and monotonous sameness across the Republic, certain of our writers found that the culture of the citizens continued untouched or degenerated under the irresistible destructive power of the great American passion for smugness, fixity, and standardization. They saw only empty-headed business men and their ingrown village wives, bolstering their egos by shouting for boosterism and hounding down their betters who disagreed, joining lodges and making money and stoning the Socialists and conforming to the vulgar pattern they thought their neighbors demanded of them, swelling with pride over winning the War and imprisoning Debs and deporting radicals and being on top of the world in the greatest country in the greatest universe in space: what a moment it was for satire! For satire is inevitable as it is necessary in an age of rapid change when concepts of culture and moral codes in the advanced group outrun the convention-bound minds of those from whom the vanguard has escaped. And the contrast could be isolated to best advantage in a small town.

All that was needed was a vigorous writer who knew the cultural poverty of an American small town because he had lived there long enough to understand it thoroughly before he revolted against it. Then allow him to escape to the world centers where the currents of modernity were running fast and high, there let him become emancipated and veneered, and then watch him tear away the veil of pretense which had modestly concealed the tawdriness of life in Gopher Prairie. Sinclair Lewis, fortuitously conjoining with the drift of the time, precipitated a formless American mood into a smash satiric attitude which set the self-conscious country by the ears.

The country might have spared itself the shock if it had kept up with its better fiction. Chapter Twenty-one of Ed Howe's THE STORY OF A COUNTRY TOWN contained much of MAIN STREET forty years earlier. One could find no publisher, the other was a best seller and brought to an intersection the curves of popular sales and the new realistic novel. Ed Howe found the public in its customary mood of complacency. It would not listen when he described with graphic realism over a Victorian plot the petty quality of life in a Western village. With concentrated fury and a hatred and distaste which he subdued with difficulty, he presented the animosity of these villagers, their ignorance, their lack of vision, their evil back-biting and their ungenerous appraisals of the neighbors so consuming that Ned, the hero, says he never formed a good opinion of anyone but what the man was immediately proved by somebody to be a scoundrel; and if any man achieved success they called him "the most over-rated man in America." There is never a real friendship among them, he declares; they are forever hunting out scandal and peddling it, their religion is narrow and bickering and expresses nothing more lofty than their black-hearted jealousy and suspicion, they have no opinions beyond sectarian quibbles, they imitate men from larger towns and pose as great rakes having affairs with the leading ladies of the town when as a matter of fact everybody is so closely spied upon that he could find no opportunity to sin. The philosopher Little Biggs offers the final word when he destroys the cherished illusion about the nobility of going West to grow up with the country: farmers follow plows because they make more at that than anything else they could do, and they deserve no credit for superior virtue. If they get rich they go East like sensible people because life there is pleasanter; if they stay West it is because they are compelled to live where it is cheap. It is only the poorer classes "who come here to grow up with the country, having failed to grow up with the country where they came from."

The country was quite unprepared for such indictments in the 1880's. It was accustomed to romance and the neighborly tradition. To go from THE STORY OF A COUNTRY TOWN to Zona Gale's FRIENDSHIP VILLAGE (1908) is like moving from Wuthering Heights to Sweet Auburn before it was deserted. Friendship Village is of course as true to life as Gopher Prairie. They represent the eternal duality of life. In Zona Gale's book we meet the gentle Calliope so full of benevolence and good will and wanting people to be happy. It contains heart-warming episodes which make human beings irresistibly interesting because of their humanity, as when Calliope compels Mrs. Postmaster Sykes to bring her guests to the poor old charwoman's début party, and Mrs. Ricker asks for her funeral flowers now when she really needs them to decorate the house, and Calliope and the pastor sigh because there are at the moment neither sick nor poor to be ministered unto. The main street is called "Daphne" and it is lined with trees because a man with a vision and an unselfish interest in posterity planted them. Although there is a woman's club named "The Friendship Married Ladies' Cemetery Improvement Sodality" and although there is some scheming within its membership, the author does not satirize it. She makes it the instrument for the most gentle and good-natured fun. The "I" has come to the village not to reform it but to accept and enjoy it.

Freud's theories had first come to these shores about the time FRIENDSHIP VILLAGE appeared. No future study of village life could ever be quite the same because of Freud. His shadowy form lies dark across the SPOON RIVER ANTHOLOGY (1915) which anticipated Sherwood Anderson's WINESBURG, OHIO. It was a tremendous success, partly because of the form and partly because of its viewpoint. In a series of dramatic monologues presenting a crucial episode in each life, Edgar Lee Masters analyzed, satirized, and exposed society, telling a story in flashes, and presenting "a working model of the big world." But this working model shocked even advanced spirits like Amy Lowell, who thought it consisted of "one long chronicle of rapes, seductions, liaisons, and perversions." Behind the goodness of the good, the ANTHOLOGY repeated, is an unconfessed blackness which the tombstone finally obliterates, and to every sin there are two sides. Edgar Lee Masters presented both, summoning from their graves for a dramatic instant the representative types of departed natives. They now have nothing more to fear from their neighbors. They lay aside their respectable citizenship and let the long suppression break the bonds. When the depositions are all taken, the village has been laid bare, the good in those whom the citizens condemned, the evil in the hearts of the righteous, and the final feeling is one of despair over a life so stale and so barren of joy or nobility, so pitifully mean and cruel. The outcry that went up in 1915 was a foreshadowing of that to come in the winter of 1920-1921 when the right satiric note was struck in a novel. And that was the mission of Sinclair Lewis.

As the whole world now knows, he was born in 1885 in the little town of Sauk Center, Minnesota. It is in the heart of the state and on the south edge of the lake he writes of with such poetic feeling. After a long period of hesitation and searching of heart, the village finally concluded that this was a great honor to it, and by 1931 was advertising itself with a banner across the street as the authorized and original Main Street. There are only a few points to the biography which contribute to an understanding of the novels.

He was the doctor's son. That gave him a certain social position, an excellent opportunity for knowing a community, and reasonable economic security, in contrast, for example, with Theodore Dreiser and Sherwood Anderson. He had leisure to read, to walk, or to drive with his father through the Minnesota countryside, and to cultivate his talent for words. The town was small enough to be known intimately (between two and three thousand) and yet large enough to present a complete picture of human nature. The banker, the merchants, the real estate men, the drummers, the women of the clubs—he knew them all, envying and despising them at the same time. The assurance with which Sinclair Lewis draws his people is the product of the early years spent among them. He shares with every other exceptional boy in a small town the distinction of being considered queer by the more normal neighbors.

He was so fortunate as to escape Sauk Center after finishing high school, and to make most of his way by himself. The point can hardly be overestimated. He was exactly of the proper age and disposition to be most affected by the contrast between New Haven and Sauk Center, between Upton Sinclair and the home-town banker. These contrasts endlessly mounted as he went through Yale, and as he made his way to Europe on cattle boats as the young men were then wont to do, to Panama, to Upton Sinclair's experimental dwelling near Englewood, New Jersey, through various newspaper jobs, to California with William Rose Benét to write, only to find that his materials were not yet available. It requires time for life to take on sufficient perspective and the understanding to reach deep enough to do an important book. But the materials were in, and after he had tried editing and advertising, and had married and spent years trying to learn how to say what he had to say, he found his stride at the most opportune moment; MAIN STREET was published in October, 1920, when the citizens were so weary of idealism and world improvement that they were turning to a small town newspaper-man senator for their new leader. While the typesetters were putting the book into print, Senator Warren G. Harding was standing on his front porch assuring a people fatigued with internationalism that "there is more happiness in the American village than in any other place on the face of the earth." And one might note in passing that before MAIN STREET was a month old with its protest against standardization, the first broadcasting station had been set up in the republic.

The long preparation for MAIN STREET and BABBITT comprised five novels which gave some little indication of the greater works to follow. They are now exceedingly interesting as records in the growth of America's first Nobel prize-winner in literature. OUR MR. WRENN (1914) has a hero who toils as a commonplace clerk in New York, but dreams of an escape into romance and adventure. He does actually escape for a time, but soon, the little journey over, he returns to his prosaic business, and slips back into dullness and repose. The opportunities for satire are not often utilized. The Outlook was reminded by this little story of H. G. Wells and at times of O. Henry—so versatile are the minds of reviewers. The spokesman for the Nation put down the book "in a pleasant frame of mind, with the feeling of having wandered awhile in an odd and delightful world of make-believe," and the Review of Reviews suggested that "the tired business man will find just the right antidote for weariness in *Our Mr. Wrenn,* a gently satiric novel by Sinclair Lewis." And thus did the author come first before the public as novelist to the world just beginning its War.

THE TRAIL OF THE HAWK (1915) was, Sinclair Lewis said, written on the train while he commuted. It is a more important novel and more interesting than either ANN VICKERS or WORK OF ART, and its opening pages contain the best its author has ever written about childhood and the feel of the countryside. The title is a symbol for the restless spirit of Hawk Ericson, who is always pushing forward for something bigger and more beautiful than he has yet seen or accomplished. The first scenes in a Minnesota town anticipate the locale of Main Street. The little Baptist Plato College to which the hero goes is a draft for Elmer Gantry's college; its president hopes "that in devotion to the ideals of the Baptist church we shall strive ever onward and upward in even our smallest daily concerns, *per aspera ad astra,* not in a spirit of materialism and modern unrest, but in a spirit of duty." And the adventures of Hawk, wandering about the world, doing odd jobs, marrying a social worker, trying to find himself in the growing automobile and airplane industry, and going off at last to manage a corporation in South America, are drawn in part from the author's own experience and represent a pattern which is repeated with variations in all the Sinclair Lewis novels. The not unkind reviewer in the Nation said that "Mr. Lewis knows the scenes of which he writes and . . . has succeeded in giving a truer picture of our puzzling United States than . . . more ambitious tales. This sane-eyed, realism . . . should win for it a multitude of interested readers." It didn't but it should have, for the author had almost found himself. It was a few years early.

There were several noteworthy things about THE JOB (1917). It was timely in its theme of independence and self-expression for women, but it was not striking enough to command the attention of a nation just plunging into the World War. A year or two later, thousands of girls were revolting against the small-town conventions which expected them to live virtuously at home and marry the most readily available man. They went into newspaper offices, editorial rooms, and advertising agencies, and lived with greater freedom in Greenwich than in Friendship Village. But Una Golden was still something of a brave pioneer with the twofold problem of making her own living and securing, even in New York, some degree of satisfaction in her private life which The Job threatened to crush. How she met those difficulties and with what degree of success are the materials for this novel. Her escape is not of that adventurous quality so familiar in novels on the same theme in the booming twenties. She is at best a wage slave in the many-towered island. The heroine is portrayed with sympathy and understanding, more convincingly a human being than the celebrated Carol Kennicott. She was praised by discerning readers as sincere and original. The middle-aged salesman is to his confrères what Elmer Gantry was to the ministry, and provoked the remark from a reviewer in the New Republic: "Mr. Lewis has put all the banality of all the American drummers into this one genial swine. . . . He is composite of all the complacent American barbarians who ever guzzled prosperity and bragged generosity and whined affliction at the first flick of nature's whip." Although Sinclair Lewis had done a good job, the world was not yet ready to hear him with that degree of seriousness necessary to establish him as an important novelist.

Nor were the next two novels strong enough to command it. THE INNOCENTS (1917) was not so good as THE JOB. It suggested that the energetic author had paused for his own amusement and had put tongue in cheek while he wandered according to the Bookman "in the pleasant flower-grown fields of sweetness and light" and laughed inwardly at himself, his characters, and the readers of Dickens for whom it was composed.

And in the last of the group, FREE AIR (1919), Sinclair Lewis concluded his apprenticeship by spinning a yarn about a girl in a big car crossing the United States and meeting love and a boy in a little car on the way. But even in this weakening effort, where in the words of the New Republic "the characters and plot are commonplace to the point of banality" there is a gusto, an energy, and an authentic feeling "for the sweep and exhilaration of the great open country."

These were the novels which preceded MAIN STREET. In one form or another they contained nearly all the ingredients which were now expanded or rearranged into the pattern of that successful novel. But there is no getting away from the element of coincidence in the popularity of MAIN STREET because, as any one who will trouble himself to read it along with its predecessors may now see, it is not as a novel enough better than THE TRAIL OF THE HAWK or THE JOB to become of itself a phenomenon. But the country was finally ready for MAIN STREET and BABBITT, and the discouraged Sinclair Lewis was prepared to write them and accept the sudden conspiracy of a capricious public to take him seriously.

The story of Carol Kennicott's plunge into Gopher Prairie and what she saw there is now known throughout the world. For the first time we paused in our hypocritical post-War narcissism and had a good look at ourselves in a mirror distorted just enough to focus attention upon our defects, and while the whole continent lifted up its voice in cries and curses and lamentations, the jealous and delighted European world which had been amazed at American efficiency in mechanics and engineering rejoiced in the picture of our cultural deficiencies, the students at the Sorbonne wrote essays on backward America as seen in the realism of MAIN STREET and BABBITT, and the eminent committee at Stockholm presented the author with a purse and a crown. It is really more interesting as a social than as a literary event.

The young firm which published MAIN STREET advertised
it so steadily and so successfully that thousands of Americans
long trained in the art of ignoring books were unable to
escape this one whether they liked it or not. It sold nearly
four hundred thousand in less than three years, and although
that is only three to each thousand citizens, and does not compete with the number of automobiles or radios, it was most
uncommon for a book.

The novel was received as a satire, as a realistic report
of small-town life, or as a protest against the absorbing poverty
of American culture. It brought to the national attention the
critical attitude of the young generation toward the home-
town life. The cleavage which had developed between the
way of life of the folks back home and this group of young
Westerners who had escaped the West, received a college education, and adopted the cosmopolitan customs of the cities,
was a shock to many people and added to the interest in this
novel. For it was an examination of Gopher Prairie by one
who was measuring it by a standard quite alien and unfamiliar
to the natives of that village, and his heroine was a college
girl educated away from village life and panting for uplift.
Both the author and the reader tacitly accept this inferred
ideal when they walk down Main Street.

The protest was against the same contemptible qualities
which infuriated the author of THE STORY OF A COUNTRY TOWN:
the smugness of the village mind lost in a rut without knowing it and venomously hostile to other values and to change,
with no conversation except gossip and no social resources
above Dave Dyer's stunt about the Norwegian catching a hen,
secure in repeated platitudes about "the best people on earth
here." The ugliness and absence of plan in the towns is especially depressing to Carol, and she analyzes this perfectly
when she discerns that the symbol of beauty in these hideous
places is old Rauskukle with his filth and his dollars and not
beautiful streets and lovely buildings. She longs for some
spark of gayety, charm and amusement to overcome the slow

contagion of the village which infects and destroys the ambitious people who have looked upon the world where these graces are in favor and then have gone back to a profession in Gopher Prairie. Her two-year escape was futile. Gopher Prairie remained the same, and in the end, Carol too contracts the disease and looks after her baby, her conforming village-doctor husband, and her conventional house, a part of the "social appendix" still far from obsolescence. And while she rationalizes her failure with the spoken thought that she has kept the faith while losing the fight, Dr. Will is thinking about putting up the storm windows—if he can find the screwdriver.

Sinclair Lewis weakened the force of Carol by making her the mouthpiece for criticizing the small town and at the same time making her futile and a little ridiculous. She is often fantastic in her discontent; her idea of reforming this country town is to replace the Thanatopsis Club program of planting trees and establishing rest rooms for farmers' wives with Strindberg plays, classic dancers, and a black, Rabelaisian Frenchman to kiss her hand. She is a silly girl, dreamy, naïve, impractical, unsettled by her "culture" like hundreds of other co-eds of her day. It was right and proper for the natives to resent her puerile superiorities and to consider her flip and stuck-up and faintly scarlet when she spoke of legs, silk stockings, high wages for servants, and B.V.D.'s in mixed company. But the finer side of village life is carefully omitted in this satire, and the people are somewhat manhandled as a result.

The truth is that every single quality that is castigated in MAIN STREET was and is as much a part of metropolitan life as of small-town life. Only it was easier to isolate it in Gopher Prairie. The Great Red Scare which figures in BABBITT was a phenomenon of New York City, Washington, D.C., and San Francisco. Jack Elder, mill owner in Gopher Prairie, has precisely the same views on labor, socialism, and the Republican party as any Eastern steel magnate with a castle on the Drive. Boston, not Gopher Prairie, was rabid on censor-ing books. Comstock and Sumner were in New York City and not on the school board in a Western town. George F. Babbitt might have been drawn out of a New York real-estate office and a Forty-fourth Street Club as well as from Zenith. Columbia University dismissed professors during the War in the same spirit that moved Blodgett or Plato College boards. And the Episcopal churchwomen of New York City, including celebrated names, proposed an organization for keeping dress and dancing modest that would have done credit to Mrs. Bogart and her neighbors in a Minnesota town. The Main Street mind was not merely small-town; it was Ameri-can. And now it was a flourishing part of the American novel.

The success of MAIN STREET was the stimulation Sinclair Lewis needed to develop the assurance and the pace which characterize BABBITT. That book was even more necessary to the American novel than its predecessor and it is as firmly a part of the third decade of this century as the Harding scan-dals, the Dayton trial, or Calvin Coolidge. The country was moving with exciting speed into the fabulous boom period after the War. The Harding administration was turning the country back to the business men for exploitation; the Reds were dramatized and hunted; the espionage system and sup-pression of freedoms developed in the War were carried eagerly into the peace; the women's clubs and the gentlemen's luncheon clubs were trebling membership; high-pressure sales-manship was getting into full swing, teaching Yale men how to sell securities, and vacuum-sweeper agents how to overcome housewife resistance by group singing at headquarters before beginning the day of bell-pushing in the suburbs; the real-estate men laid out curving boulevards in cornfields beyond the pre-War corporation lines, and laid down preposterous miles of gas, water, electricity, and asphalt; the men of vision discovered for the first time in history that values always go up in America, that if wealth could only be concentrated in the hands of a few everybody would be well off, and that permanent prosperity was assured if people would buy all the luxuries they craved out of anticipated income. After the brief slump of 1921, the country was off to a wild ride with the Babbitts of Zenith and New York. And Sinclair Lewis photographed the tribe at the moment of their taking off.

More graphically and more movingly than in MAIN STREET, Sinclair Lewis presented his view of the stultifying effect of the War prosperity on the lives of our men of business, their hypocrisy and infant mindedness, their cringing before mass opinion in the clubs and around the card tables, their race hatreds and idea resistance, their corruption in business and politics, and the pathetically shallow and standardized private lives which accompany their feverish rush into the $8000-income brackets. Poor old George F. Babbitt catches glimpses of it, vaguely understands that he is missing what he most wants because he is scared to death of the pressures his brothers can bring upon him, and confesses pitifully enough his defeat in the end. He manages to stick his neck out just once; the whack it got was sufficient discipline. The best he can do is to hope his son may have a better life.

All this is set down crisply, often with sparkling satire, always with a malicious understanding. And it is one of the few Sinclair Lewis novels which pleases the reader with its nice structural proportions. Most of the novels are sprawling chronicles. BABBITT has form. It lays a strong base in the first hundred pages as it gives minutely everything of interest in a typical day, unbelievably commonplace and banal, from the guest towel and razor blades in the bathroom, through the morning conference on the possibility of wearing the pants another day before having them freshly pressed, the breakfast quarrels, the journey down town, and the oft-repeated imbecilities which serve as greetings, lunch, swindle, browbeating the underlings, bickerings, and the final bored hours of the tired business man at home between dinner and bedtime. The body of the novel rises easily from this foundation through the career of futility to the appendicitis operation, final defeat, and dull conformity to dullness. And behind every page of the satirical portrait is the implied world of charm, gayety, and amusement for which Carol Kennicott also fruitlessly sighed.

Always in these novels the good life is inferred but not charted. In his next novel, ARROWSMITH (1925), Sinclair Lewis fronted it directly and wrote vigorously and convincingly of a man so devoted to an ideal that he gave only a fleeting glance to the right and the left as he romantically pursued it. Martin Arrowsmith has his failings; his injustices to Leora, his single-minded worship of science, his desire for a flannel shirt and gruff, he-man eccentricities to separate him from the suave administrators, are by-products of his egotism and his vanity; but he is a man after his author's own heart and the author exalts him. The inevitable element of satire is reserved for the pretenders and the stuffed-shirts who furnish the contrast for Martin and Gottlieb and Terry Wickett. They are a diverting crew: the pretentious dean of the medical school; the pompous university president and his board who dismiss Gottlieb; the small-town ass who is his brother-in-law banker in Wheatsylvania; the hilariously caricatured Dr. Pickerbaugh, health maniac of the Nautilus board of health, and his flowering daughters; each successive fake-scientist, publicity-hunting, social-climbing director of McGurk, officialdom and the cracked-brained evangelist in the West Indies, and the parasitic bores who surround Joyce Lanyon Arrowsmith—they are all superb creations. But our true men of science resist the shallow values of these impostors and labor on through day and night, success and failure, sustained through terrific hardships and personal sacrifice by the integrity of their purpose. The author was aided in his presentation of these laboratory workers by Dr. DeKruif, who himself was later to do a splendid piece of work on the same theme.

Behind the long quest of the country doctor is the honest and unaffected soul of Leora, whose devotion to Martin Arrowsmith from the day she looked up at him from her disciplinary pail of scrub water in the Zenith General Hospital to her pitiful death on the epidemic-smitten island of St. Hubert whither she had devotedly gone with her now famous husband, gives human warmth to the story. She could not arrange her hair neatly, or keep buttons on her dress, or work out a color scheme for the flat, but she could be courageous and quiet and free from cant and not too ambitious and an unaffected companion to a husband with a flannel-shirt complex. The memory of her was poignant enough to affect Martin's second marriage. In the end Arrowsmith achieves in the improvised laboratory among the Vermont hills the serenity and the peace which Carol Kennicott and George F. Babbitt and even Joyce Lanyon could never quite capture. Sinclair Lewis had written directly of the things he admired, and produced a book satisfying in style, development, and proportions. With MAIN STREET and BABBITT it placed him securely in the front rank of American writers in the twenties who were creating the modern American novel.

The height to which the author had risen was difficult for so restless a spirit to maintain. Instead of relaxing for a time while the stream deepened again, he plunged into the composition of three novels considerably below the standard of his best work: MANTRAP (1926), ELMER GANTRY (1927), and THE MAN WHO KNEW COOLIDGE (1928). ELMER GANTRY succeeded in rousing the country with its strident satire on its preacher-hero who was a composite of every objectionable characteristic in the entire profession. Its unrestrained lampooning of hypocrisy, its mock romanticism in the sections on the lady evangelist, and its continued violence got for it as wide a reading and as much animosity as any novel in our day.

DODSWORTH (1929) was fortunately more perfectly done, and its theme was nearer to the heart of the times. For it told of the pathetic attempt of this likeable business man to retire from his labors and cultivate "culture" in Europe with his shallow wife, Fran. The consequences were as inevitable as they were disastrous. The years of bartering in the market place had unfitted Dodsworth for the ultimate peace in retirement of which he had dreamed. And the snob "culture" of Fran left him with a wholesome, masculine disgust for all affectations. The problem with which the book dealt is still alive, Dodsworth is a true American type, and Walter Huston and Sidney Howard made a successful play of them in 1934-1935.

DODSWORTH was not quite great enough, however, to prevent the American public from thinking that the award of the Nobel prize in 1930 to the author of BABBITT was something of an anomaly. And when it was followed by ANN VICKERS (1933) and WORK OF ART (1934), two novels not quite up to the standard unconsciously expected of authors distinguished by such an honor, one could not avoid the question of the relation of Sinclair Lewis to the thirties. The new novels seemed less a part of contemporary life than their great predecessors. New cross-currents had plainly set in toward the end of the twenties, and they were reflected in novels like GALAHAD, DEATH COMES FOR THE ARCHBISHOP, and THE BRIDGE OF SAN LUIS REY. The world depression had destroyed most of those absurdities of the newly rich and the newly educated which Sinclair Lewis had so hilariously satirized in the earlier day. ANN VICKERS and WORK OF ART brought no new departures which could touch vitally an alien period. It seemed that the scornful rejector of the Pulitzer prize had already performed his most individual function for American letters and had now entered a changed social situation in which his genius was less potent. Even the celebrated realism of the talk in the earlier books came into question. Many interested persons, who had long taken it for granted that Sinclair Lewis was adept at reporting the vernacular, looked again at the attempt to record the talk of children at play at the beginning of ANN VICKERS, and then went back to the works of 1920 and

1922 to discover that the realism consisted chiefly in omitting pronoun subjects and otherwise truncating spoken sentences.

ANN VICKERS and WORK OF ART were not so pertinent to the times as were MAIN STREET and BABBITT, but they did have their moments of vigor. ANN VICKERS came into the glow of life while the horrors of the Copperhead Gap Penitentiary were recreated. The author has never been considered a deep thinker on the social issues with which he has dealt, but he often introduced words of wisdom in his own striking fashion, as in the remark: "The more punishment there is, the more things there are to be punished, and the general philosophy of the whole business is that of an idiot catching flies."

Although Sinclair Lewis had not found the right tone or material to speak to the 1930's, it was evident that he was groping toward an integration of the confused spirit of the times. Whatever one's judgment may be on these later books, the fact remains that the work of Sinclair Lewis's middle period was the most stimulating in our literature. The omissions in it were too glaring to be long overlooked, but the 1920's cannot be thought of without his novels. Their range is not wide in proportion to their acclaim, they have been external and on the surface, seldom probing into the sources of human character and illuminating it—as though one walked endlessly up and down Main Street noting the cat sleeping on the lettuce in the window of Howland & Gould's grocery store. But when reservations have been made to include any and all of his limitations there remains a solid accomplishment. His notes on some aspects of American life acutely in focus in the post-War America were indispensable to the literature of his country, so long satisfied with being smugly content and optimistic. By the sheer energy of his mind he helped the modern American novel into maturity and recognition.

Chapter Ten

THE CRITICAL SPIRIT

I

UPTON SINCLAIR

THE literature of satire and remonstrance extended in both directions from the Sinclair Lewis triumph in 1920-1922. Other writers had done much to straighten the way for this triumph by persistently criticizing the shortcomings of American life in season and out for nearly two decades. The simultaneous development of the mode of realism and the critical spirit gave added power to the novels of protest. The attention given to books which revealed the corruption in American cities, so unjustly and inappropriately labeled "muck-raking" by one who should have been more honest, had, through the early years of the twentieth century, accustomed readers to the stronger discipline of a dissenting and censorious literature. The critical attitude was so pungent that modern novelists could not entirely escape it, even when protest was not their primary purpose. A few important writers turned frankly to the attack on social evils.

Among these novelists Upton Sinclair (Baltimore, 1878) is in a class by himself, only a little below Sinclair Lewis in literary art, and, at his best, even a little above him in narrative skill and zeal for honesty and decency in living. For, whereas Sinclair Lewis uses the terms gayety, charm, amusement, Upton Sinclair repeats justice, unselfishness, temperance, humanity. That is, Sinclair Lewis is a satirist and a social historian with great literary energy; Upton Sinclair is a reformer and a humanitarian with the most vigorous propagandistic pen. And whereas Sinclair Lewis, after a brief boyish fling at socialism in Upton Sinclair's own colony at Helicon Hall, has maintained a detached aloofness from any attempt to reform American life, which he found so unsatisfactory, and has been content to describe it and poke fun at it, Upton Sinclair has been a tireless worker for reform, always ready to risk everything in a brave effort to put into practical function the ideals he pleads for in his fiction. The thirty thousand dollars which THE JUNGLE (1906) earned for him he invested in a socialist colony in New Jersey. The venture failed and the money was lost. He earned more and spent it trying to improve the sorry conditions of coal miners in Colorado.

Most of his contemporaries were only literary radicals who disdained politics and did their reforming in books or private talk. But Upton Sinclair has never shirked political strife. He has been in the thick of the fight for a better America, running for Congress as a Socialist in New Jersey in 1906, in California in 1920 and 1922, and in 1934 winning the Democratic nomination for governor in the reactionary state on a platform to "End Poverty In California." It is clear that Upton Sinclair means, and has always meant, business when he criticizes the injustices growing up in the American system. He has been more concerned with facts, ideas, and results than with abstract literary values. In his opinion a novel is not an artistic end in itself, but a means to touch the minds of his fellow citizens with a desire to abolish inequality and to create a better life for all. He has shown that in a mechanical and industrialized world where the American tradition of freedom and equality of opportunity is under continuous assault because of the unequal powers of different competing groups, at least one wing of a vigorous literature must be dedicated to social and economic ends. In this capacity Upton Sinclair has been the greatest and one of the most indispensable writers in the development of the American novel.

In 1932 he published an engaging account of his life in

AMERICAN OUTPOST. A BOOK OF REMINISCENCES. It is an important book because of its intrinsic interest as a record of a colorful career, and also for the illumination it throws on the hard-working, idealistic character of a man who has never been discouraged by defeat, and who has managed along with other activities the amazing toil necessary to write on the average more than a book a year since the turn of the century. The memoirs make clear what an informed person should naturally expect, that the many novels of the last three decades were forged in the heat of an essentially artistic nature overflowing with a powerful feeling. This intense creative emotion has never been wholly subordinated to the intellectual activity which has engaged his restless spirit. AMERICAN OUTPOST is also a record of his devotions and a clue to the ideology which sustains the novels.

He believes that a greater degree of happiness is possible to men on earth; that the commonwealth should be used for the common good; that cruelty, selfishness, and the violent taking away of justice should be destroyed; that the greed of the unscrupulous should be curbed—in a word, he has taken seriously the doctrines of Christianity and believed that it might profit a country to put them into practice. From these questions of wider import he has sometimes relaxed to speak his mind on the compensations of Puritanism in an age of indulgence, on the desirability of restraint in a period of moral relaxation, and on matters of diet and the evils of alcohol. And volume after volume has come from his pen, zealously exposing and attacking evil, and exhorting his fellow citizens to a more passionate concern for human welfare.

The nature and the extent of his work can best be seen by noting the materials and the themes of a dozen of his more important novels. THE JUNGLE (1906), exposing the malpractice of the meat-packing companies in Chicago, made his name a household word and brought him confidence and a small fortune. In THE METROPOLIS (1908) he studied the unsocial life and business practices of millionaire New York, and set them over against the Socialist ideal of equal shares among those who produce the wealth. THE MONEYCHANGERS (1908) carried on with the story of the panic of 1907. LOVE'S PILGRIMAGE (1911), a sensational book in its day, was exactly what the title implied, and was drawn largely from the personal experiences of the author which culminated in divorce. The comparative daring in its handling of the sex theme, and its wide reading, helped to break down the crumbling taboos and give to newer writers a wider freedom in selecting their materials. The autobiography, AMERICAN OUTPOST, supplements this novel with mature reflection on the benefits and the disadvantages of his virginity at marriage at the age of twenty-two. KING COAL (1917) was a bitter indictment of labor conditions in the coal mines, here localized in Colorado, presenting the natural hazards of the occupation, showing the selfish greed of the owners who permit trapped workers to be destroyed so that their coal may be saved, and proving that in the capitalistic scheme human life is the cheapest of all commodities.

THE BRASS CHECK (1919) went behind the scenes to uncover the duplicity of American newspapers and to maintain the thesis that they are owned and fettered by financial interests and advertisers, printing or withholding news at their behest, and devoid of freedom. He has returned to this thesis at various times, in common with many another modern novelist. *100%* (1920) told the story of Tom Mooney and divulged the methods by which he was condemned, in the hysterical days of espionage and Red-baiting following the War for democracy, the period which gave inspiration and title for John Dos Passos's *1919*.

THE GOOSE-STEP (1923) and THE GOSLINGS (1924) criticized the education of American youth in college and high school in a social atmosphere under the dominance of modern business ideals. MAMMONART (1925) arraigned the lack of personal integrity among artists who have, he charged, always been willing to sell out to mammon. OIL! (1927) was a highly successful novel read round the world, in which Upton Sinclair attacked the social and economic primitivism of industry and finance centering about the production of oil and speculation in the money marts, posing against this un-Christian system an ideal of justice and freedom for the laborers.

BOSTON (1928) was one of the best novels he had ever written, a long two-volume creation unflagging in its interest and breathless in its pace, reconstructing the characters, the backgrounds, and the story of the trial and death of Sacco and Vanzetti, blazing with controlled passion against the frame-up and the perjured testimony. MOUNTAIN CITY (1930) showed with simulation and restrained ridicule the methods and the psychology by which Jed Rusher, the poor worker in the beet fields of Colorado, made good in the approved American fashion and became wealthy and individual and selfish.

In this manner, the genius of Upton Sinclair has probed into the various evils of American capitalistic society and brought forth a series of novels unique in our literature for their uniform excellence within their *genre*. It is a significant comment on his powers as a writer that his last three novels have been his best. BOSTON runs to seven hundred and fifty pages, and it narrates not only the celebrated case of the two Italians, but gives a social, political and financial history of the period, concentrated in Boston and the Back Bay society, that anticipated ONLY YESTERDAY. Yet its energy is so great, its passion for honesty and truth so flaming, its partisanship so appropriate that the narrative seems short. It is alive with characterizations, with probings into motives, and with a biting irony in its style. OIL! and MOUNTAIN CITY share these qualities.

Since Upton Sinclair has declared that he has written exclusively for human welfare, it is idle to measure him by other standards. The result is, doubtless, what he aimed for: propaganda first, good stories second, and living people last of all. His natural ability for narrative and his interest in people, however, sometimes make him a novelist in spite of his practical aims. For a third of a century he has been at the front,

tireless, provocative, passionately sincere, original, and incorruptible. These are notable qualities, and they mean simply
that in the order of fiction he has chosen to write he has no
rival. He has been rewarded next to Theodore Dreiser by
the condemnation of more people who have not read his
books than any other American novelist.

2

JOHN DOS PASSOS

*T*HE critical spirit settled heavily upon American letters
after the Peace and along with the great disillusion. We
have seen how it laid hold upon essentially romantic minds
like Willa Cather's and kept them in the mode for many
years. We have seen how it revivified the work of established
authors like Edith Wharton, Ellen Glasgow, Zona Gale, Booth
Tarkington, and others. We have seen how it sent a multitude
of writers in every medium to scrutinize life through newly
awakened eyes and to analyze it in every nook and corner of
the Union: biographies in the new Strachey manner, poetry
in the Masters-Eliot-Robinson traditions, dramas in the WHAT
PRICE GLORY mood, essays and critical articles in the Mencken
style, and novels in the MAIN STREET vogue. The period between
the Armistice and October, 1929, was dominated by the spirit
of censorship and protest and the cynical mood into which the
world was plunged after its orgy of idealism erected on the
foundation of blood and muck. In much of the writing which
we have already examined, these qualities were conspicuous
though not always supreme. But with many of the younger
men who had reached maturity during the War, and who had
turned to writing under the ascendancy of MAIN STREET, THE
BRASS CHECK, 100%, and THE WASTELAND, the point of view was
central and compelling. And among the best of those who
have carried it on and actually advanced it is John Dos Passos,

the most conspicuous of the group, the one who has fully arrived and is established beyond the stage of promise.

He was one of the dozens of young American geniuses formed by the War period. He was born in Chicago in 1896, and graduated from Harvard University in 1916 just in time to plunge from those quiet halls where reflection and peaceful living are cultivated into the crash of modern civilization in the World War and the general chaos which followed. Like many of his contemporaries, he volunteered for ambulance service, first in France, then with the Red Cross in Italy, and finally with the United States army until his discharge in 1919. Such a violent transition accelerated the growth of sensitive young men, and it had a profound effect upon many of them who were to turn to literature. John Dos Passos saw clearly from the outset that letters could not be cultivated in a vacuum and that young literary men ignore this truth at their peril. He was made to understand that the structure of modern society is precarious, and may at any moment convert the most civilized age into the most chaotic and barbaric. He turned naturally and inevitably to the conditions of contemporary life and their casual background as the essential material for a vital literature.

He brought to his writing an indignation against all pretense. He is a poet, as most realists are, keeping a sensitive love of beautiful things under the exclusive discipline of realism. His poetic nature and his painter's eye are revealed again and again in vivid passages in the travel diary, ORIENT EXPRESS (1927) and IN ALL COUNTRIES (1934), and in the novels which are usually rigidly objective in their point of view. The stark realism of the novels is, by a curious paradox, a complement to the poetic wish for its opposite. The need to express this side of his nature more directly is one reason for the experimental character of the Dos Passos novels. It results in the brilliant, sharply phrased, personal expressions in the prose poems at the chapter heads of MANHATTAN TRANSFER ("In Constantinople the minarets flame like great candles round the Golden

Horn . . ."), in corresponding positions in THE 42ND PARALLEL
and 1919, and in passages set down in the midst of grosser
materials. One needs to keep this quality firmly in mind
when approaching these novels, for no one has surpassed their
author in tracking down in honest observation and report the
wretched elements, the dreary scenes, the sore spots of contemporary life.

As a novelist of protest, he is somewhere between Upton
Sinclair and Sinclair Lewis. He does not use the novel to work
out a social theory or to propose direct reform as Upton Sinclair does. On the other hand, he rarely resorts to caricature
to point his satirical portraits of the people whom he dislikes.
He is too much the literary artist for the one, and too deeply
concerned with accuracy and a vision of a better life for the
other. He writes novels which live by their own merits as
literature and for their virtues as histories of a period; he
relies upon implication to point to the reforms he might welcome. You must deduce them for yourself from the mood and
the materials of the novels in the same way that you would
arrive at them from life itself outside of books. They are not
thrust at you but are suspended in the pattern of life which
the author is weaving. He therefore escapes the limitations
as novelist of Upton Sinclair by beginning not with a thesis
or an ideal to which the characters must conform but with
life as a spectacle in flesh and blood moving before his eyes.
And he likewise avoids many of the distortions necessary to a
trenchant satire.

The result is not by any means a complete picture of all
the qualities of rounded, living, human beings. The hatred of
unfairness and the espousal of the cause of the common man
lead him to bear down much harder on the evils of society
than on its virtues. The principle of selection enters, as it
always does, and we get in these pictures of the age a larger
portion of cruelty, meanness, hypocrisy, bribery, injustice, indifference, suffering, criminality, and general wickedness than
the proportion of good and evil in real life would warrant.

Pity and sympathy among his characters are inconspicuous and action beyond self-interest is rare. This disproportion is the modern way of stating the gospel which cannot be uttered directly or positively. Behind the confusion, the shabby vanities, the shallow compensations which he reveals may be discovered by those who have eyes for the mood and the method the things in modern life John Dos Passos hates and feels are dangerous to our welfare. It is only another of the paradoxes of contemporary psychology that an author like John Dos Passos can picket the Boston State House and suffer arrest and imprisonment along with Michael Gold and Edna St. Vincent Millay to protest against injustice, but that in the act of writing a novel such a direct attack would violate the credo of art. In post-War America an author had to be indirect and work from opposites.

Because John Dos Passos has been active as a champion of the oppressed, he has often been described as a Marxian or a proletarian novelist. But it must be remembered that while he has written extensively in books of travel, in articles and essays of his views on politics and economics, and has definite ideas about the nature of the more perfect state, these things are not directly stated in the novels. They may be deduced from them, and their author would probably be the last to object, but the novels are, first and last, novels. Nor is their author a Communist. He is a powerful writer, with strong sympathies for the efforts of workers toward improving their lot, who has added three or four novels to the growth of American fiction. He remains precisely that, as a novelist, although he believes in his other capacities that the profit motive feeds on selfishness and exploitation and breeds hardship and chaos, that those who produce should share the wealth, that economic conflict under capitalism results in wars which make huge profits for a few while destroying the common soldier under the hysteria and the subterfuge of patriotism, and kindred tenets which he holds in common with many of his contemporaries, with Amos and the prophet

Isaiah who said in a moment of vision, "And they shall build houses, and inhabit them; and they shall plant vineyards, and eat the fruit of them. They shall not build, and another inhabit; they shall not plant, and another reap." Such an ideology furnishes the latent reference points for selecting materials for the novels and gives barb to the passages of denunciation and satire which enliven their pages.

Excluding the preliminary attempt at recording the experience of an ambulance driver, autobiographical in nature, in ONE MAN'S INITIATION—1917 (1920), and a study of the dilemma of modern youth in STREETS OF NIGHT (1923), he has written four novels: THREE SOLDIERS (1921), MANHATTAN TRANSFER (1925), THE 42ND PARALLEL (1930), and 1919 (1932).

THREE SOLDIERS was among the first American novels to debunk the romantic and adventurous attitude toward war. It took for its heroes three private soldiers representative of three broad social groups: a young Italian, a Mid-Western farm boy, and a cultivated young musician and college graduate. These boys are thrown into the filth and degradation of modern warfare, the corrupting life enforced upon them is accurately detailed without any reserve or squeamishness, the tragic effect upon their personalities is driven home, the incompetence and confusion and arrogance of the officers are mercilessly exposed, and the disillusion with the whole sorry mess is complete.

MANHATTAN TRANSFER is a portrait of New York City and a novelist's record of an epoch in its life. It flashes a scrutinizing glance at a hundred or more people from every social station as it hurries along from scene to scene trying to arrest for one instant the rush and confusion of life on Manhattan Island. Sometimes it is muddy in style, relaxed and sluggish, the very diversity of talent and the rapid shifting of scenes, weakening the cumulative power that develops in less impressionistic, more firmly cohering structure. But John Dos Passos has made his choice deliberately, preferring the nervous rapidity, the sense of breathlessness and confusion it conveys,

like a cavalcade or a midnight walk in New York through
fleeting scenes. It is the spectacle as a whole, not the development of a hero, which he strives for, and he differentiates it
only because in literary art you must dwell on one thing at a
time. He tries every possible device—headlines, scraps of history, news flashes—to break down even such separateness as
remains in this complex milieu.

Many of the brief sketches are quite perfectly executed,
creating the individual life of the Ellen Thatchers, the Jimmy
Herfs, the Bud Korpennings, of politicians, Babbitts, returned
soldiers, milkmen, etc. Some of them are introduced and immediately disappear; others recur. The style is pliable, sometimes sharp and hard, sometimes colorful and warm with a
feeling for the city, its wet asphalt streets full of light and
hurry at midnight and the life of its towers at dawn. And
everywhere is the sense of humanity not completely hidden by
the realism, or the honest description of a confused population.

THE 42ND PARALLEL and 1919 are conceived in sequence
although the connection is tenuous. They extend the technique
and the types of MANHATTAN TRANSFER, and the satire and war
background of THREE SOLDIERS. In each the title is illuminating.
The forty-second parallel cuts across the United States on the
line of cities from Salt Lake City, Omaha, Pittsburgh to New
York. It is also the line of the eastward moving storms. Under
this symbolism the novel describes the disordered industrialism of the present century, and the intricate unfoldings of
the destiny of contemporary life. This destiny has for its
agents the powerful forces of a capitalistic economy. They beat
upon the five principal characters and press them all, however
diverse, into the common pattern of contemporary America;
and John Dos Passos does not find the pattern desirable. In
addition to the fictional characters the author has included
brief, merciless biographical sketches of nine American figures
who directed the period—including Bryan, Carnegie and
Edison.

A few of the characters are continued in 1919, but without reference to the preceding novel. They do not interact, but they are all caught in the same maelstrom and swept into the focal point of the year 1919. Among them is Joe Williams, the baffled sailor moving just above the dregs of society, having an occasional desire for decency but never getting away from the bestiality of the fo'c's'l for more than a brief interlude. There is Richard Ellsworth Savage, the young college man so carefully brought up, only to be corrupted by the War and unfitted for civil life. There is the pathetic Ben Compton, beaten and sent to jail for pacifism. There is Eveline Hutchins, the new "arty" female who goes to France and generously looks after the Boys. There is her friend Eleanor, the lover of the dollar-a-year patriot who is in France to keep the Red Cross going straight. There is the tragic case of Ann Trent of Dallas, Texas, who finally commits suicide after her seduction by Captain Savage. There is a continuation of the "Camera Eye" and the "News Reel" and the biographical sketches which include "Meester Veelson," Joe Hill, Jack Reed, Wesley Everest, Paxton Hibben, Randolph Bourne, and The Unknown Soldier. And about them all is woven the author's theme of the hysteria and insanity of the world during the War, the disastrous effect upon the mass and the individual lives herein recorded, the snobbishness and impertinence of all officialdom, the loss of all moral values, and the sickening disparity between the ideal of the War and the cruel hunting down of all dreamers or seekers for a better world who refused to surrender their integrity in 1919.

John Dos Passos has shocked many readers with his violence of scene and vocabulary, and his emphasis on sex as animal experience with no spiritual overtones. He has irritated others with his moving-picture technique. His chief fault, artistically, is that his books are sometimes foggy, sometimes lacking in selectivity, and that he does not always transcend his material. But his materials are legitimate, he is in dead earnest, he is honest and hard-hitting, and he belongs to the generation taught by War to refuse escape into a dream world while this one is in danger of burning about us. His work is a logical extension of preceding tendencies into the world of the War generation.

Chapter Eleven

EXPLOITING THE NEGRO

*T*HE WAR gave a new direction to Negro life in America. It brought on one of the great migrations of modern times. Thousands upon thousands of Negroes, unsettled by the dislocations of the War and accustomed for the first time to free movement from place to place, quit the restrictions and coercions of their life in the South and hurried North in search of freedom and high wages. They crowded thick into apartments in Harlem, and rapidly overflowed into the entire district immediately north of Central Park. With Lenox Avenue as its Broadway, the swarming Negro city began to develop an exotic life of its own, full of gayety and high spirits. And out of it there soon emerged the "new" Negro and the long-awaited contribution of the colored race to American culture.

The Negro affected all the arts. He had already achieved considerable repute and a certain favor during the War when he fought side by side with his white brethren to preserve civilization. The famous Negro band under the direction of James Europe Reese had acquired great popularity with the American Expeditionary Forces and had captured the imagination of the French with its syncopations. These rhythms were soon elaborated into modern jazz, blues, and like variants which swept over America and caught the ear of Europe. The Negroes established their own cabarets and night clubs, jazz orchestras and dances, which for a time set the pattern for the white world. Negro revues, Negro and African art—everything Negro commanded attention. Negro spirituals were revived, and native artists like Roland Hayes and Paul Robeson won international acclaim interpreting them on the concert stage. Charles Gilpin created a sensation as the Emperor Jones in 1921. The Negro magazine, Opportunity, was established, and social organizations for the betterment of the race were founded. Many of the best young Negroes distinguished themselves in the arts and sciences at the universities. A large group of young and gifted poets, several of whom have attained national reputations, expressed their race in terms of poetic art. Toward the end of the twenties a number of talented novelists appeared upon the scene, and the Negro became a vivid part of the literary activity of his country.

This dramatic rise of the Harlem Negro was a social phenomenon which the New Yorkers could observe at first hand. Some of them were for a time absorbed in the strange life going on in the north end of their city. They cultivated the interesting Negroes and explored Harlem life, and they wrote books about it, as we have seen in the work of Carl Van Vechten. At the same time a number of authors were examining into and revealing the conditions under which the Negro lives and suffers and sometimes finds happiness in the South.

T. S. Stribling, Du Bose Heyward, Julia Peterkin, and others imbued with the realistic spirit and the common desire to present neglected aspects of American life, found an untouched mine of material among the Southern Negroes. And while they were working it into the novel, Paul Green was taking the same materials to the New York stage in his Pulitzer prize drama, IN ABRAHAM'S BOSOM, written in 1925 and produced in 1927; and Marc Connelly was following it with THE GREEN PASTURES (1930), dramatizing Roark Bradford's OL' MAN ADAM AN' HIS CHILLUN (1928), which became the success of the decade. Everything, indeed, seemed to combine at the right moment to exploit to the limit the American Negro, North and South, and to include his life and problems, old and new, in the expanding American novel. And in 1934 the interest was still strong enough to warrant an award of $10,000 to L. M. Alexander's CANDY, a novel of Negro life along the Savannah River and the conflict between the old established ways of living and the promise of the North.

This movement in literature was begun simultaneously by Eugene O'Neill in the play THE EMPEROR JONES (1921) and by T. S. Stribling in the novel BIRTHRIGHT, first serialized in The Century Magazine and then published in 1922. The dramatist made only one other attempt with ALL GOD'S CHILLUN GOT WINGS (1924), a distressing play set in lower New York "years ago," and dealing with the problem of miscegenation which became prominent in the mid-twenties when cultivated Negroes were invited to white social gatherings. It showed that intermarriage could not produce happiness. But Maxwell Bodenheim defended the opposite thesis in his novel NINTH AVENUE (1926) by permitting his white heroine to marry with prospects of success a Negro who was in every way superior to the white men she had known in her own circle on Ninth Avenue.

In the novels of T. S. Stribling, however, there is no thesis except that of a sociologist and historian attempting to report the truth. For this work he has a talent of a very high order. He understands the peculiar social problems and the attitudes of the South, and he is able to present them in readable fiction enlivened by wit, irony, a concern for truth and a sense of humor as well as of tragedy. But his work has by no means been confined to the Negro. Two of his novels, TEEFTALLOW (1926), and BRIGHT METAL (1928) were penetrating studies, closely documented, of the poor whites in the Tennessee hills, showing their ignorance, their lack of enterprise, their religious bigotry, their hatreds and brutalities. BACKWATER (1930) transferred the interest to Arkansas. And there was a series of novels and stories with a Venezuelan background.

In his most celebrated novels, however, his central interest has been in the Negro and the social problems created by his presence in the South. They are BIRTHRIGHT (1922), and the trilogy, which is his greatest effort so far, THE FORGE (1931),

THE STORE (1932), which received the Pulitzer prize, and UNFINISHED CATHEDRAL (1934).

T. S. Stribling is especially fitted for the work he is doing. He was born in southern Tennessee in 1881. He spent several summers with relatives in Florence in northwestern Alabama, about fifty miles from his birthplace. He later went to the Normal School in Florence, and became for a time the kind of disciplinary failure as a teacher that he pictures in J. Adlee Petrie. The contemporary life he portrays in UN-FINISHED CATHEDRAL is drawn directly from this background, and the tri-cities on the Tennessee River near Muscle Shoals—Florence, Sheffield, and Tuscumbia—are undisguised as the setting for Colonel Vaiden's story.

BIRTHRIGHT was a direct study of the Negroes. It centered about the character of an intelligent mulatto who had been educated at Harvard University. He returned to the South in a missionary spirit to improve the lives of his people, but they were unsympathetic toward cultivated members of their race and resisted his efforts. Although this trained and capable man was defeated, it is perfectly clear that he and others like him are gradually altering the life and the way of thinking of his people and accustoming them to resistance.

This new type of Negro reappears in various roles in the trilogy. In those three novels, T. S. Stribling gives a lucid picture of Negro life as a vivid background for the white characters whom he portrays. Although Colonel Vaiden and his family occupy the spotlight, the presence of the Negroes is felt in the house, the yard, the town, all over the South, inextricably woven into the tapestry of wider life of which they are a suppressed part. The author has several points which he insistently drives into the foreground of the trilogy. In some of the most dramatic episodes in the books, he pictures the Negroes' exact social status from the lowliest servant to the educated mulatto, and he is often at pains to make perfectly clear the superiority of some Negroes to many of their white masters. He shows the race prejudices and hatreds which result in economic exploitation and in lynchings, and he protests against it. He sets down in some of his best pages the effects of this particular social system on the character of the people, both white and colored, and reproduces in detail the reasoning behind a request for "jury lynching" instead of mob lynching. The slumbering hatred against the educated Negroes is made especially vivid in UNFINISHED CATHEDRAL in an episode which brings a white minister and a colored bishop together in a crisis created by a Scottsboro case. And Colonel Vaiden is made to voice the opinion of his class when he declares in THE STORE that education does colored people more harm than good.

This conflict between the new educated Negro and the decaying aristocracy represented by Old Pap Vaiden of Civil War times, and continued into the contemporary scene by his son, Colonel Miltiades Vaiden, leads the author into the most delicate of his themes, the intermingling of the races. He attacks it forthright. In the genealogy of the Vaidens, Gracie, the quadroon, is the daughter of Old Pap and the slave Hannah, and therefore a half-sister to white Colonel Miltiades Vaiden. Toussaint, the "white nigger" lynched in THE STORE for demanding his rights, was the son of Colonel Miltiades and Gracie. And finally, Toussaint's grandson is one of the little boys held in the Florence jail and charged with rape.

It is clear that most of the modern social problems created by the two races are touched upon by T. S. Stribling. His novels have, as a matter of fact, more interest as social studies than as great fictional works of art. They are more serious in purpose than most of those written on this theme by other white novelists. For while T. S. Stribling has been scientifically at work on his materials, these other novelists, the finest of whom are Roark Bradford, Du Bose Heyward, and Julia Peterkin, have discovered picturesque districts where the black folk are unique in their customs. They have written about them in the spirit of interested exhibitors, saying: Here are some very quaint Negroes and this is the way they live, love, worship and entertain themselves. They are seen not as a grave

social problem, a threat to white economic supremacy, or a
danger to racial purity. They are under much the same kind
of observation as an explorer would give to an interesting tribe
in interior Africa.

Roark Bradford was born in Tennessee (1896) not a hundred miles from T. S. Stribling. But the two men could hardly
have been more different in their approach to Negro life. For
Roark Bradford belongs to the old, pre-War tradition which
thinks of the Negroes as "darkies." He has looked steadily for
the picturesque and singular qualities of the Negro's spirit as
revealed through his religion and its lore. There are no "problems." His work is represented by his novels THIS SIDE OF
JORDAN (1929) and JOHN HENRY (1931) which deal with customs and credulities among the Negroes in the lower Mississippi regions. THE GREEN PASTURES, based upon his book of
sketches, has made his work a household word.

Du Bose Heyward achieved fame with his novel PORGY
(1925). It was dramatized in 1927, and became one of the sensations of the post-War period. It appeared near the height of
the vogue for Negro literature, at the moment when the
literati of New York were most deeply absorbed in Harlem
life. And it happened to be a work of high order. Its author
was a native of Charleston, South Carolina (1885), who had
been placed by fortuitous circumstances where he could observe the life of the Negroes among the cotton warehouses of
the Charleston waterfront. After an apprenticeship in poetry,
he retired to the Great Smokies and wrote PORGY, picturing
these Negroes of Catfish Row. It centered about the crippled
Porgy and the crowded tenement row, and it succeeded in
giving to this primitive life the illusion of complete realism
without losing the sense of awe and wonder and pathos which
belongs to romance.

His second novel ANGEL (1926) dealt with the moun-
taineers of North Carolina, among whom the author was so-
journing for the second time, the same district so powerfully
realized in Lula Vollmer's drama, SUN-UP. But in MAMBA'S

DAUGHTERS (1929) he returned to the now famous Catfish Row to create another great fictional character in Mamba. The point of view and interest were similar to that of PORGY. His PETER ASHLEY (1932) presented old Charleston in the romantic days before the Civil War, and was not concerned with the Negroes.

Julia Peterkin, also of South Carolina (1880), is the most considerable of the women who have written of Negro life. Her volume of sketches, GREEN THURSDAY, appeared in 1924 without exciting wide interest. Then her novel, BLACK APRIL, was published in 1927. Its success was very great, and SCARLET SISTER MARY, which appeared the following year, was awarded the Pulitzer prize in 1929. Julia Peterkin has continued her writings in BRIGHT SKIN (1932), and in ROLL, JORDAN, ROLL (1933), a book of sketches beautifully illustrated with photographs by Doris Ulmann showing in pictures the life so effectively described in the novels and the stories.

Julia Peterkin's work offers an entertaining ethnology of the Gullah Negroes who live by the hundreds on the Peterkin cotton plantation near Fort Motte in the center of South Carolina. As seen by "Cap'ns wife," it is a romantic survival into the modern age of an old and exotic group of Negroes. They are untouched by the mechanized and changing world; they belong somewhere in the golden days of happy servitude before the Slavery War.

In complete contrast with T. S. Stribling's point of view, Julia Peterkin has remained thoroughly objective, with the interest of a painter rather than of a moralist or sociologist. Instead of exclaiming, How unjust! How cruel!, she has observed, How quaint the Gullah Negroes are! and has proceeded to exhibit them in the spirit of a Southern hostess on a large plantation showing her northern guests her unique collection. She has lived intimately among these people, she has doctored and judged and cared for them, and she knows them in all their moods from the authoritative commands of the giant Black April and his dying wish for a "man-size box" to Jinny disciplining her fickle lover with a butcher knife. Her purpose is to make known the peculiarities of a group, showing where and how they live, how they work, what they eat, how they marry and unmarry, breed and rear children, what their religion and recreations are like, and the nature of their funeral customs. There is no spirit of criticism or reform, there are no social problems which extend beyond the plantation. The people, for the most part, are reasonably happy and content, and at the farthest remove from the "new," educated, assertive Negro of T. S. Stribling and New York. The mode is realistic, and the structure of the novels is just tight enough to make a narrative of separate episodes which she has taken directly from the life. She simplifies the dialect so that it can be understood but without actually falsifying it, and she catches the easy, relaxed pace of the life she describes. The Julia Peterkin novels, particularly BLACK APRIL, are a definite part of American fiction.

Among the Negroes themselves, the excitement of modern life soon found expression in literature as well as in music and the dance. They turned first to poetry. They seemed to express themselves naturally through the medium of verse in various forms in which colorful words and the themes of personal and racial oppressions, emotional introspection, and self-pity were appropriate. Many of their best authors who later turned to the novel began with poetry, notably Claude McKay, Langston Hughes, and Countée Cullen. Although Charles Waddell Chesnutt had written realistic stories and sketches of the South and had published in 1899 his THE CONJURE WOMAN (reissued in 1929), the real interest of the Negro in the novel began around 1924, the year of Walter White's THE FIRE IN THE FLINT, Jessie Fauset's THERE IS CONFUSION, and the year following Jean Toomer's CANE for which Waldo Frank had written an introduction. These efforts were not immediately followed up, and it was not until 1928 and 1929 that the Negroes turned definitely to the novel as a creative medium. In 1928 were issued William E. B. DuBois's DARK PRINCESS; Rudolph Fisher's

THE WALLS OF JERICHO, followed by THE CONJURE-MAN DIES (1932), a mystery tale of Dark Harlem; Claude McKay's HOME TO HARLEM, followed by BANJO (1929), GINGERTOWN (1932), a collection of short stories, and BANANA BOTTOM (1933); Nella Larsen's QUICKSAND, followed by PASSING (1929). In 1929 was issued Wallace Thurman's THE BLACKER THE BERRY, followed by INFANTS OF THE SPRING (1932). Since 1929 new novels have appeared in increasing numbers and each year sees fresh talent emerging. There now exists a considerable body of novels by Negroes which is worthy of observation.

These novels are all created under the strong discipline of the realistic method. They have been written by a group of keen, educated, traveled, observing, thinking Negroes who understand their materials and have a racial self-respect. Walter White is a distinguished authority on race questions, and his book ROPE AND FAGGOT (A BIOGRAPHY OF JUDGE LYNCH) (1929) embodies a ten years' study of lynching in the South. Claude McKay, Jamaica born in 1890, was educated at Tuskegee and Kansas State College; he traveled in Russia and lived in Europe. Langston Hughes, born in Missouri, 1902, attended high school in Cleveland, Ohio, taught English in Mexico, had a year at Columbia University, and then wandered about the world. Countée Cullen, New York born in 1903, is a graduate of New York University, and has an M. A. from Harvard. Jessie Fauset is a graduate of Cornell and attended the University of Pennsylvania and the Sorbonne. Zora Neale Hurston, the latest arrival with her JONAH'S GOURD VINE (1934) was born in Etonville, Florida, the first incorporated Negro town in America, was graduated from Barnard College in 1927, and is a researcher in and an authority on Negro folklore. These and others like them are creating the Negro novel in America.

Inevitably these writers have been concerned with the problems of their race. In contrast to the preoccupation of most of the poetry with analyses of the humiliations to which the Negro is subjected and with assertions that a Negro is also a human being with sensitive feelings, the novels, while often emotional, are more objective in their methods. This is doubtless because they come after a decade of purging and readjustment in the post-War atmosphere. But they are none the less strong in condemning the cruelties of their oppressors and the limitations imposed upon the race, and subtly glorifying the dignity and self-respect of the Negroes who, in the words of Claude McKay, "possess the courage and the grace to bear my anger proudly and unbent."

Naturally the greatest bitterness centers about the outrage of lynching, and the wilful destruction of Negro property by the whites. Some of their most powerful work is directed against these conditions. They show how the blind, jealous fury of mobs, like those described by T. S. Stribling, William Faulkner, and Waldo Frank, hunt down innocent Negroes, tar and feather them, lynch them, and burn their houses. Walter White's THE FIRE IN THE FLINT details these events to the final sickening conclusion. Langston Hughes's NOT WITHOUT LAUGHTER (Harmon award, 1930), although primarily concerned with other themes, tells the story of the wanton burning of an entire Negro village because one prosperous Negro bought an automobile and others had neatly painted their cottages. They were getting too "uppity." Some of Langston Hughes's best short stories, notably "Father and Son" in THE WAYS OF WHITE FOLKS (1934) deal with the same question. Welbourn Kelley's fine novel, INCHIN' ALONG (1932), telling the story of the slow rise of a thrifty Negro against the tyranny of the whites, culminates in a lynching and the gruesome burning in tar and feathers of an innocent Negro farm hand.

The Negroes have, like the white novelists, written at length of the economic hardships of their race, of the exploitations through peonage, share cropping, and the "nigger pound;" of the exclusions from the better jobs and from politics, of the cruelties of white children repulsing Negroes with hatred and the word "nigger," of the humiliation of the "Jim Crow" cars, segregation in or complete exclusion from public theaters, and all those well-known practices by which

the Negro is "kept in his place." They have been interested in
the psychology which causes white folks to take kindly care
of a "good nigger," and to break the head of an "uppity" one.
Again, like the white novelists, they have shown their
concern over the mixture of their race with white blood. In
fact, one of the most common characters in their fiction is
that of a Negro child by a white father. Their novels explain
the emotion of restrained rebellion in which the Negroes regard these white men, and they frequently describe the relationship between the white man and the Negro woman. The
relation of a white father to his colored son, which often
enough culminates in a lynching, has been a common motif
in fiction since Chesnutt's story, THE SHERIFF'S CHILDREN, and
is equally dominant in many stories by white authors. As Zora
Neale Hurston causes a Negro mother of a white man's child
to say of her son John-Buddy, in JONAH'S GOURD VINE, "He
ain't de onliest yaller chile in de world. Wese uh mingled
people."
Particularly since the growth of Dark Harlem, the
Negroes have written much about the color line and the "passing" of those who are white enough not to be challenged.
Occasionally the theme has been treated satirically, as in G. S.
Schuyler's BLACK NO MORE (1931), wherein a Negro scientist
discovers a serum which obliterates the color line, with the
obvious result. Usually the theme is tragic, as in Walter White's
FLIGHT. Two women have done most with the subject, Nella
Larsen and Jessie Fauset. They have explored a strange and
little-observed world made up of those attractive women who
are not suspected of Negro blood. In Nella Larsen's PASSING,
it is Clare Kendry, barely touched with color, who married
out of her race with tragic results to her own soul. Jessie Fauset
has brought style and maturity to her novels on, or not far
removed from, the same theme: PLUM BUN (1929), wherein
an attractive woman goes to market for a bun and releases the
forces which change her life; THE CHINABERRY TREE (1931)
with an introduction by Zona Gale, wherein is handled a

subtle psychological relationship among intellectual Negroes; and COMEDY: AMERICAN STYLE (1933), a closely knit, often brilliant, study of Olivia Cary, daughter of superior Negro parents, who was bitterly humiliated as a little girl, and thenceforth determined to "go white" and to rear her children to the advantages of white people. How she placed them in white environment, and the resulting effects upon them of their struggle between two loyalties, furnish the materials of this novel. Jessie Fauset is the most important of the women novelists of her race. Unlike the stories of the common Negroes where the interest is in social conditions and the characters are only types which could be moved from one book to another with little disturbance, these novels are concerned with psychology, motivations, and the life of cultivated people with intellectual interests.

Some of the Negro novelists have been interested in picturing Negro life for its own sake rather than for its problems. Countée Cullen's ONE WAY TO HEAVEN (1932) deals with religious life in Harlem. JONAH'S GOURD VINE is, in its best pages, a painstaking record of manners, customs, speech, and the life of Negro children in the South. Langston Hughes's NOT WITHOUT LAUGHTER (1930), among the good novels, pictures the life of a poor family in Kansas and the cleavage between the hard-working, religious, conservative older generation, and the young people coming to maturity in the jazz age, leaving the church and the submissions of the race for a freer life. And in the novels of Claude McKay, the best of the men and master of a crisp, poetic style, we are taken into the heart of Harlem life in HOME TO HARLEM (1928), to the waterfront of Marseilles in BANJO (1929), and to the banana orchards and shipping yards of the Caribbean in BANANA BOTTOM (1933).

In books like these a new body of fiction has recently been added to an expanding American literature. While few of them have that power and distinction necessary to enter the list of permanent works of art, they have created in narrative form a new and significant phase of American life, and they give a bright promise of greater things to come.

Part Three

FREUDIAN PSYCHOLOGY AND THE SEX AGE

Chapter Twelve

SHERWOOD ANDERSON

SHERWOOD ANDERSON belongs with Theodore Dreiser and Sinclair Lewis as the three most stimulating and influential authors in the creation of the modern American novel, and most of the significant work of the twenties and thirties stems in one manner or another from their work. Sherwood Anderson began to write during the fruitful period of Theodore Dreiser from 1911-1915. His first novel, WINDY MC PHERSON's SON, was printed in London in 1916. Although this book was at first refused by American publishers, and has always been subjected to antagonisms and critical attacks, the author did not have to fight as his predecessors did for the right to report in his own way what he had seen or experienced in the Willard Hotel and heard over the yard fences and among the drummers in Winesburg, Ohio. It was fortunate for the American novel that this brooding and dreamy genius was able to go his own way to his chosen work without these annoyances and distractions. Like his great contemporaries, he looked at life in a typical village of the vast Middle West, but his eyes were different from theirs and he offered his report in a new and individual manner. The product forms one of the most interesting chapters in the growth of our modern fiction.

Sherwood Anderson (Camden, Ohio, 1876) was and still is a man of his times. His life and his career are a pictorial history of the unique mood of the modern America which produced them and made them possible. Should some curious soul hereafter be moved to learn by what subtle alchemy we achieved that degree of difference which set the modern day

apart from previous ages, he might well begin with WINDY
MC PHERSON'S SON, A STORY TELLER'S STORY, and TAR.

These autobiographical books are convincing testimony
to the contagion of the creative spirit at the beginning of the
second decade of this century. They show how the singular
psychology of the day caught up restless and desiring young
men and women from the farm lands and the expanding mill
towns and set them to writing about themselves. They were
the sons and grandsons of the pioneers who had tried to escape
to the West. This new generation came back from the West.
Like their forefathers gathering for encouragement and protection within the nightly circle of covered wagons on the
flat grasslands, they banded together for mutual stimulation
and support in little groups in Bohemian quarters in the cities
to voice their creeds and formulate a craftsmanship to embody
them.

They did dramatic things. Carl Sandburg, son of immigrant parents, rose with the times to sing a vision for Chicago
and the wheatfields of the West. Fannie Hurst traveled steerage to Europe to get exact detail and local color for her story
of an immigrant servant girl in LUMMOX (1923). Edna Ferber
on the Chicago Tribune followed the same methods in her
study of poor girls in that thriving city. Vachel Lindsay went
abroad in the land preaching the gospel of beauty and trading
rhymes for bread. It was a great day. There was a *Cause*
around which the creative energy of a generation could be
concentrated and released. It reached into most unexpected
places and freed talent which might easily have been lost in
less hospitable times.

Among others it exalted one of Ohio's native sons, Sherwood Anderson of Camden, Clyde, and Elyria, interpreter of
the secret places in the hearts of queer villagers. In his native
state, where politicians are normally accorded first honor, his
fame is not abundant and people have been known to burn his
books; but England published him, and in France his reputation was so great that a distinguished critic and author,

Régis Michaud, accorded him two chapters in his published lectures on American literature presented at the Sorbonne.

In some periods in the history of this republic, Sherwood Anderson might have gone on managing his paint factory and accumulating dollars as a respectable Ohio citizen should. But the War decade was so unsettling, and the new materials for fiction were so compelling to a man whose soul was left dry in the mercantile process, that he finally capitulated to the urge to create something more colorful if less tangible than house paint.

The decision was sudden and irrevocable, and it is completely revealing. In A STORY TELLER'S STORY he has reported that the crisis came one day while he was dictating commonplace letters to his stenographer, declaring with typical American candor that "The goods which you have inquired about are the best of their kind made in the——" At that point he was overcome by the feeling that mere financial success as a paint-maker was prostitution and this routine of buying and selling was self-destruction. He abandoned the unfinished sentence and convinced the astonished girl that he was insane by looking at his feet and saying, "I have been wading in a long river and my feet are wet." Then he laughed and took up his hat and walked out into a new and adventurous life without once looking back even to put his house in order. A decade later he returned to see what had become of the old factory and nearly got shot by the night watchman.

That impulsive act terminated a period in his life that was typical of a large portion of the population in the United States before the War, and is sharply stamped upon much of our contemporary fiction. His family was poverty-stricken and unhappy and their life was hard. The future author went desultorily and with little profit to school. He carried papers in his native Ohio village, and later worked in the factories at whatever offered. He spent his idle hours at the stables or the race tracks and among the villagers at the bar-room corner. In those days he was hurt and humiliated by his father. He has pictured him again and again with all his absurd vanities. He drank too much, bragged too much, and strutted too much, and he worked at his trades of harness-maker and painter too little. The gulf between his pretense and his real position made him ridiculous. The distress of the family grew more acute while the jaunty father hunted drink and an audience for his wild tales of his Southern ancestry and his heroism in the Civil War. He is embalmed in two episodes in WINDY MC PHERSON'S SON: the bugle-blowing fiasco where the vain Windy had no better sense than to pose as a bugler when he had never in his life put his lips to a horn; and the attempt his son made to murder him for making drunken noises when his mother was dying. How deeply Sherwood Anderson was affected by his story-telling father is evident from the recurrence throughout his work of this theme in similar episodes. So also is its contrasting counterpart, an affectionate and sentimentalized regard for the patient, tender, hard-working and ill-used mother who kept the family together in the face of adversity. Her life was difficult and her struggle with poverty heroic, and her son has woven these qualities and his affectionate regard into many passages in the novels and the autobiographies.

Following the death of his mother when he was fourteen, Anderson wandered about Chicago for several years, went to the war in Cuba, then married and entered the paint factory at Elyria, Ohio. In this undirected manner he spent nearly half a lifetime in unsatisfactory pursuits, rich in nothing but experience, before he found himself and attempted to record the life he had led and the meaning of his existence. He possessed that fortunate oddity which enabled him to use and to interpret these apparent commonplaces and to try to discover the obscure motives behind his actions. He has tormented himself continuously in the search for the illusion of ultimate truth. He followed it to a cabin in the Ozarks, to the towers of Manhattan, to the salon of Gertrude Stein in Paris, to a workingman's section in New Orleans, back to

New York, then to the Hello Towns of the Virginia mountains, and again to New York, coming up with it now and then only to see its illusive form retreat before the searcher. It has been a long quest for some intangible Nepenthe.

The record of this great adventure, transformed into fiction, now comprises six American novels: WINDY MC PHERSON'S SON (1916), MARCHING MEN (1917), POOR WHITE (1920), MANY MARRIAGES (1922), DARK LAUGHTER (1925), and BEYOND DESIRE (1932). With only a little expansion of the definition of a novel one might also include WINESBURG, OHIO (1919), A STORY TELLER'S STORY (1924), and TAR (1926). Their materials are much the same and the form and technique are not dissimilar. His work is, in truth, all of a piece, whether its form is a novel, a sketch, a short story, a poem or chant, an essay, a note book, or an autobiography. It is always the baffled and dreamy boy caught in the toils of poverty and crudity in any small town; the bewildered men thrust from old freedoms on the land into factories and industrial life too complex for their understandings; and the sex-starved villagers defeated in their private lives because of their evasions, their repressions, and their erotic perversions, and because they lack the courage to live out their potentialities in spite of the hostility of their neighbors.

Some of the best writing about village life from the point of view of the under dog has come from Sherwood Anderson. No one who has yet written in America can surpass him in handling those materials offered to a mind with a Freudian bent by the poor but sensitive boy in a small town. His contribution to this subject may best be studied in TAR and in the first parts of WINDY MC PHERSON'S SON and POOR WHITE, where the scene shifts and the name of the hero is altered, but the character and the conditions are unchanged. This world pictured by Sherwood Anderson is one of astounding limitations. Conditions of life are crude and vulgar. They are filthy within and without. It is an animal existence untouched by beauty or joy. It is symbolized in the persons of Hog Hawkins, who could be distinguished from the hogs because he wore a hat;

by the lonely old woman who died among the pack of hungry dogs on her way home from the store; by the drunken John McVey lying in a stupor in a river shack; and by dozens of such types drawn from the life with a sure pen. It is a rough frontiersman's life devoid of all cleanness and nobility. Imbecilic clerks, drummers, town loafers, drunkards, and farm laborers in town for Saturday night sit and jest, tell stories and spit, and make ribald remarks about the passing females. The curious boy stands on the edge listening. He is being educated to carry on in the village.

The religious life of the town is in these novels an instrument for extending the drab, gossipy, and sometimes vicious spirit of the people under the comforting sanction of their God. The stones fly, for there is no one to finger the sands in tolerance and humility. Every aspect of the environment seems diabolically arranged to produce a tedious and narrow life divorced from all joy of living, and few there be who survive it. And the emotional evangelism which reaches out and traps the adolescent, makes him, if it holds him at all, just another village church member.

More sickening than all else because more consuming is the degraded regard for sex among these Anderson characters. Sex is bestial and evil, a subject for the barnyard and not a part of beautiful and natural living. Yet the code is strict, and woe betide the poor woman who gives the empty tongues the slightest excuse for action. The women are the plague carriers. They are laid bare in a great passage in WINDY MC PHERSON'S SON. They form a group in every community, he says, "the thought of whom paralyzes the mind." Love to them is an unclean thing "with kisses in a darkened room by a shame faced yokel. . . . Something touching the lives of such as walk in the clean air, dream dreams, and have the audacity to be beautiful beyond the beauty of animal youth, maddens them, and they cry out, running from kitchen door to kitchen door and tearing at the prize like a starved beast who has found a carcass." In such an atmosphere the young boys and girls of

American towns, with dreams in their heads and their bodies suddenly and mysteriously astir, come into knowledge of sex. There is no way of calculating the loss to those intangible values of the spirit effected by the episode related in TAR where the birth of a litter of pigs is linked in a sordid bond in the mind of the boy with the birth of a child. And each generation builds these attitudes into the one that follows catching it before it has the power to escape.

It is such things as these which are stamped forever into the mind and become formative in the character of the boys in these novels. But it is not for knowledge of this fact that Sherwood Anderson deserves homage. It is for the truth and the variety of significance which he finds in it. For he does not merely heap contumely upon it as many others have done, and he does not offer an objective report of "the facts of life without rearrangement." Indeed he is not a realist at all in the usual sense of that word, or as Theodore Dreiser is. He is a poet and one of the few first-rate symbolists in America, and he deals with material so native that it smells of the cabbage farms and cultivator factories of northern Ohio. The realistic detail in his work becomes a base for the overtones of dreams and puzzlement, and for the fears and torments which accompany them. Objective reality is only a starting point on the road into the psyche where its meaning must be sought. It is to be sifted, analyzed, and arranged until it yields this truth on a more difficult plane than the one which describes accurately the ugly buildings along Main Street. To label this difficult quest, which by its nature lends itself to no easy and final precision of statement, a "mystic stammering" is to obscure its merits.

For Sherwood Anderson believes that there is no sharp division between the event that befalls a character visible to the eye, and the brooding upon its meaning long after the moment of action is past. He holds that life moves from one instant of experience to another and that the interval between is not connective tissue in the outward and plot sense of connection, but is filled with fancy and brooding.

The internal world of fancy is just as real and more important to Sherwood Anderson than the external world of newspaper fact. This quality distinguishes his fiction. The perplexed mind of the boy, and later of the man, gropes about in life, never able to get it all straight. The emphasis therefore falls upon the relativity of truth when referred to dreams. Always, everywhere, the Anderson character is alternately hurt by the crude facts of life in an Ohio, Iowa, Missouri village, and then granted an escape through a glimpse of beauty into this private dream world. So with Tar, particularly in his sex experiences, so with Sam McPherson contrasting the vulgarity of farmer-boy denials of life, and their half ashamed moments of love, with the stir in himself among the long corn rows and the sensual beauty of the sun rising hot and red over an Iowa field.

In like manner, the two sides to village life dawn slowly upon these boys. Sam McPherson, Tar, Hugh, Sherwood Anderson—was for the most part kindly treated by people as he moved among them selling papers, or as a stable boy or factory hand. Then suddenly there came one of those outbreaks of cruelty and jealousy and these kindly souls were consumed with unaccountable viciousness. "I guess that'll bring her down." Sam never recovered from the shock of accidentally hearing these people attacking the neighborly and sympathetic Mary Underwood, and with unprovoked malice trying to destroy her life because she did a good turn for a desperate boy when his mother was dying.

These boys became fathers to the men in Sherwood Anderson's novels. The unsatisfactory condition of their lives felt dimly in youth becomes clear in maturity. The wanderings of an adolescent into the creeks and roads outside the village grows into the extended vagabondage of the adult. They are always hurrying off to another place to think about something. They are bewildered, grown-up children walking on and on through by-roads and side streets, avoiding people but longing for their companionship, peering out at them from behind fence rows and lilac bushes, trying to think, and then going home at last with their loneliness to try to find sleep. They are tormented by the vacuity of their lives, but they can never come quite clear as to the reasons and the remedies. They are all pilgrims pursuing the illusion of "truth."

Sam McPherson accepts the common belief that truth consists in making money for the sake of the power and luxury it brings, and in becoming a superman. He follows the career of Cowperwood, though much less convincingly. For Sherwood Anderson has created in Sam a duality of desire the conflict of which destroys the possibility of the superman; and he neglects or disdains the painstaking research and accumulation of exact detail which made Theodore Dreiser's creation a masterpiece of its kind. Sherwood Anderson was not interested in that; he was hurrying on to the lack of satisfaction which these activities produced and the revolt of Sam McPherson. After his long wayfaring up and down in the land, more of a symbol than a reality, Sam McPherson also discovers that social reform of the sentimental and paternal type is impossible, that the endless districts of submerged life are full of revolting evil, that vice in all its forms is repulsive and young men should be taught the fact, and that perhaps he can find peace as foster father to the three children of a wayward mother. In varying degrees, the heroes in the other books follow the same pattern.

Inevitably Sherwood Anderson's work soon encompassed the inescapable theme of modern times: the destruction of the craftsman by machine processes, and all that this implied in further restricting the satisfactions available to men in our day. These themes, first suggested in WINDY MC PHERSON's SON and interwoven into the wanderings of its hero "in search of truth," become more engrossing in MARCHING MEN and POOR WHITE. Both deal with themes which have engaged the talent of many of the best young men in the 1930's, and the line of descent is direct. Even before the War Sherwood Anderson had seen enough of industrial life to know its sorry limitations which Americans are so reluctant to face. He had seen the independence and the pride of craftsmanship of a harness-maker destroyed in a few years by the expansion of machine processes. He had seen the vicinity of Clyde, Ohio, grow dark with factories, and the farm hands transformed into factory slaves without suspicion or forethought. Somewhat blindly and sentimentally he resented the monstrous thing the country was growing into. How could men, brought up in a new and clean land like America, develop in their own lives so many unclean and ignoble qualities? Will mankind, he asks in WINDY MC PHERSON'S SON, "never shrive itself and understand itself, and turn fiercely and energetically toward the building of a bigger and cleaner race of men?"

He has no exact course charted for the adventure. But he is clear on a few of the requirements. America has produced so many of the trader-type millionaire because she has offered no better outlet for the energies of quick-acting and audacious men. By her success publicity she built their emptiness into the supermen of business which a more experienced and cynical age has deflated with a single epithet: stuffed-shirt. And she has spawned their antithesis in the mass of enslaved workers who have no vision of independent men in beautiful free cities, who have never learned to coöperate, and who do not really want reform because their minds are too inert to be deeply moved by a dream. The two opposing groups, the few with the will and the power to hurt and to underpay the many whom they control, have moved farther into hostility. Beaut McGregor in MARCHING MEN forsees a day when the curse on the country will be lifted and the working men will begin to march together by the hundreds of thousands. On that day, these marching men will parade straight into the consciousness of their oppressors and make them afraid. And he thinks that when this symbolic marching has made one great body of its members, a miracle will happen and a collective brain will grow.

This kind of marching, however, has not yet begun in POOR WHITE. The hero of that book, although a blundering inventor who advances technological unemployment and the industrialization of Bidwell, Ohio, has no clear notion of what it is all about. By trial and error he builds machines, by craft and dishonesty the local townsmen manufacture and sell them, and the people creep in from the fields to "grow thin and haggard with the constant toil of getting food and warmth" in the dark houses they do not own. The blight of their lives is vividly symbolized in the fable of the mice which opens Chapter Seven. The steady advance of this commercial spirit and its devastation forms the central theme of the novel. It is sounded in the three distinctive pages comparable to those in ARROWSMITH on the dispersal of the plague, describing the spread of the new spirit as it captured and confused the minds of all men, sent the young out of the moonlit roads into technical schools, and swelled the population and the ill will of the village. Poetry and dreams died. The result is concluded in the flaming symbolism of Joe Wainsworth, the last of the old craftsmen, cutting the throat of his new-era helper, slashing to bits the machine-made harness he had bought in defiance of Joe's wishes, and with his last energy of protest shooting Steve Hunter because he typifies this mad new world. The episode is finally pointed through the mind of Clara, for whom "the harness maker had come to stand for all the men and women in the world who were in secret revolt against the absorption of the age in machines and the products of machines. He had stood as a protesting figure against what her father had become and what she thought her husband had become." But the bewildered Hugh got something of a vision from the disease of thinking. He discovered that growth was not in itself good, that the new towns were like colorless pebbles thrown on the ground, and that there was some kind of unformulated release and satisfaction in the presence of his pregnant wife as he walked with his arm around her into the farm house.

The program of "marching men" is too vague to inspire any labor movement, and the solution of Hugh McVey's problems is too nebulous for a gospel; but in a day when most writers are so wise and messianic about what should be done, and confuse literature with "the coming revolution," it is not without pleasure that one reads Sherwood Anderson's brooding pages. They vividly realize the confusion as an end in itself and profess no easy formulas for ordering chaos. But he does catch in simple words the effect of the confusion on minds equally confused.

The experiences of the intervening years have done little to dispel the confusion; it still permeates the last novel, BEYOND DESIRE, issued at the beginning of the fourth year of the depression. In this story of the workers in a Georgia mill town, we meet in the central character, Red Oliver, the familiar Andersonian hero. He does not engage in the strike and regrets his failure; but he does learn that there is "something beyond desire" (after desire has been satisfied) and that "there's something worth living for—dying for." And Red Oliver does die in a neighboring town in the cause of Communism. Sherwood Anderson and his hero have achieved that degree of clarity or confusion in the fog of a vast bewilderment.

The sex question, latent in all the earlier novels, became explicit in the WINESBURG, OHIO stories, and was central in MANY MARRIAGES and DARK LAUGHTER. It soon overshadowed all other qualities in Sherwood Anderson's work. His great and damaging popularity in the early 1920's was based upon his use of this theme. He became novelist to sex-obsessed post-War America, the man of Freud among the villagers. This confused and brooding man to whom the secret dream was more real than his actual experiences, wanted passionately to understand and get straight the crooked lives of all these eccentric people he had met. Why were they so odd, so lonely, so melancholy in their sense of aloneness and separateness, so unable to break out of their confinement to establish free contact with other human beings? Why were they driven to moon about in the rain, to lie in a cornfield, or to stand before the door of a woman with hand uplifted to knock, only to become suddenly inhibited and run away, like Hugh McVey on his wedding night? The answers to all these questions and the explanation of all conduct were in the early days of Sherwood Anderson's writing to be had from Sigmund Freud.

Sigmund Freud dominated American literature for exactly two decades. He provided Eugene O'Neill in drama, Robinson Jeffers in free-verse tales, and Sherwood Anderson in novel and stories with the proper clues for understanding their collections of failures, misfits, and wild men. It is one of the strangest and most fascinating chapters in the history of our literature. The literary men had found truth, and it was as intriguing as it was simple. They accepted the belief that behind the civil front presented to the censorious world every man conceals a part of himself where his dark thoughts and desires dwell. In this subconscious world he lusts and longs and murders and broods on forbidden things. In most cases, he is successful in keeping the evil imprisoned in the subconscious, and in finding compensating releases in accepted modes. But when such driving impulses as those behind sex are forced down into this section of one's being and become warped with repressions, the whole life and personality may be imperiled. This, they believed, is most likely to happen to the more sensitive and less courageous and natural men and women in small towns and villages where the communal mind seems to be perverted and abnormally interested in all matters related to the sex code. And if one does not unfold naturally through adolescence, he may become the victim of a "fixation," or he may develop one of many possible "complexes" which become linked with the springs of all his actions. The problem is, therefore, to diagnose the libido of the patient and explain his peculiar psychosis. Edgar Lee Masters had united these elements to make the explosives in SPOON RIVER ANTHOLOGY. Sherwood Anderson brought them together in WINESBURG, OHIO.

The materials in that collection and the use he made of them were and are unique in our literature. Without benefit of plot or story in the old sense, he sought out the pathos behind the lives of these townsmen, prying into the secrets of their hidden selves to find the reason for their twisted personalities. One by one the concealments are made plain as this strangely gifted artist tries, as he says in his NOTEBOOK, "to really call up before ourselves . . . something of the inner quality of lives." Wing Biddlebaum alias Adolph Myers, once a gentle and gifted school teacher, now a poor, terrified fugitive from Pennsylvania, so small, so white, so pitiful with the sensitive hands always in motion, wrecked in mid-career by the perverted imaginings of a half-witted boy and the community's revenge, now at the age of forty a decayed and frightened recluse on the edge of Winesburg; Tom Foster, whose adjustment to sex is twisted by the sordid exhibitions he witnessed in degraded sections of Cincinnati; Kate Swift longing for love; Belle Carpenter out to seduce; Joe Welling, the man of ideas, whose prototype warms a cracker box in every crossroads store in Ohio; George Willard and his withered and suppressed mother—they are all there. But the reader moves through a village he never visited before because he is seeing laid bare those private corners in men's souls which they try so hard to secrete from the eye of their neighbors.

Many good people who were accustomed to meeting these characters every day at the post office were horrified and outraged when they met them in a book. There was an outcry, because they felt that their reticences were being violated. But the Dial awarded it a prize, and two thousand dollars; and Americans have little resistance for things which win prizes. Although it was too theory-ridden to become a book for all time, it was distinguished by its sympathy, it was often bril-

liantly written, and it sometimes lifted into poetry the overtones of the great mystery behind human lives.

Both Sherwood Anderson and America grew more sex-
conscious as the third decade unfolded. The frontiersman's
fear of sex, his naïve madonna-worship of the pure and in-
violate female, and the tragi-comic effects of these attitudes
upon his conduct, were present in POOR WHITE. In MANY
MARRIAGES these elements overshadow every other. The novel
appeared in 1922 when the sex theme was nearing the height
of its popularity, and no doubt that fact is partially responsible
for the overemphasis and the resulting failure of MANY
MARRIAGES.

DARK LAUGHTER was published in 1925. It was more restrained in its materials, its story of the escaping journalist
who wandered away from Chicago and the shoddy life he was
leading to become a wayfarer and finally the lover of Aline,
his employer's wife, was better narration, and its symbolism
of the *clean, noble, natural* life in the healthy laughter of the
Negro women below stairs as they watched the intrigue of the
less spontaneous whites, made fewer demands upon the
reader's credulity than the erotic orgasms of John Webster,
the washing-machine maker in MANY MARRIAGES. The book
was a success. It left the happy couple eloping, leaving behind
them the helpless husband and the dark laughter. Since this
too is an Anderson symbol for the need for free and brave
living, they are permitted to go off into the land of romance
where their bold solution of their problem need not confront
the prosaic fact that neither has an income.

Sherwood Anderson shared with D. H. Lawrence the belief that life could be made happier by a more beautiful understanding of love and its functions, and a more natural and
a cleaner acceptance of it. In his first novel he had caused his
young hero to understand that his shamefaced and secretive
attitude toward women was a distorted and perverted one.
" 'Sex is a solution, not a menace—it is wonderful,' he told
himself . . . " But when he tried to show the exact working

of the solution in MANY MARRIAGES and DARK LAUGHTER he was not convincing. It can justly be said that his contribution to this subject in the American novel consists in his sympathetic delineation of men and women acutely conscious of their separateness from other beings and of their inability to attain any sense of oneness with them; of their emotional disturbances and ecstasies; and in his attempt to lean with the reader beyond the edge of words where there are meanings which both can feel but never completely express. Compared with the casual matings in much of our fiction, Sherwood Anderson's lovers seem to be caught up in a mysterious agitation of the universe itself. He has been moved to ask again and again for the ultimate *Why* in a baffling world too fragmentary to permit of ultimates. He has been unable to reason about it, but his instincts are keen and honest. Many readers have mistaken this honesty for a greater weakness than it is. On the contrary, it is the source of his strength. He has always been willing to trust these instincts and let them bring into his novels the unaccountable tumult of the soul which defies all reason.

The passing of the Freudian obsession with which much of his work is identified has carried with it for the time being some of the great pages of our contemporary fiction wherein he has recorded the fragments of experience which have most forcibly touched and molded human life. For these extensions of our knowledge of the people who live among us and consequently of our sympathy and tolerance, he has and deserves an important place in our literature.

He has also contributed to the style and the form of the novel. Ernest Hemingway and William Faulkner came under his personal as well as literary influence, and they do him honor. He himself has paid homage to the experiments of Gertrude Stein for aiding him in that part of his technique which depends upon a feeling for simple words in fresh arrangements, and for the trick of skillful repetition of words, phrases, and ideas. He wrote an introduction for her GEOGRAPHY AND PLAYS praising her preoccupation with words, and he

has furnished ample evidence of his own pleasure in manipulating them and tossing them about like colored pebbles to see
their hues. Under his hand they issue in the novels under a
severe discipline which has ordered them into simple combinations that are often poetic and sometimes on the verge
of finality. The apparent simplicity which conceals the art
often intensifies the total effect of a passage. Gertrude Stein
said another Gertrude Stein kind of truth when she observed
that "Sherwood Anderson had a genius for using the sentence
to convey a direct emotion . . . and that really except for
Sherwood there was no one in America who could write a
clear and passionate sentence."

The novels as a whole give the reader a curious sensation
that the form is always about to fall to pieces although it never
does. It is the exact opposite of the crisp precision of a W.
Somerset Maugham story. It advances, retreats, anticipates,
turns back upon itself, pauses for an apparently unrelated
digression, in itself often a perfect short story, soars into tightly
wrought essays and breaks into cadenced chants; and yet it is
never haphazard but is skillfully managed through all its
intricacies. His work seems to be firmly built into the structure
of modern American fiction, and from him proceeds one or
two of the important groups of contemporary novelists.

Chapter Thirteen

EROTICISM AND THE PSYCHOLOGICAL NOVEL

*T*HERE was a period of several years while Sherwood Anderson's popularity was at its flood, during which both the novel and the drama threatened to surrender outright to the dominance of psychological analysis and theories of motivation inspired by Freud, Jung, Adler, and Havelock Ellis. Both novel and drama were rather taken by storm, and for many seasons they interpreted dreams as symbols of concealed lust, and presented such a diversity of twisted human attachments between mother-son, father-daughter, son-daughter-mother's lover, son-father and a common love, etc., that a normal person was a rarity and the simplest expression of family affection was a clue to unsuspected abnormalities. For the romance and spiritual elevation of a great self-giving love there was substituted a cold, scientific, matter-of-fact attitude which reduced it from divinity to a biological function common to all animal life.

The temporary triumph of this harsh pose was as much a social as a literary phenomenon. Few of the novels which affected it provoked more than an ephemeral sensation. They have perished and we shall make no effort to revive them here. But the insistence of Freudian psychology on the role of the unconscious in human behavior directed the interest of the novelists toward that prolific and riotous well. They tried afresh to extend the province of the novel by probing into this subterranean level of human activity. The resulting product was the new psychological novel. And since, according to the theory, so many of the motives to conduct were entangled beyond separation with "the life urge" in the region of "libido," these psychological novels were, for the most part, written around that problem.

There are at least three writers who have achieved especial distinction in handling such materials. They are Waldo Frank, Evelyn Scott, and Conrad Aiken. This is by no means to suggest that the work of these writers has been confined to a single vein; only that the central drive in most of their writings is so closely related to this theme that it is convenient to examine them under this general classification.

I

WALDO FRANK

WALDO FRANK was born in New Jersey in 1889, and is therefore thirteen years younger than Sherwood Anderson. But as novelists they are exact contemporaries. Waldo Frank issued his first novel, THE UNWELCOME MAN (1917), a few months after the appearance of WINDY MC PHERSON'S SON (1916). The publication dates of his next five novels almost paralleled those of Sherwood Anderson, and the first stage of each career ended in 1925. These facts are important as chronological evidence that Waldo Frank is an independent genius who shared with his better-known colleague the honor of pioneering a new type of American fiction.

He has written, in addition to critical works which have had international attention, seven novels. THE UNWELCOME MAN was the story from birth to maturity of young Quincy Burt, whose artistic spirit was unwelcome to a business family and to an era of industrial materialism. THE DARK MOTHER (1920) was a study of mixed human relationships and their consequent problems involving Tom Rennard of New England, who had come into New York from a Freudian father-mother-son background, his sister Cornelia, also touched with a complex, and David Markand, subtly entangled with Tom and Cornelia. The "dark mother" has many implications, the central one being enigmatic Life itself, whose mystery illudes the searches of men. RAHAB (1922), bearing the author's notation *1916-1921,* followed the gradual descent of Fanny Dirk Luve from the day of her seduction by a young Southern gentleman, through the story of their marriage, his desertion, moral degradation, reform, and separation from Fanny, and of her slow journey "falling *upward*" from her first idyllic happiness to the house of ill fame of which she is mistress at the time of the story. CITY BLOCK (1922, reissued 1932) was a series of fourteen impressionistic short stories, separate from one another and yet tenuously related into a whole, giving the final effect of a novel. It explored the lives of typical dwellers in one commonplace block in New York City: a policeman, a governess, a politician and his wife, a priest, a Negress and her white lover, Mrs. Fanny Luve, and others pursuing their secret ways. HOLIDAY (1923) was a prose-poem novel probing into the psychology of a group of whites and a group of Negroes representing the ultimate source of the race problem. It culminates in a lynching following "the Freudian fever dream" built up in the unspoken stream of consciousness of the races. CHALK FACE (1924) went further still in destroying the novel form to create in its stead a symbol in poetic prose.

Whether Waldo Frank had reached the limit of experimentation with CHALK FACE, or whether his growing interest in criticism and travel intervened, he at any rate put aside fiction for ten years. Then in the autumn of 1934, he resumed where he had left off and published THE DEATH AND BIRTH OF DAVID MARKAND, a character who had been previously introduced in THE DARK MOTHER.

The first two of the novels, while often brilliant in passages, were not complete as works of art. In RAHAB his materials, his style, his point of view, and his technique were definitely defined. It was then clear that he was concerned with the feelings behind action, not in mere objective activity. His attack therefore is always inward, and although there is a precise narrative development, it is always subordinate to the drama within, which takes form by association in the mind of the reader. Long passages become unspoken monologues which reveal the turmoil in the soul of a person being acted upon by events but betraying little or no outward sign of the effect of those events upon the soul. The characters are substantial, but they carry about them the haze of this subconscious world in which their lives are rooted.

Waldo Frank continually underscores the mental impressions of his characters in order to give them priority over the source of the impressions. He accomplishes this by using a poetic style, heavily weighted with images and metaphors. The images are often deliberately chosen to suggest morbidity and fevered nerves, as in RAHAB where the carpet is *acid* green, a person is sensitive like the *antennae of a bug,* flowing at rest like *a red worm through water,* fingers trailing like *grey worms through sawdust,* and hands *corroded* in cleanness. When the narrative threatens to become too visual and objective, he shatters it with metaphorical language pointing it inward until people become insubstantial shadows of an excited mind.

"Fanny walked up the street into the Winter sun. It was morning. The sun stood low in the street's square gap: its heatless dazzle was in her eyes as she walked. She walked with sight blurred by the sun among the men and women wa'king like her to work. They were the substance of their shadows, long and black upon the sunglazed City. They swarm like wraiths, remnants of warm houses, warm sleep, in the inhuman brilliance of the sun."

The books are framed in that way: a moment of action, followed by a connective interval of feeling and of thought that is not logical cerebration but an undifferentiated series of flashes and fragments mixed with emotion. The result is a highly impressionistic novel, suggesting more than it says, sometimes overburdened with an excess of psychoanalysis.

Waldo Frank is a poet. He has attempted the difficult task of writing realistically of illusive things and at the same time preserving both their outward form and their spirituality. He has contended that religion in its universal sense is necessary to life, and he has attempted with considerable success to introduce this concept into the novels. Some passages in them are elevated and warmed by a religious fervor breaking into psalmlike chants. He repeats again and again the symbolism of Jesus, of the church shutting out the sun from Fanny's room, of trees rooted in the ground and reaching skyward to the wind, and of a mystical concept of cleanness.

Like the "mystic stammerings" of Sherwood Anderson, these symbols and their religious meaning never come quite clear. Perhaps they were intended to be illusive. But the view of life behind them, organizing and proportioning the author's material, is reasonably plain. Life is pain. Men and women are aglow with ecstasy and purpose beautiful deeds. The insensate cruelty of life beats them down. They are moved not by their wills but by their fate, doing what they would not, leaving undone that which they would do. They float "upon the viscid surface of a stream they have no weight to pierce." They are hurt and can find no meaning in the wound. They pass it on to others no more protected than themselves. Some use the words of Jesus as a subterfuge for their cruelties, others for personal comfort. Some of those whom the world counts lost—Rahab and her sisters—retain beautiful souls through acts of charity to each other, growing wise and clean, like the symbolic trees stripped of leaves but not uprooted. It is, however, misleading to state it so precisely, because it is all a wondering and not an assurance; a mysticism not whole in its faith.

This mysticism is closely involved with sex in the broader implication of "the life urge." It is an experience of the spirit as well as of the flesh, and even at its lowest it does not become solely biological. By vague suggestion he implies in RAHAB, and in several stories in CITY BLOCK, that it may be redeeming and purifying in a religious sense. He seemed to be seeking in these realms for a new kind of faith to replace the loss he felt in THE DARK MOTHER (1920), when he said, in words like those F. Scott Fitzgerald was using at the same moment in THIS SIDE OF PARADISE (1920), "We have no Gods. We have lost the old ones. We have won no new ones." He has been searching out new ones for more than a decade, and the quest has led him to the ambitious and thought-provoking novel THE DEATH AND BIRTH OF DAVID MARKAND (1934).

THE DEATH AND BIRTH OF DAVID MARKAND continues the unusual combination of realism and mysticism, in a prose firmly wrought and often poetic. It shows the drift of intellectualist thinking as the depression lengthens. The social criticism merely implied and never emphatic in his post-War books takes full possession in the new novel. How is a man to understand himself as a personality in a confused world? how is he to make peace within himself? and how is he to relate himself to the world that is now in death and to the one that must follow it into birth? In pursuit of answers to these problems, Waldo Frank constructs the provocative allegory of the well-favored and richly placed David Markand and his long, uncertain pilgrimage. His emotional adjustment to his business and his family collapses; he wanders back to his old home in Connecticut, but understanding is not there; he journeys about the United States injecting himself into the focal points of unrest and rebellion among the workers, hoping always to discover the personal secret of peace and harmony and a relation to life about him which tantalizes and illudes him. His wife Helen had found the secret in the Catholic Church. Tom Rennard was able to do without it. Lois tried hard, sensual abandonment. John Byrne and Jane Priest found it in vicarious death in the coal fields fighting sacrificially for a better life for the miners. And it is the martyrdom of working-class John Byrne and Jane Priest which, in a moment of great spiritual yearning and insight, reveals to David Markand the clue for which he is seeking. He meditates over their mountain graves, thinking:

—When I stood here before, I envied you but I could not think
of you. Now, let me not envy you; let me understand you.

—Your death was not unhappy, because you wholly lived, and
even your death was of your life. . . .

—I envied you, knowing how different I am. I will no more
envy you. I will be like you. I will do like you. . . .

—I embrace your class. All men who want to live today must
embrace it. My own life needs it to live. I have only the dead
body of a class that dies: I need, that I may live, the living body
of the class which now is life.

—I accept the language of your class: Bread. I accept its arm:
War.

In this symbolic way he is presumed to die and be reborn
to become a living Man in the world, not in "meek acceptance
of all life" but to act and "make its place and its deeds within
the world." It is a modern-day Carlyle crying the reformed
gospel of repentance and work from the platform of a com-
munistic ideology. And it is the summation of Waldo Frank's
work. The striving for significance and profound poetic meanings often makes the act of reading difficult but the retrospect
is always definite and pleasing. And if one ultimately is left
with a sense of great tumult on a surface beneath which he
is unable to penetrate very far, perhaps the reason is that not
even so serious and gifted a mind as Waldo Frank can go
far beyond the partial wisdom of his day.

His contribution to the novel is now definite. He has
grappled sincerely with the problem of the novel turned inward, extending its bounds. He has elevated the discussion
of sex and the emotions surrounding it. He has reasserted the
importance of a fervid spirituality in a material-minded age.
He has evolved an impressionistic technique capable of expressing these new facets of experience. He accomplished these
things at the beginning of the great tide of fiction which made
use of his experiments. And he has enlarged his dimensions
and justified the experimental period with THE DEATH AND
BIRTH OF DAVID MARKAND and the large and eternal concerns

with which it wrestles but does not subdue. On these grounds he has established himself in a prominent and honored place in the creation of the modern American novel.

2

EVELYN SCOTT

*E*VELYN SCOTT began her career as novelist in 1921 when the interest of writers in a scientific, psychological analysis of motives and emotions originating deep in the life urge and expressed in an experimental technique was in its first enthusiasm. We have seen how Sherwood Anderson was suddenly made famous to a not unpleasantly shocked America, and how Waldo Frank was elevated by a smaller band of the initiates. Many gifted young people, following the custom of the young in most ages, were both living and writing in the relatively new, unconventional style. Some of them, as we have also seen, frankly exploited the bolder freedoms in human relationships. A few were interested more specifically in the result of these relationships on the personalities of those involved. In this milieu the gifted young Evelyn Scott did her first work: THE NARROW HOUSE (1921), NARCISSUS (1922), and an autobiography, ESCAPADE (1923), made of the same goods as the two novels. Were these books not important in their own right and for themselves, they would still be interesting as a record of the state of mind produced by those first feverish years following the War.

A reader interested in the formation of the artist as a modern young woman should begin with ESCAPADE. Evelyn Scott was born in Tennessee in 1893. While a student at Tulane University, at the age of twenty, she suddenly eloped to Brazil with C. Kay Scott. They spent three exiled years there in happiness, poverty, and misery. The record of that difficult adventure in love and economics and revolt in terms of the author's mind and emotions is the substance of ESCAPADE.

The narrative background, while distinct, is deliberately subordinated to the psychological implications of the events. The touch is so sure, the truth and sincerity are so palpable, the balance between objective reality and the febrile imagination of the perceiver is so delicately kept, and the style is at once so poetic and yet so tight and firm, that ESCAPADE is, in the opinion of many, the most brilliant and satisfying of the books Evelyn Scott has yet written.

The early novels are obviously an extension of these qualities in a minute study of other lives. The parallels with the psychological autobiography are many, and though they are palpable they are not always superficial. The point of view from which the characters are chosen, and the circumstances in which they are placed, are suggested by the author's own experiences. And the overwrought mental state of the people in the novels is similar to that of the author of ESCAPADE. The background and temperament of Evelyn Scott, conjoining with the temper of experiment and rebellion in the early 1920's, help to explain the distinctive achievement in THE NARROW HOUSE and NARCISSUS.

The novels are two parts of the same story. THE NARROW HOUSE (symbolic title) tells of the complicated and pathological family relationships of Mr. and Mrs. Farley, their neurotic, unmarried daughter Alice, their son Lawrence and his invalid wife and their two children, May and Bobby, who live with the Farleys. It ends with the death in childbirth of Lawrence's wife. NARCISSUS continues with an equally tangled domestic situation involving Lawrence; his second wife, Julia, and her lovers; May and Bobby; and a brief glimpse of Mr. and Mrs. Farley and Alice. The background is suppressed, leaving the interaction of the characters upon one another's nerves exposed in all its stark, jangling irritation. As in the Waldo Frank novels, the narrative is suggested by brief, carefully selected episodes woven into a story by association in the reader's mind.

The people are all morbid and a little mad. The "narrow

house" is a sanitarium housing a group of neurotic patients. The author diagnoses each with a penetrating, merciless detachment. She indulges in no brooding, no mystic stammering, no striving for significance. For poetic feeling she substitutes a sharp, scientific eye riveted on truth. Sometimes she is frankly satirical in a dry manner. She deftly cuts away the protective illusions and exposes the withered souls of people.

Every motive springs from or entangles with sex. Every event is colored and distorted by the mind of some character unhappy because of a maladjusted sex life. In this family everyone is dull and querulous. They irritate and depress one another. Mr. Farley has an illegitimate son and his mother to look after. This reacts upon the resigned Mrs. Farley who takes refuge in a morbid sense of duty. Alice is a sex-repressed old maid, unbalanced by repression and a desire for her employer, taking it out on her mother whom she despises, and by periodic attacks upon everybody around her. Lawrence's wife is neurotic, excitable, weepy, sickly, sensuous, and cringing. And in NARCISSUS are added Julia, not very different from the first wife, an artist, an adolescent school boy, and a middle-aged Babbitt. There is a preoccupation with nakedness and dreams but they are not symbols as with Waldo Frank and Sherwood Anderson. The atmosphere is, in the words of Alice, that of "a moral cellar." But even in NARCISSUS, where there are three adulteries, there is no sensuality. Attention is always directed to the sensations in the mind, not to the deeds. There is no objectivity. Each person tries to dominate the others, to command their admiration, and to make them dependent emotionally upon him. They reach out for other people only to take to themselves something they want. They give only enough to attract satisfactions for their own narcissism. And everywhere the impressionistic technique, the unspoken monologues, and the tireless, minute probings into the subconscious, point the interest toward sensing what the author called in NARCISSUS "the *psychological essences* of those about him."

After these three books, Evelyn Scott developed, or at least changed with the times. Two transitional books followed: THE GOLDEN DOOR (1925), and MIGRATIONS (1927), a novel laid in the South with attention to background and social problems involving miscegenation. The second phase of her career began with THE WAVE (1929), just as the renewed interest in the past was beginning to develop. THE WAVE was a Literary Guild selection and brought its author into popularity. She had gone from "the narrow house" to the great panorama of the Civil War, which tossed up individual lives like corks on a wave but did not advance them. It was a technical triumph in craftsmanship. It created unforgettable snapshots of hundreds of people, from the lowliest slave girl to President Lincoln and General Lee, as they were caught up, modified, and set down again by the upheaval. By limiting herself like John Dos Passos in MANHATTAN TRANSFER to compressed episodes briefly illuminating the lives and fortunes of separate individuals, she was able to give a new kind of suggestive record of the four complex years of private sorrow and bloody battles in the field without undue prolixity. It was a high point in her career, combining her technical equipment, her intelligence, and her scholarship, with a significant theme.

One cannot feel that she has added to her stature or contributed greatly to the American novel in the three books which have followed. A CALENDAR OF SIN (1931) records certain activities of several families from the Reconstruction to the World War, arranged by year and day according to the calendar as a means of keeping time and people straight. It is not a moral treatise. It is an unsentimental, thoroughly objective, and quite voluminous study of human behavior in various parts of the Union beginning in the day when old Cadwallader Sydney left his family and eloped with the young school teacher and ending with the experience of life through which his grandchildren are still muddling.

EVA GAY (1933) is a long, detailed "romantic" biography of the awakening of a young girl from the false notions of life given her by her parents to a realization of the physical facts as they really are. BREATHE UPON THESE SLAIN (1934) tells the story of the lives of a family who had once lived in an English cottage now occupied by an author who tries to re-create them imaginatively from the photographs and other clues they have left about the place. It is long and unmoving, defeated in part by the method employed.

Evelyn Scott has done some brilliant work, although she has not yet completely realized the great promise which her facility as a novelist warrants. Her later work is too diffuse, and the analyses and the minutiae make it tough reading. There is little warmth about it, and it is too confined in its intent to command a wide reading, or to be greatly satisfying. But THE WAVE was an accomplishment, ESCAPADE was something of a classic of its kind, and THE NARROW HOUSE and NARCISSUS, firm in their experimental technique, stand out distinctly in the growth of the American novel in 1921-1923.

3

CONRAD AIKEN

THE greatest accomplishments yet made by an American in the psychological novel are to be found in the work of Conrad Aiken. He was born in Savannah, Georgia, 1889, tragically orphaned when still a child, reared at New Bedford, graduated from Harvard, and awarded the Pulitzer prize in 1930 for his SELECTED POEMS.

He is first of all a poet. And the intimate understanding of human nature and the processes of the mind which has always distinguished his poetry is the very quality which enriches his novels. The masterly technical facilities which he has cultivated in his poetry since 1916, concomitant with but not dependent upon other experimenters, in the quest for an instrument capable of exploring the life of the mind, served perfectly in his hands for a prose as well as for a poetic medium. All that was necessary to turn his genius into the novel form was the will to modify his art to suit its peculiar demands. This he did in BLUE VOYAGE (1927) and again in GREAT CIRCLE (1933). The necessary modification was less than it had ever been before because the boundaries of the novel had been extended to include poetic fancy, psychological materials, psychoanalysis, visions and phantasmagorias, stream of images, unspoken monologues, and such technical devices which Conrad Aiken was using in poetry at the time James Joyce and his disciples were developing them in fiction.

BLUE VOYAGE and GREAT CIRCLE have only the barest minimum of objective narrative. The actual story could probably be written in a few hundred words. BLUE VOYAGE tells how William Demarest, author, sailed second class for England to see the woman he loves, only to discover by accident that she had been in New York without seeing him and is now returning first class to England on the same boat engaged to another man. She and her mother cut him, and he goes to his cabin to think it over, while the boat sails on. Then he rejoins the passengers, and the boat sails on. GREAT CIRCLE tells how Andrew Cather, scholar, returned to his apartment unexpectedly to find his best friend in the bedroom with his wife Bertha, and how he drank, slept at his club, talked with his friend Bill, and finally worked out a solution of his problem.

From such a simple base Conrad Aiken proceeds to orchestrate in the most intricate but carefully disciplined manner the variant themes suggested by Coleridge's question, "What is there in thee, Man, that can be known?" What men actually *do* is told daily in the newspapers. They do all the things that human beings do. But to discover what there is *within* him is difficult. Conrad Aiken has tried to find out, and he has disclosed an amazing number of secret things. It will be observed that, brief though the narrative framework is, it presents a critical moment of cataclysmic importance for William Demarest and Andrew Cather. They are caught at the instant of their greatest agitation, and in that crucial moment their souls are laid bare and a whole lifetime is brought to a burning focus. For this reason the novels are concentrated in place and time, one being limited to three days on an ocean liner, the other to an equally brief period in Cambridge, Massachusetts, and each pours forth from the mind or the lips of the hero himself. A remarkable sense of verisimilitude and intensity results. Because he is concerned with the mind, he does not build up any interest in the relationship of either man with the woman before the crises. This destroys the poignancy of the personal tragedy but sharpens its psychological results.

And what does he discover within? Again, Coleridge, quoted in BLUE VOYAGE, is the clue:

> "Dark fluxion, all unfixable by thought,
>   A phantom dim of past and future wrought,
>   Vain sister of the worm——"

With determined honesty, Conrad Aiken probes the hidden corners in the souls of these two men and ruthlessly exposes the last cherished vanity. It is a self-analysis that flinches at nothing. It is conducted by the device of having the hero discovered in the act of introspection. He is merciless with himself, taking a sadistic pleasure in pricking the old wounds he has reopened. And he is by turns grim, sardonic, facetious, frivolous, and deadly in earnest. He is trying to find an explanation for his present catastrophe. That explanation is the structure of the universe itself and the agglutination of impressions and experiences reaching back into childhood which now determine the behavior of maturity. Under the impact of the dramatic moment both Demarest and Cather become aware of complexes formed in youth which handicap them as adults. Cather has a mother fixation, resulting from the circumstances leading up to and surrounding her death in a storm during an illicit intrigue with her husband's brother. Demarest has an inferiority complex born of a fear of his father which left him incapable of direct action. In their moments of crisis each is the victim of these experiences and a dozen lesser associated ones.

For Conrad Aiken emphasizes the complexity, the confusion, the dim border lines of reality in those misty regions of the subconscious where it merges with fancy and unreality. He does not simplify, nor impose upon the chaotic flux of things definiteness, order, or pattern. In each novel he has begun with the unquestioned world of the senses, only to push gradually down through the different planes of being to the "well" where the world of atoms, heart, blood and digestion entangle with spiritual abstractions like love, honor, hope, beauty, and God. The contradictions meet there, not to be resolved into unities and simplicities, but to remain contradictions under illusive names like *good* and *evil, purity* and *lust, love* and *hate, advance* and *retreat.* Round and round the analysis goes downward in a spiral and back to resolution, opening up vistas at each turn as we rush past, vistas we do not stop to explore. It is impossible even to suggest the extraordinary diversity of these novels, and the perfection of their form.

Both novels are built on the same plan. It is suggested by the title GREAT CIRCLE, signifying not only the long journey of Cather and Bertha from separation to reunion and lesser concentric circles from the formation of the complex to release from it, the storm, etc., but also the nature of its physical structure. Each deepens rapidly after an objective beginning, and reaches its spiritual climax in a stream-of-consciousness dream or monologue. Each attains resolution by a flight of fancy around the intricate symbolism of Cynthia transformed into a stained-glass window, and the cuckolded Cather into a crucified pig. Demarest regains resignation by sublimation through literary composition, Cather by confession and a visit to the region about Duxbury where his youth lay buried. And in each book, some of the most brilliant passages (the best of their kind in any American novel) recreate the glamour and the wonder of childhood.

There are not many novels in the language that satisfy the mind and nurture the heart by a union of rich materials with perfection of artistic design. Conrad Aiken has achieved it. The apparent difficulty of the form and the allusiveness of the matter necessarily limit the number of his readers to a small, but highly select group. He has chosen to write, not of small-town folk or rude peasants, but of men of learning and cultivation, like himself. Their problems are in part his own. When such a mind pours itself out, its wealth is amazing, and it legitimately floods the pages of the novels with tags of poetry, learning, and the topics written and talked of in our day by cultivated men. He pays his readers the compliment of making demands upon them. His work has justified the experimentations conducted in recent years. BLUE VOYAGE and GREAT CIRCLE must be read, if one wishes to see the extraordinary richness of which the new extensions of material and technique in the type of American novel suggested by this chapter are capable.

Part Four

ROMANCE IN A REALISTIC AGE

Chapter Fourteen

JAMES BRANCH CABELL

*T*HE novelists so far considered have been more similar than different. Their materials have been basically alike and their points of view, while individual, have been related. They are realists interested chiefly in the recent or the contemporary scene. James Branch Cabell, later Branch Cabell, is by all odds the most important and the most distinguished of American novelists in a realistic age deliberately to cultivate romance. He has made it acceptable to a large number of people by his jaunty spirit and by weighting its light frame with urbane and often profound observations on the import of the human comedy. He arrives at truth not by making a documented report on the lives of men in Richmond, Virginia, but by projecting carefully selected samples of their amusing antics into an imaginary world of Poictesme where the exaggeration makes them grotesque through simplification. The reader has the double-edged pleasure, if he cares for it, of laughing at the world while enjoying a temporary escape into an imaginary and diverting realm.

James Branch Cabell was the height of fashion immediately after the War. This exaltation followed upon the unexpected good fortune which befell him when the censors temporarily suppressed JURGEN. True to custom, this ill-advised agitation put the book into the hands of every literate college boy. James Branch Cabell, who had already written eleven books without seriously interrupting his cultivated obscurity to the wider public, was at once a national figure. It is a vagary of fame in the arts. It was not improper in that day to divide the world into Cabellians and non-Cabellians.

There was often violence between them, and there was no half-way house. One had to be of the fellowship, or one was beyond the pale. The fact is significant, because it is necessary to a complete picture of the creation of the American novel which needed its James Branch Cabell as badly as its Sherwood Anderson.

He was the only purveyor of the only kind of romance in books possible to the post-War age. Some romance is necessary to support life, and every age has had its portion either directly in action or vicariously through its literature. America adopted a hard-boiled pose after the peace, and found romantic outlet in the excitement of life in a time of inflation. Young men and women of parts no longer found it necessary to resign themselves to the limited opportunities of the home community and solace themselves with Zane Grey stories of the glorious West where men were men. There were jobs in the city, and the population was erect and confident of its ways and its destiny, and knew all the answers. The age which first acclaimed James Branch Cabell was secure in its new prosperity. It was not to be quieted with stories about heroines of old romance who were usually at best condemned to a guarded life in the castle garden within the walls, or the lover's walk under the mimosa trees and the Carolina moon. Romance of that kidney might do for the outmoded Rossettis and Swinburnes, and the Miniver Cheevys who were homeless and afraid in the new world. The intelligent moderns were trained to self-assurance among the bold facts of life. The tougher-minded were more susceptible to the romance of the vast claims of science, the concept of parallel lines meeting in infinity in a universe contracting upon itself (or perhaps expanding) and the projected vision of applied science transforming the world and all our ways of living. Many of the best minds went into these scientific fields, or the equally romantic occupations of building miraculous bridges, Holland Tunnels, waterways, dams, skyscrapers, airplanes and dirigibles. And for the less successful and unsophisticated there were

the Alger-story magazines devoted to the glorification and
canonization of the success heroes from Ford, Chrysler, Dawes,
Young, Coolidge, down to the George F. Babbitts.

Even in so colorful an age, our men of letters did not use
these materials for a great fiction as writers in other countries
have done. H. G. Wells of England was able to take the dreams
of a mechanized world and build them into romantic literature by extending the promise and the tendencies of the present day to an ultimate conclusion. And Aldous Huxley has
done a masterpiece of a more complicated and searching type
on the same theme in BRAVE NEW WORLD. The American novelists have not bothered with it and the field still lies curiously
barren. They have been content to leave Jeans and Eddington
in possession. But in the work of James Branch Cabell we
do have another kind of up-to-date romance, keyed to the new
freedom and the sex interest, and made agreeable to the
moderns by sly and mocking reminders that everybody was
only playing with "beautiful nonsense." It is brittle with urbanity and aloofness. Its carefully polished double meanings
became the despair of the censors, and the rapture of the
zealots.

James Branch Cabell, born in Richmond-in-Virginia,
1879, and, unlike most of his contemporaries, still dwelling
in the city of his birth, is one of the few authors in America
whose work is not greatly illuminated by his biography.
Granted the genius of Theodore Dreiser, Sherwood Anderson, Sinclair Lewis, Willa Cather, their lives ran a straight
course into their work as novelists. The most notable fact
about James Branch Cabell's manner of life has been its quiet
detachment from the struggle in the market place. It contrasts
markedly with the life of most of the great realistic writers.
The few years (1899-1901) he spent reporting on the New
York Herald and the Richmond News seemed to leave un-
harmed the scholarly reserve of the Phi Beta Kappa William
and Mary student and instructor in Latin and Greek. A brief
experience among the coal mines of West Virginia just before

the War (1911-1913) did not make a proletarian of the man who had already written, among other things, THE EAGLE'S SHADOW (1904), GALLANTRY (1907), CHIVALRY (1909), and THE CORDS OF VANITY (1909). His services as genealogist to the Virginia chapter of the Sons of the Revolution followed after convincing evidence from Poictesme of a genius for that quaint calling. And none of these matters suggests any great significance in relation to the novels. They sprang from a private world unrecorded in biographical data. Probably the best clue is to be found in the two indisputable classics from his pen: BEYOND LIFE and THESE RESTLESS HEADS, wherein he has affirmed his belief "that romance [controls] the minds of men," and his refusal to get excited over questions of large social import or "burn with generous indignation over the world's pigheadedness." Thus serenely remote from the panting spectacle of the moment, he has found it congenial to explore the more diverting activities of the Count Manuel and his people, utilizing as a background, he confesses, the life he had observed at Rockbridge Alum where young gentlemen of breeding affected the usual ideas of feminine delicacy and purity but found them no barrier to successful approach and experiment. Since 1904, uninterrupted by the passing taste for exposing the shame of the cities, by the nature-cult and strenuous-life period, by the War, by the era of sex, jazz, satire, and Freud, by the boom, or by the collapse, James Branch Cabell has steadfastly maintained his own counsel and averted his head.

Recognizing his own singularity in a world of conformity, he has in THESE RESTLESS HEADS (1932) offered his own comment on the character of his labors. He was deliberate in his refusal to view "with remunerative scornfulness the American doings of my own muddled and tumultuous era . . .

Throughout the last some and twenty years, in the while that my more temerarious fellows have with untiring typewriters assailed and derided her [Aesred, the goddess of mediocrity and conformity] notions, I have written on sedately in praise of monogamy in *Jurgen,* and of keeping up appearances in *Figures of Earth,* and of chastity in *Something About Eve,* and of moderation in *The High Place,* and of womanhood in *Domnei,* and of religion in *The Silver Stallion:* and indeed throughout the long building of the Biography I have at every instant upheld, in my own unpresuming way, all that Aesred endorses as the more comfortable fetishes for a man to believe in."

The shrewd reader will not, of course, be misled by the sly simplification of the passage, nor miss the Cabellian wit in the affected innocence of purpose in the themes.

Having chosen, then, to avoid the immediate scene in favor of unrecorded moments in the intimate history of great men and women of the past, and the adventures of imaginary characters in Lichfield, Fairhaven, and the fabulous Poictesme, he called upon all the resources of his art to make them agreeable to a realistic age which would laugh any solemn or pretentious romancer from the bookstalls. He made them gently comic, and recalled from disuse a flock of adjectives long inappropriate to the description of American novelists: shrewd, witty, ironic, urbane, suave, sly, trenchant, saucy, jaunty, sedate, adroit, and kindred words for Cabellianism.

The continuous theme through more than a score of the books is that of sex and love. Not a study of its tragic power as in AN AMERICAN TRAGEDY; not a record of twisted misfits as in WINESBURG, OHIO; not a eulogy of maternal fulfillment as in MY ÁNTONIA; but a light toying with its charm and gayety, and an intelligent resignation to its vanity and disillusion. It was this quality more than any other which communicated itself to the age.

James Branch Cabell cultivated the art of writing freshly and beautifully about the oldest of human experiences. It was not without some struggle, he has said, that his generation of the advanced writers in the twenties developed the courage to talk in mixed company of sex matters which in their youth they were taught to avoid in drawing rooms, and some of them never learned "to approach the obscene with genial levity" without betraying their self-consciousness. But he was soon the greatest master in America of the art of engaging the interest of a reader in this subject through the medium of words childlike in their innocence. And much of the vogue for his works after JURGEN was based upon this treasure-hunting. The skilled reader found his amorous way among the accumulating symbolism of swords and lances and daggers, of candles and triangles and church spires, and of carefully phrased talks and comfortings. The charming pastime of deciphering the double meanings was an interest in itself without suggesting a careful examination of the importance of the meanings.

The novels are twelve in number. One records them in this final way because James Branch Cabell announced that THE WAY OF ECBEN (1929) was his final novel, and bade farewell to the land of the disillusion and accompanied it symbolically with a portion of his name. Five of them, beginning with THE EAGLE'S SHADOW (1904), are in the Fairhaven-Lichfield group, tenuously related to Manuel through his descendants who carry on the most primary of his interests in a later day: Robert Etheridge Townsend, poet, in THE CORDS OF VANITY (1909); Rudolph Musgrave, genealogist, in THE RIVET IN GRANDFATHER'S NECK (1915); Felix Kennaston, philosopher, in THE CREAM OF THE JEST (1917); and Gerald Musgrave, adventurer, in SOMETHING ABOUT EVE (1927). The intricate breedings by whose vagaries this group of amiable and amorous philanderers sprang from Count Manuel, the Redeemer of Poictesme, may be followed by the curious in the book of the visitations, THE LINEAGE OF LICHFIELD (1922). The biographies of Count Manuel and Jurgen are contained in JURGEN (1919), the story of the pawnbroker; FIGURES OF EARTH (1921) devoted to the count; DOMNEI (1920), a reissue of THE SOUL OF MELICENT (1913), Melicent being the daughter of Manuel and Niafer; THE HIGH PLACE (1923), concerning Florian de Puysange of

Jurgen blood; THE SILVER STALLION (1926), concerning the legends accumulating about the deceased Count Manuel; and THE MUSIC FROM BEHIND THE MOON (1926), the music coming from the witch woman, Ettarre, the daughter of the count.

These are the novels. But the collections of short stories under the titles of THE LINE OF LOVE (1905), GALLANTRY (1907), CHIVALRY (1909) and THE CERTAIN HOUR (1916) are also fitted by their nimble-minded author into the complex edifice and become a part of the whole which his work finally attains. They are only a little more loosely connected than the episodes in some of the novels. Even the books of essays and disquisitions, the incomparable BEYOND LIFE (1919), STRAWS AND PRAYER-BOOKS (1924), THESE RESTLESS HEADS (1932), SPECIAL DELIVERY (1933) and SMIRT (1934) are hewn from the same quarry into different forms. It would be idle to individualize each of these volumes, and disentangle the complex but diligently formed geography and the lineage of its inhabitants. The always courteous author has, in addition to the genealogy, very generously drawn a map of the region for those tourists who would know by an X the exact spot where Poictesme was redeemed, or who might wish to find the shortest route back to Paris from Storisende. Any journey into these novels makes certain demands upon the reader. They are often elaborately equipped with the trappings of romance which, for long intervals, occupy the space at the expense of more serious concern. And in describing the equipage and the upholstery the gifted stylist is often betrayed into the lame phraseology of spurious romancers. Equally serious is the distended symbolism which sometimes baffles the reader. It even grows turgid and suddenly lets him down, as in the ceremony of the Pink Veil in Anaïtis's chapel in JURGEN. And yet, when a balance is struck against the excessive admiration and the indiscriminate praise of the votaries, and when certain characteristics distressingly on this side of perfection have been regretted, there remains enough uncommon excellence in the novels of James Branch Cabell to make any man rejoice in his contribution to the American novel.

He is, curiously, one of the very few novelists in America with a philosophical point of view. Our way of life has not engendered the philosophical novel so characteristic of European literatures. We have been limited to a realism, envigorating at its best, and naturalistic in its point of view. The work of Theodore Dreiser can stand against OF HUMAN BONDAGE with its picture of cruelty, of bitter loneliness, of betrayal, with its demand for the meaning of life, its end and purpose, and its answer in the symbol of the Persian carpet that there is no neat design except as and if the individual soul can impose upon the flux a pattern to live by. But we have had nothing quite like T. F. Powys's MR. WESTON's GOOD WINE, with its symbolism of the two wines of life and death against a realistic background of an English country village full of beauty and sin. And we have had nothing like THE MAGIC MOUNTAIN creating the scientific and philosophical texture of the world, unintegrated and shapeless, which blew up in 1914. But we do have in the American novel a kind of Anatole France in the person of James Branch Cabell. The tenets are not unfamiliar, but they are freshly phrased. The wise man is resigned. He knows that the world is full of lovely things, but that they are temporary and at the mercy of an impermanent illusion. When the ecstasy is over, the dusty commonplace returns. The novels show the process by which man is made wise and resigned and inexpectant. In THE CREAM OF THE JEST it is Felix Kennaston, adequately respectable gentleman-author of Lichfield, who, through the miracle of dreams, finds a transitory escape from conformity. Through this harmless medium the boredom of this world may be exchanged for the imaginary delights of the world of reverie. Kennaston can arrange the dreams but not Lichfield. A man who tries to dwell in these two opposed worlds must be prepared for the difference in values when they are transposed and accept the cream of the jest; for the burnished talisman in the world of

Ettarre is only the top of a cold cream jar in the prosaic world of Mrs. Kennaston. The sly author without doubt intended to shadow forth the comedy of the human race constructing its romantic heroics out of the poor materials of life as experienced.

In much the same fashion, one after another of the Cabell heroes makes the journey and brings back the same report. Gerald Musgrave makes it in SOMETHING ABOUT EVE, and the dream adventures with Maya lead only to the acceptance of comfortable domesticity, and, so the author said, to a praise of chastity. Out of the same dream land where he was free from the limitations of the world came Manuel in FIGURES OF EARTH to accept the same bonds of the commonplace. Jurgen, reversing the route, ascends with a youthful body and a mature mind from the world of a pawnbroker to the realms of romance, but returns with the year wiser still and a little sad from the society of Guenevere, the Lady of the Lake, and fair Helen of Troy, to the plain little Philistia of the pawnbroker's wife. The dream pilgrimage of Florian in THE HIGH PLACE, encompassing a marriage, among others, with the Sleeping Beauty of the Wood, leads at last to resignation, a mild regret, and the wisdom of being inoffensive to one's neighbors. The evidence of the heroes is finally confirmed by Branch Cabell writing in his own person in THESE RESTLESS HEADS in praise of Aesred, the goddess of comfortable mediocrity and conformity, in whose will is our peace. Like Koheleth before him, he has gone the whole round of creation and found it vain.

There is no grave importance even in the writing of books except to the degree it affords diversion to the author. For the purpose of his art, it becomes necessary for the writer to indulge his illusions that literary values are not mostly humbug, and to encourage if possible "a kindly conspiracy to take him seriously." In the interest of contentment he will find it best to practice "a sedate pessimism." The phrase is inspired. As nearly as so illusive a spirit as James Branch Cabell's can be imprisoned in a phrase, it is "a sedate pessimism." It is born of an understanding of earth-born men seeking escape from worldly tedium in the adventures of the imagination. That is the proper escape for sagacious mortals. Imagination was given for that use, and books were invented to facilitate the recreation of another world more congenial to contemplate. And while you are about it, there is every reason for doing it in the grand style. But at the heart of each adventure there lurks the suspicion that after the brief flight the world of disillusion waits to receive us. And after love which furnishes most of the dreams, and after adventure with its ultimate ashes we grow calm and shrug our shoulders, skeptical of the conventions and the codes, but accepting them as the simple sureties of the happiest life obtainable in a universe where the central mysteries are forever sealed against the searchers.

It is obviously not with concerns of morality that we are engaged, but with the degree of pleasure in beauty permitted to man. The heroes are genial rogues, for the most part, often displaying the most joyful disrespect for the "comfortable fetishes" in which more prudent men have believed. And so uniformly in the novels does the author offer his approval for these Jurgens who finally give up because they have no stomach for a continuous moment of ecstasy, that one suspects him of irony even in his frequent praise of Aesred.

For James Branch Cabell is one of the great satirists. He has wasted no energy in denouncing the lack of art in domestic architecture, or the failure of prairie-village shopkeepers to rise to the high level of Carol Kennicott's betterment program. Rather he has with the most urbane control of his irritations pricked at the eternal follies of all men everywhere in all ages. His keen and graceful mind has seldom failed to preserve its decorum, and a joyous wit has never been far absent from his polished prose. In the most satirical passages the trenchant comment on life and letters is touched with a barb so sharp and seemingly gentle that we are compelled by it and fail often to realize how fatally we are wounded.

The more serious aspect of his work is to be found in

one of the classics of modern American prose, BEYOND LIFE.
It defines both the ideology and the temper of the only romance possible to our day. "Romance controlled the minds of
men; and by creating force-producing illusions, furthered the
world's betterment with the forces thus brought into being:
so that each generation of naturally inert mortals was pro-
pelled toward a higher sphere and manner of living, by the
might of each generation's ignorance and prejudices and follies
and stupidities beneficently directed." Such a philosophy, devoid of great passion and faith, is still invulnerable before the
assault of logic. It was in the temper of the day, and it spoke
to the eager young listeners in a mechanical age who liked
to contemplate a hedonism offered with cunning mockery,
who enjoyed seeing the dullards baited and roundly trounced,
and who were diverted by the spectacle of the heroes being
lured and then duped by their nympholepsy.

It has been James Branch Cabell's calling to remind
prosaic men, in season and out, that they are creatures of
two moods; that beyond the rigid world of commonsense
there is a pliant and controllable land of dreams; and that
they ought to "keep faith steadfastly with all those impossible
things which are not true, but which ought to be true." The
novels which urge these delightful dogmas are already aloof
from the out-of-print commoners and preserved for the ages
in the Storisende edition. They are unique in our literature,
and they have contributed to the American novel a type without which it would be poorer and incomplete.

Chapter Fifteen

FACING TWO WORLDS: JOSEPH HERGESHEIMER

JOSEPH HERGESHEIMER is often and with partial truth set beside James Branch Cabell as the other purveyor of romance to a realistic age. But it is a matter of fact that Joseph Hergesheimer has been a jovial wanderer between two worlds: a realistic present in which people are not so great or heroic as once they were, and a romantic past in which men now appear heroic by virtue of a halo of years and where the bric-a-brac is more diverting. The materials for his art are drawn from an observation of a life in which the problems of primary concern are not economic but personal and artistic. These materials are molded into form by a writer whose first interest is in the settings of his people and in the select details that seem to him to point and explain their character. He himself has the true collector's instinct. With great charm he has related in FROM AN OLD HOUSE (1925) the origin and growth of his hobbies and the long pleasure of restoring and furnishing the old Dower House near West Chester. Many of the physical details of the novels were modeled by this house and the open country and golf course around it, and by the careful selection of hinges, bottles, and old furniture which has sharpened his eye and made him wary of the unauthentic. In minute detail of this kind—the color of the upholstery in a lady's motor car, the brand of cigars on a gentleman's table, the texture of the lingerie, and the quality of the rye—he seeks and discovers the clue to the understanding of the personalities and the breeding of his people. This interest gives his novels a certain romantic flavor and the people an air of fastidiousness even when he is ostensibly dealing with a serious problem. He is quite singular among American novelists in this method, and from it derives some of the strength and much of the weakness in the emphasis of his work.

The novels are now twelve in number. They have been written methodically through the years to a production scale in which the ideal stint was three thousand words each day divided equally between the evening and the morning. Behind these dozen novels lay fourteen years of unsuccessful but persevering effort made possible by a small inheritance which freed him from pressing economic worries at the age of twenty-one. He had been born in Philadelphia in 1880 and had lived in a house which preserved into the modern period an atmosphere of an older way of life, encompassing bells for morning and evening prayers and a regard for fine old furniture. He responded naturally to these things, and when in after years he began commuting into West Chester for the daily quota of words, he tried to recapture their quality in the stories. After the years of effort his first novel was published in 1914, and since that day he has been one of the figures in the American literary scene.

The twelve Hergesheimer novels present one of the dilemmas of the modern artist: a natural, emotional longing for beauty and romance that is immediately inhibited by the assurance of the intellect that they are not now to be had. The author, therefore, is torn between the impulse to write realistically about contemporary life and its problems, and the desire to create in the past a life more satisfying to contemplate than the one immediately experienced. Six of Joseph Hergesheimer's novels face one world, and six the other, and his success in each group has been about equal.

Fronting the realistic and contemporary world are THE LAY ANTHONY (1914), MOUNTAIN BLOOD (1915), LINDA CONDON (1919), CYTHEREA (1922), TAMPICO (1926), and THE PARTY DRESS (1930). Each of these novels has its own individual problem, but one theme is most insistent and is never far from absorbing all other interests into itself. It is the old, old quest for the illusory ideal of escape through the image of beauty that continues to seduce the generations of men. It was developed by Plato in the SYMPOSIUM, and by the poets from Spenser's HYMNS to Shelley's EPIPSYCHIDION. It is stock in trade to James Branch Cabell, who weaves a dream fantasy into which the hero escapes and from which he eventually returns to the world of commonsense. Joseph Hergesheimer tries to make a realistic problem of it by confronting the restless unsatisfaction of tormented souls not in Poictesme but in Eastlake, Shadrach Furnace, East Sixty-eighth Street, and Cuba. These people long for a completeness denied them by their immediate world. Unfortunately, as the theme develops it seems gradually to lose its potential strength and its relevancy to ordinary worldlings in fantastic symbolism and separation from reality. Exceptional power is required to convince the American mind that nympholepsy is the most stubbornly persistent of all character traits and motivating forces in human experience. And this exceptional power is not always available to Joseph Hergesheimer.

The first of the novels, THE LAY ANTHONY, was concerned with a conflict between the nympholepsy of Anthony Ball and the economic barriers between him and his love. It is more frankly realistic than many of the later novels. Written through "grey winter by the uneasy grey Atlantic Ocean," it held rigidly to the view that virtue is not always rewarded and that the individual even when on fire with young love is often unable to triumph over all opposition. The author later felt that this point of view was unfavorable to its sale, but there were other reasons. In this story, Anthony Ball had somehow preserved his chastity amidst the vulgar companionship and the tawdry life of the small eastern town of Ellerton. When he fell in love with the exquisite Eliza Dreen, the ideal of purity became involved in his devotion to her. Before he could break down the economic obstacles between them, Eliza died and Anthony was thrown into violent despair. In a moment of rebellion against defeat, he carried his cherished purity to a place of ill repute and left it there with his life.

MOUNTAIN BLOOD told of the rise and fall of Gordon Makimmon, stage-driver. He struck a young gentleman passenger with his whip for molesting a girl in the coach. That act released a chain of events which cost him his place and his property, married him to Lettice Hollidew and her wealth, caused her death, and returned him finally to his original job and accidental death. It was rather a grim little tragedy in which the author had not found room for his most characteristic talents.

LINDA CONDON was more complete, and it remains one of the best of the Hergesheimer novels. It is concerned with the problem of a romantic temperament in a frowsy setting. Linda lives in second-rate apartment hotels with her widowed mother whose means of support are best described as invisible. Linda as a young girl hears the incessant repetitions of her experienced mother that women are nasty and jealous and men are a woman's tool. "Pick out what you want and make for it. Don't bother with the antique frumps, the disappointed old tabbies. . . . If you like a man, be on the level with him— give and take. Men are not saints and we're better for it; we don't live in a heaven. You've got a sweet little figure. Always remember mama telling you that the most expensive corsets are the cheapest in the end." She instructs her that love and marriage are different things and must be kept apart. "You can't do anything with a man if you love him; but then you can't do anything with him if he doesn't love you. That's the whole thing in a breath." These views make self-giving love impossible for Linda Condon.

Against this cynical realism is set the ideal of one old man who talks to Linda of the beauty of love in the poetic imagery of a lady on a snow-white mule, or a yellow-eyed leopard, of silken tents with poles of gold, of forests and black castles.

These two opposed ideals set up a conflict in Linda's soul

difficult to resolve. The cold realism of her mother is victorious when Linda marries Arnaud Hallet; the romantic dream
of the old man is victorious in her relations with the artist
Pleydon who identifies her with the statue of the Winged
Victory because she, too, is "art the deathless," and art is
"simply permanence given to beauty." But Linda, like her
creator, is never fully adjusted to either world. In the desperate resolve to vindicate beauty in a vulgar world, Joseph
Hergesheimer is led to exclaim in words more arresting in
1919 than when Browning phrased the celebrated couplet,
"Downige and the individual babies are unimportant compared to the vision of perfection, of escape. As long as men
live, if they live, they'll reach up; and the gesture in itself
is heaven." But he is too modern to rest in the reaches of
sentiment. He remembers the world of the mob which destroys
the fine Downige statue. "The drunken fools! . . . That is
the disturbing thing about what the optimistic call civilization
—the fact that it is always at the mercy of the ignorant and
the brutal. There is no security; none, that is, except in the
individual spirit." And at the end of the book, Linda is as-
sumed to have acquired this security through a mystical experience before the statue.

The individual spirits in CYTHEREA are, however, far from
secure. They are troubled by the old illusion of permanence
and fulfillment, here localized as a problem of the post-War
unrest. The important characters—Lee Randon, his wife
Fanny, and his "Cytherea," Savina Grove, are in their forties,
and they have suddenly realized that life is slipping away
without yielding up complete satisfaction. Life demands too
little of them. They have much more to give than their limited
routine can receive, and this surplus causes the trouble in
middle life. The modern relaxation of the moral codes com-
plicates their discontent. Fanny Randon is just beginning
to understand the strain put upon her generation in 1920 to
become "modern" in the specific sense of gin, short skirts,
cigarettes, and sex, and she resists it. But Savina Grove has

gone modern and is now eager to elope with Lee Randon and "to burn up with a red flower in my hair and not cool into stagnation." Lee Randon is also afraid of stagnation, and in a moment of mystic carnality identifies Savina with the image of the doll, Cytherea. They both pursue the illusion into its ultimate dust in Cuba.

Their choice, however, is neither deliberate nor free. Joseph Hergesheimer makes it plain that they were not responsible for their conduct in the moment of crisis. Some power greater than individual will moved them to their destiny. Lee Randon objectively but helplessly watches the events that befall him as though he were remote and ultimately uninvolved, a mere spectator at his own adultery with Savina Grove. "A swift conviction fastened on him that here he had been overtaken by fate. . . . It was exactly as though, struggling to the limit of endurance against a powerful adverse current, she had turned and swept with it. . . . We are not to blame ourselves too much . . . the thing happened within itself. . . . And ignorant, careless, of me, it was moving to its own end." That end was considerably short of the moving vision, but Lee Randon is abandoned by the author with a flow of unspecific words just when the real issue should be met.

THE PARTY DRESS presents a similar problem as experienced by a woman, nearly a decade after CYTHEREA. Its heroine, Nina Henry, is forty-two, and she is living the routine society and country-club life at the height of its frivolity in the late twenties. Her children are grown, "her detachment from her family was absolute," and she is longing for something vital enough to absorb the capacities to which her family is indifferent. She tries flirtation and clandestine love. In CYTHEREA such unconventional conduct caused a violent explosion, but in THE PARTY DRESS the jumbled relations in the Henry household are accepted with bored unconcern. Nina Henry, lovely and modern, is transformed by her party dress at the Eastlake club into a Cytherea. The symbolic identity is made more emphatic by repetition of the fact that the gown is by Ishtarre of Paris, derived from Ishtar, the Babylonian Aphrodite. Out of her desperate clutching at life comes no satisfaction, but the suicide of the man who, like Lee Randon, was tormented by the nympholeptic dream of the unattainable Ishtar personified for him by Nina Henry.

These novels seem at first to be seriously concerned with great matters, but it finally turns out that Joseph Hergesheimer is not deeply perturbed by the problems of these middle-aged folk in a final restlessness. He is more interested in Wilson Henry's tired legs and fat belly after a round of golf than in his emotional relations with Cora Lisher. And Nina Henry's love problem is no more important than the flimsy gown which she tears in pieces to make a climax for the book. Our eye is so frequently caught by curios, the brocades, and the salad dressings, that we forget to enter into the pain or the tragedy implicit in a theme. The characters are as smug and empty as the trivialities that occupy their hours. There is no tough-minded grappling with issues or conclusions, and the symbolism of a statue, a doll, and a dress is too commonplace to carry the emotional depth necessary for significance. Excellent as the novels in this group sometimes are, it is a surface excellence and it does not wear.

The peculiar genius of Joseph Hergesheimer is less at home in the unmanageable present than when it escapes into the past where its deficiencies are less apparent. That is why, except for a brief time during the sex vogue, most readers have preferred the second group of novels made up of THE THREE BLACK PENNYS (1917), JAVA HEAD (1919), THE BRIGHT SHAWL (1922), BALISAND (1924), THE LIMESTONE TREE (1931), and THE FOOLSCAP ROSE (1934). It seems less inappropriate to dwell lovingly on small details in a novel resurrecting a day that is far past and unfamiliar. And that is one thing Joseph Hergesheimer does superlatively well.

Around the general thesis that the modern age has progressively lost the virility and rebellion of its ancestors, he

recreates in THE THREE BLACK PENNYS the minutiae of life and
manners of the eighteenth and nineteenth centuries and
finally of the present. The theme of the gradual change in the
Penny blood which brought it from rough fire and iron to
effeminate love of the music of Gluck, and the strong characterizations of the "black" Pennys are vigorous enough to
carry forward the many pages devoted to old furniture, glass-
ware, laces and colored frocks. In this novel the author almost
succeeded in uniting his two worlds.

The approximation was also only a little short of fulfillment in JAVA HEAD, where the poise and simplicity of heart
of Taou Yuen and her heroic living and dying are powerful
enough to support the historical details of old Salem. Nowhere
has Joseph Hergesheimer put into his antiquarianism so much
feeling and so much vividness as in this novel of old days on
the New England seaboard when the China tea ships sailed
the seas. It lacked only one thing to make it a masterpiece of
its type in American fiction and that was form. It was the
opinion of Stuart Sherman, expressed in a letter to an asso-
ciate, that "it is not firmly constructed; there are loose threads
dangling—for example all that development of the young
girls in the first part; and the ending struck me as being pretty
futile." It was on this ground that the Pulitzer Committee refused it in 1920 and made no award for the year.

BALISAND must rank fairly close to these two novels in
its successful recreation of the past. For it, too, has a theme
solid enough and of sufficient interest to its author to give it
strength. The time is just after the American Revolution, and
Richard Bale was, in the author's intention, typical of the aris-
tocratic class during the struggle between Jefferson and the
Tories. Richard Bale was killed in a duel, but he "kept to
whatever fatality might overtake him, . . . his end was
happy."

THE BRIGHT SHAWL, however, lacks the ballast of an important theme. THE LIMESTONE TREE, a historical and genealog-
ical novel about a Kentucky family from the Revolutionary

period to the end of the nineteenth century, is buried under the notebooks which JAVA HEAD barely survived. And THE FOOLSCAP ROSE, suggesting THE THREE BLACK PENNYS in its plan, carries along the fortunes of the Wigtons and the Kinzers as their handicraft paper mill develops through the years into a big industry with the usual consequences. Like the story of the Pennys, this one is lightened with romance and unified by the theme of disintegration of the tougher fiber of the earlier period. The title signifies the watermark on the fine paper from the mill on the Brandywine.

There is much to praise in these studies of the past, but it is the superficial elements made up of the depthless beauty of color schemes, ornaments, and menus with appropriate wines. Joseph Hergesheimer has made only the most half hearted efforts to touch the heart of life which might put depth under the surfaces. He has a feeling for this something more, but he seldom gets his people disengaged from things. As he himself has put it, "In the effort to disentangle the reality, to mark it off, from mere show I found that, more often than not, it was the show which was regarded as important; reality was nothing against appearances." So he has enmeshed himself among appearances behind a style in which ornamentation won out over a more simple realism in the effort to arrange rows of glittering sea shells emptied of all life. And even in the beautiful past he has found the texture of the lace on a lady's drawers (as he quaintly labels the garment) more engaging than her fate in the machine age.

Chapter Sixteen

FANTASY AS A WAY OF ESCAPE

*T*HE romance of both James Branch Cabell and Joseph Hergesheimer was unheroic, disillusioned, and a little pale with melancholy. But it could hardly escape conspicuity in an era devoted so exclusively to realistic records of the disagreeable. It was not a vigorous romance, as we have seen, but it did succeed in keeping alive the pale flame against the day of greater favor. In this important endeavor it was supported by the work of a few novelists who chose to express themselves through the less assertive medium of fantasy. By a frank adoption of this mode they were able to escape the rigid and resisting world of immediate commonsense outside of one's control and enter the more supple realm of the fancy where one may exercise complete authority and rearrange at will. The best of the writers in this manner are Christopher Morley, Elinor Wylie, and Robert Nathan. Donn Byrne (1889-1928) had great success with his tale of MESSER MARCO POLO in 1921, and with half a dozen other stories in a manner which he liked to think was in the good old Irish romantic tradition. But one could hardly make a claim for him as an important creator in the American novel, since he was American only by an accident which he resented, and since his fiction was exceedingly slight.

Christopher Morley is one writer who has displayed an unflagging zest for life in a time when few seemed to find anything in it to enjoy. He was born in Haverford, Pennsylvania, in 1890. A few years later his father moved to Baltimore to become a professor of mathematics at Johns Hopkins. But Christopher Morley returned to the cultivated seclusion of

Haverford College, where he graduated in 1910. He then went to Oxford as a Rhodes scholar, and, on his return to America, entered upon his varied career as publisher's reader, high-spirited columnist, and genial essayist to a responsive and de-lighted nation. Deprived though he was of poverty, family unhappiness, personal maladjustments, and experience of war which are associated with so many modern authors, he has none the less succeeded in creating a few important books. He has usually preferred the personal essay for his expres-sion, but it is doubtful whether any one form could fully contain the outpourings of a talent so rich, so varied, and so alive. It has filled up many volumes of essays with contagious enthusiasms uncommon in our day, it has spilled over into poetry, and there has been left more than enough for several novels cast in the attenuated form of fantasy. In fact, the thin walls of that slight form are often hard put upon to contain the timed explosives with which they are charged.

These novels are among the few worthy creations in that mode in our times. They began with PARNASSUS ON WHEELS in 1917, just at the moment when Sherwood Anderson, Waldo Frank, Willa Cather and the rest were first commanding at-tention. This delicate and short novel had nothing to do with Freud, or frustrated villagers, or Western farm life, or war, chaos, and marching men. It was a timeless fantasy, ballasted with poetic phrases and wise observations, about a bookshop on a wagon, presided over by a bald little Victorian (or Georgian) bookseller. And in 1922, ignoring Babbitt, the new psychology and the younger generation (of which he was one), he presented WHERE THE BLUE BEGINS, a subtly philo-sophical story about the dog Gissing tracking down the Infinite.

THUNDER ON THE LEFT (1925), the best of his fiction to date, was under a stronger discipline of realism than its prede-cessors. It profited by it. It begins realistically with a children's birthday party and a childish wish to know the future; then by the alchemy of a moment of fantasy, the children are projected into maturity where they experience the very realistic unhappiness that awaits them. At the end, in a burst of fantasy once more, the adults are returned from their problems and their sorrows to happy childhood and the birthday party from whence they departed in the dream. It is a neat device, like the theophany in Job, and it enabled the author to ring down the curtain just before he disclosed the great dénouement of life which to discover, we must, he says, witness for ourselves. The finest section of the book is that which creates the tremulous mystery of childhood, and the haze of its wonder always a little darkened by the portentous shadows of the future. The corresponding passage in Conrad Aiken's GREAT CIRCLE is the only thing of its kind that can stand beside it. SWISS FAMILY MANHATTAN (1932) is a satire touched with no bitterness. It is full of shrewd observations on the national character and the American scene, exposing the foibles but not the baseness of mankind as seen by the Chief of Available Reference to the League of Nations after he had landed from the air on the unfinished mast of the Empire State building. HUMAN BEING, also 1932, has many of the same qualities: poetically acute observations and illuminating insights and appraisals of the domestic and business life of Richard Roe, and the multitude of forces that beat upon this wayward and often bewildered human being. It is first-rate Morley.

Christopher Morley has said that he chooses the forms of fantasy and fable as a recourse "to avoid the bitterness of being understood." This may mean that he has been less unaware than some suppose that an ideology and a way of life have collapsed about his ears. One suspects that he sees clearly enough, but that he has felt that he might spare himself the necessity of castigating the age for its blundering stupidity, or of joining the proletarian authors in exalting the workers, or of engaging in the officious exercise of reforming the world by writing another novel about it. He works in his chosen medium with such mastery that no one in his senses could wish him other than he is. He has cultivated an important type of novel disdained by the bolder realists of the day. And in a chaotic and futility-struck period, he contributes to the gayety of life and distills a fragile and mellow wisdom, expressed in phrases that often seem to lean over the rim of reality to eavesdrop on the great secrets which he almost heard beyond our finite worries.

Elinor Wylie (1885-1928) was a poet of the rarest genius, and she was not less so when she exercised her gifts in fantasy and romantic fiction. Her four novels elude any strict classification because they are unlike anything else in American literature. They are a rare interfusion of wit, historical fact, satire, allegory, fable, sympathy, and sheer intelligence condensed in an intensely poetic mind and set down in a style that delights and astonishes with its virtuosity.

She fled the contemporary scene for certain glamorous periods of the past more congenial to her temperament and more suitable to her design. She was concerned with the atmosphere of her fiction and took keen joy in living in the world created by her imagination. It was the same emotional necessity which returned her again and again throughout her life to England and the places where Shelley had lived. It is easy to understand why, of all available periods in history, she should prefer the eighteenth century for its wit, its formalism, its attention to the nice details of cultivated living, and the age of Shelley for its romantic passion, its search for perfection, and its excess of poetic feeling. She was compounded of both.

For JENNIFER LORN (1923) she chose the time of Warren Hastings and carried her English gentleman and his bride out to the romantic India of the eighteenth century. It was a spirited extravaganza done in elaborately ornamented prose. THE VENETIAN GLASS NEPHEW (1925) was laid in the magic city of Venice, also in the eighteenth century, so hauntingly resurrected by Robert Browning in A TOCCATA OF GALUPPI'S. Elinor Wylie created her own Venice and peopled it with churchmen and sorcerers and beautiful, living creatures in spun glass.

The book is an ode on the two lovers imprisoned in this fragile substance. It cannot be analyzed because it can exist only in the words and in the atmosphere of the completed work. But some of the rich overtones to the fantasy may be suggested by such words as these about the lovers now living "happy ever after, in Venice, in a world of porcelain and Murano mirrors." "Having forgotten fear and the requirements of pity, their tenderness becomes a placid looking-glass in which each beholds the other; the mercurial wildness which no longer moves them is fixed behind this transparent screen, lending brightness to the mirrored images."

Elinor Wylie's devotion to Shelley and the romantic age in which he lived entered into the creation of THE ORPHAN ANGEL (1926). It is more of a narrative than its predecessors and its prose is less ornate. One's interest is instantly intrigued by the fantastic conceit of an alternative to Shelley's death by drowning permitting that insubstantial orphan to become a pioneer into the American wilderness. A large portion of the joy of the novel is the charm of Elinor Wylie's own spirit revealing itself as the story unfolds. She never fails to preserve a detachment that can laugh playfully at the subject of her exuberant invention.

In MR. HODGE AND MR. HAZARD (1928) she selected the period just after the death of Shelley and Byron when the Romantic movement was dying under the assault of the hard-souled science and industrialism of bourgeois England. Mr. Hazard represents the one, Mr. Hodge the other. The book is compounded of fantasy, whimsy, and satire. It does justice to the lovable but ghostly Mr. Hazard while it laughs at his weaknesses. At the same time it points its calculated thrusts at the single-minded, prosaic Mr. Hodge and his practical outlook which admits no margin of romanticism. Mr. Hazard is driven from the country by Mr. Hodge, but not before he enjoys one last holiday. It is a subtle book, summing up in its slender pages an entire era. It is more restrained in style, and for that reason the figured language occasionally admitted seems less successful than in the earlier novels. Sometimes it even breaks the illusion with an image which intrudes into that region where prose and poetry do not fuse, as "Flashes of cool sunshine ran between the articulations of the rain like little fishes in a vast silvery net."

The novels of Elinor Wylie are choice figures in porcelain among the robust exhibits of the realistic novel. They aim primarily at atmosphere and sensuous delight. Few people have dared even to attempt such virtuosity. But Elinor Wylie cultivated it and kept her mannerisms under a firm artistic discipline. And when they threatened to break down under their very extravagance, they were saved by their author's unfailing wit which played over them with the threat of breaking into a resolving ripple of amusement at their vagaries.

A third creator of fantasy pointed with light satire who has flourished through the period of realism is Robert Nathan of New York (1894). Since 1919, when he began his career with PETER KINDRED, he has, in addition to his poetry and music, composed ten novels: AUTUMN (1921), THE PUPPET MASTER (1923), JONAH (1925), THE FIDDLER IN BARLY (1926), THE WOODCUTTER'S HOUSE (1927), THE BISHOP'S WIFE (1928), THERE IS ANOTHER HEAVEN (1929), THE ORCHID (1931), ONE MORE SPRING (1933), ROAD OF AGES (1935). They are all quite brief, running only to some thirty-five thousand words each. And they are all curiously alike. The principal weakness of his work as a whole is its narrow repetition, for he has set strict limitations within which his art must function. It is the same story of the same people over the same formula in the same mood. As a result one is never tempted to reread one book because it soon reappears in a fresh imprint. ONE MORE SPRING is as nearly a rewriting of THE ORCHID as it could be without still being THE ORCHID. This is a serious fault, and it compels his admirers to reservations when estimating his importance among his contemporaries.

He has some rare gifts. He is a master of the novelette form, and he has wisely understood that length would disturb the form and the fable it contains. It is painstaking within the confines of the formula. There is lightness but no padding. And after a few thin pages sustained only by the strength of the studied prose, there comes a burst of meaning in a concentrated thrust which does the work of many more elaborate pages of other authors. Examples are to be had in nearly any chapter. We choose one from a scene in the New Jerusalem to which the pilgrims have gone in THERE IS ANOTHER HEAVEN.

"Well, just the same," Mrs. Crisp insisted, "it's peaceful here." And she quoted: " 'Jerusalem the golden, with milk and honey blest. Beneath thy contemplation, sink heart and mind oppressed.' "
"And that's heaven enough for you?" asked Mr. Lewis.
"It's heaven, anyway," replied Mrs. Crisp. "And whether it's enough or not, don't hardly signify."

His people are like the naïvely wise old-worldly failures of Anatole France to whom Robert Nathan is most to be likened. There are Jonah; the Fiddler in Barly; the Bishop's wife, her Bishop and the Angel who came to earth as archdeacon and fell in love with her; the melancholy children; the carousel operator aspiring to opera; a street cleaner and his wife; musicians, tradesmen, innocent prostitutes—the gallery of a faëry tale from a planet unrelated to the world described by his fellow New Yorker, Michael Gold, in JEWS WITHOUT MONEY.

They are not people, of course. They are the fantastic marionettes who are moved by the author around the symbols which he constructs. They enable him to throw into more vivid relief the values of human tenderness which interest him in these delicate little flights from reality. In the best of them, THE ORCHID, the symbol of the carousel gives an inner as well as an outer perfection. It carries the theme of the momentary whirl of life which drops one at last precisely where he began.

There are many excellent passages of urbanity and incisive comment scattered about in all the books. THERE IS ANOTHER

HEAVEN is the sharpest and most consistent for these qualities, particularly in the portraits of Mrs. Meigs, the reformer, still at it in heaven, of Reverend John Calvin Crisp, whose Comstock mind has not been weakened by any influence in this New Jerusalem, and of the poor lonely Jew Lewis, born Levy, who became a Christian so people would love him and looked in vain about heaven for Jesus. The fine irony of Robert Nathan gives weight to the light texture of these fables. When they fail it is because the material or the theme is not appropriate to the form, as in ONE MORE SPRING; or because they attempt more than the slight form can carry, as in ROAD OF AGES.

The number of people in our day who are temperamentally fitted to enjoy novels in this manner is not very large. The current of which such fiction is a part was almost lost in the tide of realism and realistic satire. Yet it is an authentic art and it deserves an honored place in the story of the creation of the American novel.

Part Five

THE FRUITS OF THE WAR

Chapter Seventeen

THE WAR GENERATION

WAR enjoyed stupendous prestige in 1914 and 1917. It
was a religious ecstasy in which cleric and layman
alike could revel. It swept the world into hysteria.
Men were still quite unaware or unconcerned that Krupp
guns should be firing on all fronts and blowing up all nation-
alities with magnificent impartiality; that German boys were
being hung and ripped to pieces before Verdun on barbed
wire made at Magdeburg; that British ships were being sunk
by running against English mines, laid by German sailors.
Those bitter facts and the web of the munitions makers were
concealed from the unseeing eyes of patriotism and a militant
idealism whipped up by the mobilized forces of propaganda
in the War years. And when America plunged in 1917, it was
not because of the jeopardy of extensive Morgan loans to the
Allies, but a sudden passion to share like a votary in a holy
crusade which we were already late in joining.

It was in the spirit of religious sacrifice that the young
Englishmen hastened to France and Belgium in the early
years of the War to be destroyed by the blundering generals,
as Lloyd George has charged, in the rain and the muck, and
in fruitless assaults against the solid concrete of the Hinden-
burg Line. But in those days the church, the munitions makers,
and the politicians released an irresistible wave of propaganda
for patriotism and the desirability of death for young men
for violated Belgium. How effectively it functioned the voluntary enlistment of enough of her best men to keep full for
two years the withering ranks at the front is ample affirmation. How tragically futile the trick was, the endless lists of

the slain in Oxford, Cambridge, Eton, Harrow, and the memorial chapels in the cathedrals mutely testify. How sincere the young men were, their letters and their poems written in those years eloquently and pathetically declare.

That spirit of costly idealism still maintained in 1917. Young Americans went to battle under the blare of alluring phrases glorifying the "supreme sacrifice, if need be" "to end war and preserve democracy." American universities emulated England and sent their best men on the pilgrimage. By the sheer logic of the years, many of them were born in the mid-nineties, just in time to plunge from a sheltered, academic life in the schools of peace into the chaos of the War. Among them were to be some of the most powerful writers of our times. They were well brought up under the best civilizing influence our culture afforded. Hervey Allen, after a period of study at the Naval Academy, graduated from the University of Pittsburgh in 1915, aged twenty-six, and soon afterwards went to War. Sidney Howard at the age of twenty-six deserted Professor Baker's drama workshop to enter the ambulance service. Archibald MacLeish, aged twenty-five and fresh from Yale, enlisted in the ambulance service and later transferred to the field artillery. Laurence Stallings, born in Georgia in 1894, received his A.B. from a Southern college in 1915, and became a captain in the marines. E. E. Cummings of Massachusetts took his master's degree at Harvard in 1916 at the age of twenty-two, and departed for France for ambulance service. John Dos Passos, Chicago born in 1896, honor graduate of Harvard in 1916; Louis Bromfield, born in Ohio in 1896, whose college work was interrupted by the War; Ernest Hemingway, born in Illinois in 1898; Malcolm Cowley, Pennsylvania born in the same year, and still an undergraduate at Harvard when he went to War—all these young men and scores of others less gifted with the pen, went to France and Italy to drive ambulance trucks. And still others, like William Faulkner, Mississippi born in 1897, enlisted in the aviation corps.

Only a little first-hand experience with war in the field was required to debunk the fine phrases of the minutemen patriots far from the front who had sent these intellectual college boys across the sea. The shabby paradox of a war to end war could not hope to survive the actual meeting with the mad world that the chapel speakers had smoothly referred to as "life outside the college walls" for which they were "preparing." The War destroyed every single value for which civilized institutions were presumed to stand. These gifted young writers were not long to be deceived. As the lists of the slain continued to mount and the profits on steel reached new all-time high levels, and the selfish purposes in the skulls of the statesmen began to trickle out, thoughtful men began to suspect that army officers were not apostles of love, and that concealed machine guns mowed down the youth of all nations not in the interest of an ideal of living but for the safety of the rubber monopoly and threatened investments of business men not on the battlefields.

The effect of the disillusionment was decisive. The statesmen and the generals killed or wounded forty million men and blew up a fifth of the total property of mankind for an idea. Those who were lucky enough to survive saw that same world accept the payment with casual unconcern and promptly and with shattering indifference discard the idea. As Brunngraber puts it in his great novel, KARL AND THE TWENTIETH CENTURY: "It was hard to understand why things and institutions which, a short while back, every one had reverenced . . . should now be censured as villainous or absurd. . . . The sacrifices which he and millions of others had made, seemed unmeaning."

The young generation of writers who were victimized did not cultivate a well-bred silence in the face of such chicanery. They exploded upon the blind, easy-going world with such force that many good people who expected "their boys" to return from the horror, the blood, and the terror of war to write pretty prose about the beauty and sacredness of life are still paralyzed with shock. They find their writing bristling with vulgarity, profanity, materialism, lack of faith, and bad taste. But it is more important that these writers and the conditions out of which their work has been created should be sympathetically understood than rebuked and condemned. For their impassioned protest is one of the few hopeful profits come out of the War and should be required reading of every man who helped make or wage the War.

The vivid expression achieved by the War generation was made possible by the state of American letters at the beginning of the twenties. For our young writers were arriving at their particular attitudes just at the moment when the realistic method had, as we have seen, reached its fullest favor with an understanding audience, and it became the natural mode of expression for the new materials released by the War. It was possible, therefore, for the men who had been in the thick of the carnage to write about it frankly without restraint, and with only a slight modification of vocabulary. They first attacked the time-honored deception of war as romantic adventure. They had been at the front. They had carried the maimed back to the hospitals. They found no romance in such mad fury. They found a revolting orgy of legalized mass murder and callous torture. They saw millions of young Frenchmen, Italians, Englishmen exploding hand grenades in the faces of equally young Germans. They were schooled to do effectively all the things a peaceful society would have executed them for doing. They mastered the art (if they survived) of blowing off hands and arms and legs, of jabbing bayonets into soft bellies, and wading through mud over death and putrefaction. Such inglorious and savage brutality is not to be glorified into romantic hocus-pocus about heroic dying on the field of honor when confronted by a generation already schooled in looking life full in her ugly face.

Under this violent impact of experience a generation was speeded into maturity and its realism became hard-boiled. It said to the world: There is your dirty carnival, you fine-

souled but absentee idealists; smell it, rub your noses vicariously in its filth and see what it is like in barbed wire en-
tanglements, in stagnant shell-holes with rotting dead men,
in the death-shrieking emergency hospitals behind the lines.
And when war as romantic adventure had been disposed of,
and when the sorry failure of the peace was destroying what
was left of the world, they wrote against social idealism as
justification for war, and finally of lives wrecked and made
meaningless by war.

It must be borne in mind that the American novels about
the War were only a small part of a world literature. The
necessary pattern of a realistic war novel was much the same
in every land because the experience was common to all men
and knew no national boundaries. And from the day of Henri
Barbusse's LE FEU (1916), printed in America as UNDER FIRE
in 1917, to the popularity of Arnold Zweig's THE CASE OF
SERGEANT GRISCHA (1928) and the triumph of Erich Remarque
with ALL QUIET ON THE WESTERN FRONT (1929) and THE ROAD
BACK (1931), these important novels dealing with successive
attitudes toward the War have been nearly as much a part of
our literature as those by our native authors.

But if we limit ourselves to the American scene, there are
three novels in particular from among many that represented
the anti-romantic spirit toward war at the beginning of the
twenties. One was John Dos Passos's THREE SOLDIERS (1921),
which we have already examined. Another was E. E. Cummings's THE ENORMOUS ROOM (1922), a spirited, wryly satirical,
autobiographical novel which stripped away several layers of
the romance surrounding the ideal of serving France in the
Ambulance Norton Harjes. E. E. Cummings had been arrested
by America's ally on suspicion awakened by passages in his
letters. He was immediately taken from the Voluntary Drivers
to a filthy detention camp. Such treatment of a young volun-
teer put a severe strain upon the romance of service to others.
The young victim sat down and wrote of the episode in a
strong, realistic manner, and in a bold diction which did

not make more engaging the unsavory experience. It shocked the good Puritans who had helped win the War for idealism by making speeches about it in their local clubs. It irritated them to have their War represented as brutalizing destruction, and to be told that blowing up other human beings was not conducive to the Christian character-building visioned by the War pastors.

The third was THROUGH THE WHEAT (1923) by Thomas Boyd (1898-1935). It is one of the best of the early American War novels. It is direct, stark without omitting touches of poetry and human pity, and simple in its restraint. It records the common unromantic lot of a soldier on duty; the weary marches, the filthy billets, the poor food, the raids on French canteens, the terror of death, explosion, fear, rotting dead men at the front, cowardice and heroism, eight-hour watches in ice-cold water up to his knees, the silly and disgusting vanities of the new officers confronting exhausted soldiers back from the front and keeping them standing in line awaiting review, the crabbing, the letters from home, the humor and profanity, the meaningless mud and drill and moving from place to place: it is all beautifully set down under the peaceful title THROUGH THE WHEAT. It breathes a hatred for war and it rings genuine. And its realism reaches from the poetry of the opening sentence: "Dusk, like soft blue smoke, fell with the dying spring air and settled upon the northern French village," to the horror of one of the concluding experiences at the front: "'Answer me, damn it.' He grasped the shoulders of one of the bodies, shaking them. Beneath the clothing the flesh loosened from the body. 'Hell, you're dead,' Hicks told the body disgustedly."

The attack upon war as romance begun in the novel was immediately taken up by the drama in the full-bodied realism of WHAT PRICE GLORY (1924) by Laurence Stallings and Maxwell Anderson. The play bristled with profanity and sex and the stark brutality of a soldier's life in the War. It did more than any single novel on the same theme to define the point of view of the twenties. Although Laurence Stallings has labored continuously with materials gathered out of the experience of war, he has converted them into drama, into the scenario for the highly successful THE BIG PARADE (1925), into the "camera record of chaos," THE FIRST WORLD WAR (1933). His single novel, PLUMES (1924), has for its theme the pitiful after-effects of the War upon one of its heroes mutilated in body and soul by the carnage. With blazing resentment it attacked the system that produced such irresponsible wastage and human suffering to no end. Taking his work in all forms as a single whole, Laurence Stallings has done more than any one American author to cut away the romantic glamour of war and to expose its wretchedness.

America made no significant contribution to the type of war novel represented by Richard Aldington's DEATH OF A HERO (1929), Ford Madox Ford's SOME DO NOT (1924), NO MORE PARADES (1925), A MAN COULD STAND UP (1926), and THE LAST POST (1928), C. E. Montague's ROUGH JUSTICE (1926), or by books of poetic memoirs utilizing the same materials, as in Edmund Blunden's UNDERTONES OF WAR (1928) and Siegfried Sassoon's MEMOIRS OF AN INFANTRY OFFICER (1930). These books pictured in outspoken or restrained passion the actual life of men under fire, in dugouts, moving up and back from the front lines, bewildered by the apparent lack of any purpose behind their misery or the nerve-destroying interludes of quiet. The experience of American soldiers was seldom sufficiently extended to produce this psychological effect. But when the full tragedy behind the War and its aftermath began to dawn upon an exhausted world, America made her contributions to the novels of social criticism and protest.

John Dos Passos's 1919 is the best representative of this phase of the American novel. It condenses all the sense of betrayal felt by the men who saw the ideal perish in brazen compulsions which destroyed elementary principles of freedom during and following the War. The backdrop against which the novel flames is painted in a series of eloquent contrasts: The idealism of college-boy volunteers, against the fat, safe war profiteers; the self-sacrifice "for democracy," against the imperialistic schemes of the Allies; the glory of the flag, against the endangered two billions loaned from bankers in a neutral nation to the Allies; the peace of Jesus, against the war hate of His preachers; the fight for freedom, against the violent peace-time espionage and Red-hunting of Wilson, Palmer, and vigilance committees; the young men herded like sheep in the steerage to make the War, against the diplomats in staterooms on the *George Washington* to make the Peace; the League of Nations, against political capital and selfish party expediency; the gentle, upright life of a peaceful citizen, against the inevitable effects of tanks, gas attacks, mud, vermin, bayonets, raving hospitals, wholesale slaughter; the assertion of any scheme of values, against destruction to no purpose—carry on as far as you like. The total of these and more accounts for the novels of protest from the War generation. Far from being a sign of futility and defeat, they were on the contrary one of the most hopeful tokens of the day. Had they been supine, or romantic like those following the Civil and the Spanish Wars, then one might indeed despair.

These facts which were specific and dominant in 1919 are only a part of the general atmosphere surrounding the work of the most brilliant novelist of the War generation, Ernest Hemingway. He was spokesman particularly for those whose lives had been deprived of meaning by the War. His two novels did not touch the American scene, so popular with his contemporaries. He chose post-War Paris, sun-flooded bull-fighting Spain, the Italian front, and the romantic locale of Montreux for his settings, and placed in them extreme representatives of a war-weary generation showing how their experiences had sapped their sense of the importance of life and its occupations and left them with disillusion, bull-fighting, and absinthe; and with one very gentle flame of friendship and love flickering reticently in the hard-boiled wastelands.

" 'What's the matter? You sick?' 'Yes.' 'Everybody's sick. I'm sick, too.' "

Ernest Hemingway became the most celebrated of Gertrude Stein's wide circle in Paris of the young men not home from the War. Except for her unfortunate phrase, "You are all a lost generation," which caused many of them sentimentally to overdramatize themselves, her influence upon their work as art was beneficial. She has spoken of it without undue reticence in her autobiography. The evidence of it is in THE SUN ALSO RISES (1926). It was immediately felt to be one of those rare books which seem to preserve the mood of an age, and it was so distinctive that, with its companion piece, A FAREWELL TO ARMS (1929), it has supported one of the greatest reputations in the post-War period without further contribution in the form of the novel.

The title, taken from ECCLESIASTES, the most urbane of all gentle pessimists, signified that the world moved in an endless circle to no conceivable purpose, and that man hath no preeminence above the beasts. What Koheleth in his meditations had understood, Ernest Hemingway and the lost generation had seen as a result of the bolder revelation of the War. The people in the novel are all mutilated in one way or another. All faith has withered, all controls are relaxed, all inhibitions demolished. They are distracted but cynical, they are driven aimlessly about by a jaded unrest to no end, and the lust for distraction finds the elementary stimuli of sex and cocktails growing more feeble with each repetition. Brett Ashley, with nothing remaining to live by, drinking to forget, flitting from one vanity to the next, rising just far enough in the end to renounce the young matador rather than to infect him with her futility. Cohn, irritating, tormented with an inferiority complex, advancing and retreating, baited by his companions who suffer and then insult him. Mike, useless, careless, drunken and wasted. Bill, the agreeable companion kept afloat by a capacity for friendship sincerely felt but conveyed to the reader indirectly. Jake, maimed in the War, by a cruel joke left with nothing but a liking for Bill, fishing, and bull fights, and a pathetic attachment to Brett that is denied fulfillment by his physical incapacity. Under the hard-boiled pose there is considerable sentiment, and behind the cynical disgust is a spiritual bankruptcy, intensified by the method of narrating it in the first person as from one not too socially conscious. The resulting concentration creates vivid pictures of Paris, the sunlight of Spain, the romantic fishing trip, the bull pen, the Spaniards, the happy peasants. They haunt the memory years after reading. The contrast between these natural elements unspoiled by war and the maladjusted group of war-wrecked people deprived of all purpose is all the more arresting because, as opposed to the Dos Passos method, nothing is said about it. Its objectivity is unmarred, and its effect irresistible.

The matter and the mood go hand in hand with the style. All are necessary to explain the success of THE SUN ALSO RISES. For it is one of the tributes to the art of this novel that, while it convinces readers of its authenticity, few even of the War generation have recognized themselves in its characters. The style is one of studied, painstaking simplicity. The influence of Sherwood Anderson is strong, and though Ernest Hemingway later repudiated it, it accounts in part for the vague poetry, the romanticism and sentimentalism which color the realistic materials. But whereas Sherwood Anderson never came quite clear, Ernest Hemingway is as specific as a cablegram. His sentences are quick and moving, full-flavored as good speech without being prolix. No one ever talked quite so cryptically or repetitiously, and yet under the spell a reader willingly suspends his disbelief and asserts his faith.

The tricks are obvious—the faulty grammar, the planned repetitions, the colloquial rhythms, the trivialities which become vital through reiteration, the tone of superiority, the affected casualness. It is splendid reporting wherein no attempt is made to get all the facts, nor as many as Theodore Dreiser would want, but a few sharp and representative ones, with the eye always on the subject and on nothing but the subject. A memorable example is the story of the unloading of the bulls. And it is significant that there is a better record of bull-fighting in the brief section in this novel than in the long treatise in DEATH IN THE AFTERNOON.

A FAREWELL TO ARMS (1929) came at the apparent height of his powers. It is set in Italy during the War, and is narrated through the medium of one of the two central characters— an American ambulance driver not too intelligent or intellectual, and yet sensitive enough to see the implications of abundant slaughter. Frederick Henry and Catherine Barkley are only partially related to Jake and Brett. In some respects they are better rounded, and more fully developed. They belong to an earlier period of the War, before the disillusion was complete.

The novel falls into two parts, each in its way very beautiful. The first part is war, hospitals, and the defenses which a man sets up within himself against the assault of horror and of pain. It culminates in one of the best passages yet written about the War—the break-up of the Italian Army and the demoralized retreat along the Piave. It is epic in sweep in spite of its vivid concentration. And it catches not only the physical collapse of an army but its emotional upheaval, its hysteria, and its panic. To achieve such power and completeness through the limited vocabulary and essentially childlike mind of Frederick Henry without doing violence to his character is a triumph of language to be set beside that in HUCKLE-BERRY FINN. And always there are dropped those hammer strokes of observation, like: "The questioners had that beautiful detachment and devotion to stern justice of men dealing in death without being in danger of it."

The other part of the novel is the love story, movingly handled against the blood, the madness, and the wreckage of the War. Love becomes the one delicate and beautiful experience powerful enough to triumph over the general disruption of life. It gives center to two people victimized by their times out of normal relationships. Ernest Hemingway confers dignity upon their unmarried love. Its strength, its superiority to the world chaos, emerges from the revolting scenes in the Italian hospital, through the idyllic days on the Italian lakes while war raged about them, the Cooperesque flight up the lake to Switzerland, another brief moment of the idyl about Montreux, to the climax of love and devotion and courage in death. After the futility of the people in THE SUN ALSO RISES, this part of the story has the effect of a stirring affirmation.

But Ernest Hemingway went to the War when he was a boy of nineteen. He looked upon more slaughter and cruelty than is good for any man, and he saw it under conditions which made talk about the moral law and the social conventions appear imbecile. He can never pull himself far above the pit into which he once was thrown. He admires courage, the hard surface, and the bold front, but he does not think that even these avail much against the more powerful forces indifferent or hostile to them. And when he speaks finally of the heroic effort of Frederick and Catherine to preserve love against war and the universe itself, he says, "If people bring so much courage to this world the world has to kill them to break them, so of course it kills them. The world breaks everyone and afterwards many are strong at the broken places. But those that will not break it kills. It kills the very good and the very gentle and the very brave impartially. If you are none of these you can be very sure it will kill you too but there will be no special hurry."

Through the efforts of these writers and dozens of others who have contributed to the international war literature, among whom should be mentioned William March for his COMPANY K (1933), the old propaganda about the romance and character-forming results of war has been pretty well demolished. The writers have used every weapon and device in a developing literature to present a realistic understanding of war and its consequences. Some of the results are tracts for the times, others are literature; but they comprise one of the few assets of the War. A society may make soldiers of its plowboys and escape as it has through the centuries. This War was singular. Men of understanding witnessed and fought it. When it set E. E. Cummings to polishing the car of a dolt who happened to be an officer, when it sent Ernest Hemingway to haul back the wounded and the dying from the Italian front, when it amputated the leg of Laurence Stallings and threw him back into the peace, the results were different. They have made it less easy for the next coterie of interested chauvinists to send young men to the slaughter pens, and in so doing they have added a worthy chapter to the creation of the American novel.

Chapter Eighteen

ULTIMATE EXTENSIONS

*T*HERE is another side to the fiction of the War generation that is concerned with war only by reference or by indirection. It did not use the materials of war, but it carried over into post-War civilian life the tone, the mood, the point of view natural to young men who had gone through the violent reversal from the "humanitarianism" of the War years to the collapse into disillusion and unrest in the aftermath. It would be diverting to contemplate what our literature would be like now had the poetic impulse released in 1912 been permitted to unfold in an atmosphere of peace. But it was thrown into the hysteria of hate and its hope was blighted. One priceless if fragile portion of human values embalmed in the words *human, love, friendship, mercy, charity, peace,* and *good will* was crushed and battered from much of our literature by the fury of organized destruction and the callous indifference of men in high place as they scrambled for the profits in the boom. The inevitable result was a literature unparalleled in violence. For every noteworthy tendency in the great fiction whose development we have been following was intensified and extended to its ultimate capacity by the talented young men in the twenties.

There were many of them. Quite necessarily, since they were born in the late nineties, they began to find themselves around 1925. After his unromantic report on life in the War, John Dos Passos, as we have seen, published his MANHATTAN TRANSFER in 1925, and Ernest Hemingway's first novel appeared in 1926. In the same year William Faulkner came forth with SOLDIERS' PAY. The novel made no great appeal at the

time, and it was not until the publication of SANCTUARY in
1931 after the reputations of Dos Passos and Hemingway were
firmly established that the sensational gifts of the new author
were generally recognized. He now stands among his generation, individual and aloof, the most distinguished of the many
who have applied to civil life the "torches of violence" characteristic of the War. Every reader of contemporary fiction
can call up dozens of examples; therefore we may be permitted to center this brief study around their most brilliant
representative.

William Faulkner's first novel was provoked by his own
experience with the War and the disquiet of the peace. A
Mississippian by birth (1897), he left the university of his
state for service in the Canadian Flying Corps. Like his
Lieutenant Mahon in SOLDIERS' PAY, he was wounded when
his plane cracked up near the close of the War. After an
unsettled period of tramping about doing odd jobs, and a
journey to Europe (preserved in many of his short stories),
he anchored himself in New Orleans under the patronage of
Sherwood Anderson and began his career as novelist.

How firmly his origin was rooted in the mood and the
materials of the War is evident in SOLDIERS' PAY, the story of
the return of a group of young soldiers to their indifferent
country, told in a straightforward style devoid of the later
mannerisms. "Caught both in the magic of change they stood
feeling the spring in the cold air, as if they had but recently
come into a new world, feeling their littleness and believing
too that lying in wait for them was something new and
strange. They were ashamed of this and silence was unbearable. . . . 'It's a rotten old world, Joe.' 'You damn right. And
dying ain't the half of it.' 'Dying?' 'In his case, I mean. Trouble is, he probably won't die soon enough.'"

They are referring to Donald Mahon, the center of the
group on the train. He is out of his mind as a result of a head
injury and a ghastly wound, and he is on his way to his home
in the South unattended except for the Pullman porter,

almost blind, sick, and without his memory. The boy's father and his fiancée had been told that he was dead, a hero in France. They had adjusted their minds to the tragedy. But his father is notified that his son who once was dead is now alive and on his way back home. He rejoices. Then he sees the wreck that was his son and would be better dead. His fiancée looks upon him with revulsion. It is soldiers' pay, and the only man who gets him honor is, ironically, a cowardly rotter who shot his officer in the back for taking him into danger. The book is full of that extreme suffering without meaning that was to become characteristic of the novels of William Faulkner.

The two novels that followed were MOSQUITOES (1927) and SARTORIS (1929). They did little to enlarge the audience attracted to SOLDIERS' PAY. They are interesting now as stages in the growth of the artist and as preliminary definitions of his materials and his attitudes. MOSQUITOES, a story of a yachting trip out of New Orleans, and of the young couple who were lost in the swamp, gave the author an opportunity to try for a brittle humor and irony not unlike in tone some of the pages in the opening of SOLDIERS' PAY, and permitted him to extend his powers of description in the milieu of fear, terror, and human anguish as his people flounder in the swamp. SARTORIS, dedicated to Sherwood Anderson, was of like texture, but it was more serious in purpose, and it dealt with a section of life with which the author is familiar and to which he has often returned: a Southern family in disintegration and decay. As in SOLDIERS' PAY, the narrative centers about a returned aviator, Bayard Sartoris. He is restless and mentally unstable as a result of heredity and the death of his younger brother, who had crashed during the War. But the gradual retrogression of this family is merely accelerated by the War, for its basic causes lie deep in the life and the blood of the Sartoris breed. The novel, while never pausing in its drive toward the final tragedy, has many strangely beautiful passages about the old romantic South of mimosa trees and honeysuckle-covered fences, bridal wreath and crêpe myrtle bushes "old as time," peaceful homes and quiet streets "with a golden Arcadian drowse." But these, too, exist in a baleful atmosphere of decay and mold, a fit setting for the human disintegration of Sartoris.

SARTORIS is also rewarding as a study in the formation of the Faulknerian style, for it is laden with attempts at ornament and impressiveness not yet under complete discipline. The thrushes are "demurely mellifluous." Horace lay in the adjoining room "while that wild, fantastic futility of his voyaged in lonely regions of its own beyond the moon, about meadows nailed with firmamented stars to the ultimate roof of things, where unicorns filled the neighing air with galloping, or grazed or lay supine in golden-hoofed repose." And Harry Mitchell's "heavy prognathous jaw narrowed delicately down, then nipped abruptly off into bewildered pugnacity."

The journey from this relaxed wordiness to the magic of certain pages in SANCTUARY is long and difficult. When brought under artistic control the style is capable of becoming the thing to be described—no matter what—as in this passage in LIGHT IN AUGUST, where the prose is as slow and tortuous as the movements of Armstid and his mules. ". . . he does not see the woman sitting in the ditch beside the road until the wagon has almost reached the top of the hill. . . . And no one could have known that he had ever looked at her either as, without any semblance of progress in either of them, they draw slowly together as the wagon crawls terrifically toward her in its slow palpable aura of somnolence and red dust in which the steady feet of the mules move dreamlike and punctuate by the sparse jingle of harness and the limber bobbing of jackrabbit ears, the mules still neither asleep nor awake as he halts them."

These three novels, however brilliant in their own right, proved to be only an apprenticeship for those that were to follow in rapid succession with such extraordinary effect, beginning with THE SOUND AND THE FURY (1929), and continuing with AS I LAY DYING (1930), SANCTUARY (1931), LIGHT IN AUGUST (1932), and PYLON (1935). Leaving the theme of returned soldiers in the South, he isolated and concentrated upon those peculiarly fascinating elements of depravity, viciousness, abnormality, animalism, and horror implicit in the earlier volumes and caused them to flame with intensity. And he mastered the distinctive elements of style that were formerly unruly, and made of them a thrilling prose of such astonishing serenity that it produces the bewildering paradox of beauty in ugliness.

THE SOUND AND THE FURY was a notable advance over SARTORIS, both in the morbidity of its materials and in its technique. For it used the stream of consciousness method in a closely wrought form which often led to obscurity, to probe the mind of an imbecile, a prostitute, a suicide, and other degenerates in a run-down family with a few vestiges of its former gentility. AS I LAY DYING, among the best of the novels, again used the stream of consciousness method in a series of spoken and unspoken monologues, to exhibit the feeble minds of a poor-white family, and to tell the story of the death of Addie Bundren, and the accumulation of horrors that befell the attempt to haul the corpse a nine days' journey through the heat to Jefferson for burial. SANCTUARY told of a journey in search of liquor made by a co-ed and her escort to a sinister old house occupied by a group of degenerates, including criminals, imbeciles, a prostitute, and a blind and filthy old man, of the girl's subsequent violation and abduction by the perverted Popeye, the lynching of an innocent man, and the final ironic execution of Popeye for a crime he did not commit.

LIGHT IN AUGUST exploited the same kind of people, centering around sadistic cruelties, a peculiarly revolting murder, and a frenzied man-hunt and lynching which brought out all the nauseating ferocity latent in the human soul. It differed from its predecessors in the relief of a sub-plot featuring the calm and incomprehending pregnant girl Lena, who is so

gently stupid that God seems to look after her through all
these vicious doings.

PYLON relaxed the grip of sadistic horror to tell the tragic
story of a thin, skeletal newspaper reporter and a group of
indigent and vagabond air racers and parachute jumpers into
whose lives he enters for a few strange Faulknerian days during the celebration of the opening of a million-dollar airport
at New Valois (New Orleans) donated by a wealthy Jew.
It is charged with bitter satire, open and implied, against the
Jew and the rich crowd who are running the show. The novel
dwells nervously on the dehumanized, insensate aviators, their
common wife and ambiguous child, and on the chain of fortuitous events that befall them from the moment the reporter
meets them until the final tragedy and resolution. But behind
all the hardship and the drinking and the tragedy there is a
suggestion of recognizable human tissue, and the reporter,
physically suggestive of Popeye, is thrown into a generous,
sentimental, and feverish tumult by an infatuation for the
girl-wife-companion of the troupe. This note, almost buried
though it is in the hard and brittle cacophony of the story,
separates PYLON from the violence of SANCTUARY and links it
with the Lena motif in LIGHT IN AUGUST.

These are the Faulknerian materials in the novels upon
which his reputation is based, but it is unjust to summarize
so baldly. For they are frequently and with a curious contradiction beautiful in their poetic perceptions, and they often
handle revolting situations with delicacy without weakening
their power to stab the reader with a sense of extreme horror.
And it is the effect of horror made acceptable by masterly
presentation that William Faulkner leaves with his readers.
For beginning with sick and dying men back from the War,
he has deepened and advanced the element of meaningless
suffering by transferring it to common life and specializing
in it to the exclusion of all tenderness and gentle living. This
is a world comparable to that of the INFERNO, burning with
evil and abnormality. It is peopled with a collection of mon-

strous beings beside whom Cowperwood, Hurstwood, and Hugh McVey are apostolic. It comprises perverts, imbeciles gentle or vicious, gangsters, prostitutes, bootleggers, sadistic religiouses, and numerous pathological specimens engaged in horrific self-expression. It also includes judges, lawyers, university students, decayed plantation-owners, poor whites, drugstore clerks, and politicians. But there is little difference between these groups except a traditional social distinction. Their motives and their lusts are not dissimilar. Not since Swift's conclusion to GULLIVER'S TRAVELS (with the possible exception of some of the pages of Aldous Huxley) has humanity in all walks of life been pictured as such contemptible vermin. Nor has anyone probed with greater power into the volcanic fury, the corruption, the depravity in the black hearts of men who are only incidentally dwellers in the South, or written of such matters in more brilliant prose, or with finer control of mood and suggestion and careful spacing of atrocities. One is led to wonder whether this elaborate collection of abnormalities is not more accurately accounted for as a reversal of the humanitarian and poetic mood trampled to earth by the psychology of the War than by the jargon of the psychoanalysts applied to it by Dr. Lawrence S. Kubie. For it is the natural and ultimate extension of the materials and the moods clearly to be discerned in the literature of the contemporary period.

We have seen with some completeness the rise and triumph of realism and how it explored and reported previously neglected segments of American life. Although there was nothing in the realistic theory to preclude the presentation of beautiful living, in actual practice it commonly preferred to picture the evil and the sordidness of modern life. Almost from the beginning, therefore, the realistic movement was associated with repellent materials and motivated by the desire to strip away the hypocritical masks from the faces of men, to reveal the spiritual and moral ugliness which deforms them, and to uncover the miseries which are their lot. Its exponents rightfully insisted that their purpose was not to make anyone miserable, or needlessly to harrow his feelings with terrifying incidents, but to face life as it is, even when it is filthy and without redemption.

This was quite apparently the purpose of William Faulkner in his serious work. But it is impossible to bring any large portion of this complex life into the confines of a book and hold it there in realistic dimensions. The ugly and the vicious can drive out of focus the beauty and the tenderness that are equally true. And unless the artist is wary and incorruptible, in a period such as ours he may become absorbed with the violent and the grotesque moments in the activities of men. And such moments are appallingly frequent in American news.

If we may take at its face value the preface William Faulkner wrote for the Modern Library reprint of SANCTUARY (and why should we not?) then it would appear that the author, after attempting to state his view of the life of his period in novels that got but a limited notice, deliberately invented a tale that would give readers a more violent stimulation than the realistic stories had provoked. And starting with the worthy purpose of revealing life as it is without rearrangement, and proceeding to the cruelty and brutality of war as really experienced, we arrived at SANCTUARY with the avowed intent of exaggerating to the limit the evil of life and the grimness of death for the ulterior purpose of creating not truth but a sense of horror in the Mississippians. It is a blot on the integrity of the artist, and it is a comment upon criticism and the reading public in America. For William Faulkner's calculations were correct. His work was acclaimed, he was given a French and an English as well as an American reputation, and the Saturday Review of Literature ostensibly disapproving, has given more columns to SANCTUARY than to any three books issued since the Review was founded.

The Freudian materials were developed in the same way and apparently for the same reasons. It became clear early

242 CREATING THE MODERN AMERICAN NOVEL

in the realistic period that the limits to accurate reporting of life as it appears objectively to the eye are narrow and rigid, and omit the seething world in the dark recesses of the soul. We have seen how Sherwood Anderson and his compeers, following and contributing to the fashion set by D. H. Lawrence, James Joyce, August Strindberg, turned literature inward not to discover peace in the will of God, but to ferret out the unsuspected demons lurking behind innocent-appearing masks, and to expose incredible terrors and lusts normally kept under control and away from the eyes of men by severe self-discipline.

The external and often gratuitous horrors—the smell of putrefaction, the buzzards hovering above a too-long-exposed coffin, a broken leg set in raw cement, the absurd pairs of eyes flashing luminous rays through the dark where there is no light to reflect—these Gothic thrills are mild when set over against the emotional twistings and torturings of imbeciles and perverts. If the road is straight from the hesitant music of Sherwood Anderson's style to the brilliant and magic prose of William Faulkner at his best, it is also direct from Winesburg, Ohio, 1919, to Jefferson, Mississippi, 1931. And when you have extended the comparatively mild derangements of Wing Biddlebaum of Winesburg to the criminally perverted Popeye inflicting lacerating cruelties upon his victims in SANCTUARY, you have lost sight of the original purposes and produced a monstrosity not to be improved upon. And when you project the libidinous perplexities of Curtis Hartman until they become the confused fragments in the mind of an imbecile who has been three years old thirty times as in THE SOUND AND THE FURY, you are again at end point. For a literature of shock and horror prepares its own defeat, since it must depend upon continuous intensification to maintain its effect, and since there is a point beyond which the jolt of incest, ravishment, and pathology cannot be sustained.

The work that William Faulkner has so far done now appears to be the end of one era rather than the beginning of a new. In an age inured to horror and indifferent through repetition to the cruelty and the crudity of decadent people, he has succeeded in extending their potency for shock. He is not a novelist of ideas but of mood and action, physical and psychic. And he is at his best in the portrayal of men of low mentality undergoing the torture of fear. His work is the flaming focal point of ultimate extension of the characteristics of the literature of his time: the realism of exposure, the sinister distortions of Freudianism, the pain and the preoccupation with violent death revealed in the War literature. And he defines the farthest limits to which the innovations and revolts that were at one time necessary to the continued well-being of our literature can be carried without final self-defeat.

Part Six

NEW MODES FOR THE THIRTIES

Chapter Nineteen

POETIC VERSUS HARD-BOILED REALISM

WHILE William Faulkner was extending the realistic mode to its psychological limits of cruelty and horror, a group of talented young writers were cultivating and carrying forward to its limits the technique of hard-boiled simplicity which had so brilliantly served Ernest Hemingway. The living characters were shunted to the margin and became significant only as a single element in the unfolding of the event of which they were a passive part. The possibility of other dimensions that might include depth and thickness was barely suggested by the clipped and rigid externality of the action and the speech. The authors relied heavily upon cryptic and repetitive dialogue, usually but a little above illiteracy, and a fast-moving series of events stripped to telegraphic meagerness and freed from author comment or analysis. At its worst, and in the hands of second-rate imitators, the result is flat, monotonous, hard, and too narrowly circumscribed for great matter. At its best it makes for precision, selection, and the attempt to let the material speak for itself. These are not undesirable virtues.

Both the virtues and defects are clearly exhibited by the younger members of this hard-boiled school that still practices among us. And from many possible examples we choose three as representative of its continuance into the thirties: W. R. Burnett, John Herrmann, and James T. Farrell.

W. R. Burnett, Ohio born in 1899, crashed with LITTLE CAESAR (1929) into the literary scene at the height of the public interest in gangster life in Chicago. The story moved with the swift precision of a well-planned robbery and raced without interruption on an implied note of poetic justice to the climactic murder of Little Caesar. It held rigidly to the gangster's point of view and it made effective use of his professional lingo. Sponsored by critical authority of the Literary Guild, it swept the country. It was an achievement in hard, restrained simplicity.

W. R. Burnett has been content to repeat the easy formula, and his work in the thirties has shown no evidence of growth beyond the limits of his first novel. IRON MAN (1930) applied the stamp to a dumb prize fighter, DARK HAZARD (1933) to dog racing, etc. The method is well suited for portraying stupid or illiterate types. It is inadequate to the different milieu of GOODBYE TO THE PAST (1934). In this attempt to create the character of old William Meadows of the robber-baron era from 1873 to 1929, the manner is soggy, and the backward-moving technique, so well handled by Rex Stout in SEED ON THE WIND (1930), is self-defeating. The novel tries to keep the hard-boiled flavor, but the material is not adaptable and the style lacks the clean vigor of the gangster story. Part of the failure of the book is brought on by the method, and the relaxation of the drive of narrative, and part by an inadequate understanding of the economic theme and the mind of the industrialist.

John Herrmann (1900) is strongly sympathetic with the point of view of the proletarians and their protests against injustice to the farmers and the workers. But his fiction, so far, has eschewed these themes. His work is represented by the short novel (or long short story) THE BIG SHORT TRIP, which shared the Scribner prize in 1932; and by his novel SUMMER IS ENDED (1932). The novel deals with an uneducated girl and man from Michigan, and carries their story out of cheap and sordid sections of the Middle West to the Left Bank where the last sorry disillusion occurs and their futile flight in life is ended. The narrative is stark and the expression laconic; it achieves occasional flashes of power and many stretches of flattest monotony as these obtuse creatures are permitted to reveal themselves through their own speech. And it is a warning that there are limitations to a realism that strains and distorts itself in the too eager effort to be ironic and hard.

The work of James T. Farrell (Chicago, 1904) in the same tradition suffers from similar limitations and achieves an equal, sometimes greater, degree of effectiveness. His achievement in the novel is represented by YOUNG LONIGAN (1932), GAS-HOUSE MC GINTY (1933), and THE YOUNG MANHOOD OF STUDS LONIGAN (1934). GAS-HOUSE MC GINTY tells the story of the decline into incompetence and defeat of the chief wagon dispatcher for the Continental Express Company of Chicago. The Lonigan novels are studies of the young, athletically ambitious Chicago boy, a rung above the gangster level, and of his decay from health and vigor into a dissipated wreck at the age of twenty-eight. These novels are stripped to essentials. They rely upon realistic dialogue and upon some of the newer experimental methods evolved from expressionism to convey the sense of confusion of modern life. The language is bold and uncompromising, weighted with racy speech and accurate reporting of the obscenity and profanity characteristic of men in this circle of society and of the conditions under which they live.

Much of the hard-boiled writing was effective, but its limits are, at best, excessively narrow. It excludes too much, and it is not sufficiently pliable to convey a rich inner life of literate adults. It was becoming evident even in the twenties that objective realism carried to the extreme had laid a heavy hand upon the American novel and that younger men were in danger of trying to carry on in an overworked vein whose boundaries had already been set. Some reaction or divergence from its limitations had come to be indispensable to avoid sterility and to afford a new approach to life through fiction. When a movement in literature has done its work, it must be replaced with a fresh creative impulse or perish in fruitless imitation. There is still a healthy vigor in the novel, and its expression, reacting from the hard-boiled and the horror traditions, has taken various forms.

The first might be called for the sake of convenience poetic realism. It has held itself to a strict regard for truth, but it has purposely chosen subjects with elements of beauty in them, or it has softened the native harshness by cadenced prose and poetic feeling. Among those whose accomplishments in the new direction are already sufficient surety for their future are Elizabeth Madox Roberts and Thornton Wilder.

Elizabeth Madox Roberts, born in Kentucky in 1885, published her first novel, THE TIME OF MAN, in 1926, the year of the great success of AN AMERICAN TRAGEDY (1925) and the publication of THE SUN ALSO RISES, a year before the Lindbergh flight which symbolized romance to a hard-boiled generation. Its success was arresting because of the poetic mood she had created out of materials that were starkly realistic. She wrote of a family of poor whites from the hill regions of Kentucky and showed them moving about in their shiftless poverty, drifting, sinking no roots in any one place. Ellen Chesser, the center of the novel, was, however, endowed by her creator with a soul and a confused sense of beauty. It was precisely this feeling for beauty that gave the novel its distinction. For it conveyed not so much the harsh, external realities of Ellen's life with her poor farm-hand husband (although it did that, too), but rather an imaginative world created by the poetic mood of the author and made to seem more real than pure objectivity. It was written in a slow, dignified, carefully cadenced style embedding localisms and archaic expressions to suggest dialect. It was a highly mannered style, and in those places where the narrative flagged and the author relied too heavily on strange word orders for her effects, it seemed self-conscious to those who lost the mood. At its best, however, it was new and haunting and its poise and tranquillity were moving in the midst of the realistic reporting about the vagrant poor.

MY HEART AND MY FLESH (1927) has been much admired
by the discerning young writers and for the same kind of
quality that distinguished THE TIME OF MAN. By the delicacy
of her perception, by her willingness to share the spiritual
response of unaffected people in a pastoral setting, she has
restored to the novel some of the human warmth not often
emphasized in the work of the twenties. Her people are not
destroyed by lusts, they are not defeated by economic ills, and
they are not morbid with melancholy and despair. JINGLING
IN THE WIND (1928) and A BURIED TREASURE (1931) did not
advance her stature. Nor did HE SENT FORTH A RAVEN (1935),
although it was nobler in attempt and passed from poetic
realism into fantasy and symbolism to create a modern para-
ble. THE GREAT MEADOW was an advance. It appeared in 1930
along with William Faulkner's AS I LAY DYING. It was a great
success and it was worthy of it. It appealed to the same interest
in the rich historic past of the nation that Willa Cather's
DEATH COMES FOR THE ARCHBISHOP had satisfied in 1927. It
developed the softer mood that had made a Pulitzer prize in
1930 of Oliver La Farge's LAUGHING BOY dealing with love and
ideals among the Indians of the Southwest. In THE GREAT
MEADOW Elizabeth Madox Roberts, after creating a vivid and
sensitive impression of the established way of life in old Virginia, moved her heroine into the wild but picturesque Kentucky country of the eighteenth century. She peopled it with
essentially noble pioneers, and set them to the epic struggle
of winning the land from the Indians and the canebrakes.
The novel profited by and further stimulated the growing
favoritism for these materials long neglected by a period
interested solely in contemporaneity.

In a style that extended the distinctive features of THE
TIME OF MAN, but was strengthened by a firmer and more
romantic narrative, she concentrated in the person of Diony
and her frontiersman husband the epic of the westward-
moving peoples over the passes from Virginia into Kentucky.
It ranged in emotional appeal from the struggles with the

Indians and the wilderness to the most private emotions of Diony in the days of the bitter and often doubtful contest. The perfection of its mood and its structure which were paced for a steady progression to a triumphant artistic resolution was interrupted by the concluding Enoch Arden melodrama, but it remains a beautiful book. It is one of the best of the recent novels recreating the past in a romantic mood but under a realistic discipline. It confirmed the shift in the creative mood, both in spirit and in the choice of materials, that had begun to be evident around 1927.

Thornton Wilder has cultivated a poetic realism of a different texture. He has shown little interest in the contemporary scene, or in the problems that have concerned the War generation of which he is by the calendar a member. His experiences have been varied. Wisconsin born in 1897, six months before William Faulkner, he spent some eight years in China (1906-1914), attended Oberlin, served in the coast artillery, graduated from Yale and from Princeton, studied for two years in Rome and taught French at Lawrenceville. He is a poet and a musician. Neither the native endowment nor the training was likely to constrain the author to a great realistic prose.

His first novel, THE CABALA (1926), was a flight from the contemporary American scene and its problems to a specialized milieu in Rome that was able to include the present day and the death of John Keats in the same time setting. It was episodic in form and was told in the first person. The effect it produced upon a certain public can best be seen in the immoderate words of Herbert Gorman in his preface to the Modern Library edition in 1929. "Now when we look back on the event we may see that THE CABALA appeared at the proper moment as an unconscious disciplinary warning to those younger writers who were running amok." Herbert Gorman was presumably talking as a responsible person. And yet, as a matter of simple fact, THE CABALA dealt with a group of degenerate people familiar to the fiction of the day, and its chief episode was the suicide of a young pervert after an incestuous scene. The "disciplinary warning" was not, evidently, against unpleasant substance but against a too robust frankness in presenting it. The materials of Thornton Wilder have not really been essentially different from those handled by the least restrained realists: a drunken old woman trying to dominate her daughter, an actress of easy virtue, an unfortunate monk, a courtezan, an illegitimate child fathered by a respectable Greek boy and the young Roman of THE CABALA. The difference lies in the atmosphere of classic restraint which the author creates about them, and in the graceful inoffensiveness of the words in which these potentially disturbing matters are couched. In this respect the work of Thornton Wilder was another of the signs of a shift in mood toward the end of the twenties. For it is undeniable that the poetic method of writing transmutes the ill favor of a naked realism into softer and less disturbing patterns.

THE BRIDGE OF SAN LUIS REY (1927), after a short period of neglect, achieved enormous popularity in 1928. Its theme was intriguing because, with all the advance in science through the years, people still knock on wood, observe omens, and in various ways pay tribute to the uncertainty of chance. It raised again the question of Job and a million others: Do events befall by accident or by design? And it isolated the problem with the specific instance of a bridge in Peru breaking and destroying five persons in the year 1714. A naturalist would have answered with no hesitation that it was not by design and suggest an inspector of bridges. To a Christian mind the implications of the question could not even arise. The author quite wisely did not answer yes or no, but perhaps. And he suggested that, accident or design, Love was nurtured by it and the accident (if it were an accident) tended toward some beneficent end.

The thesis was happily not too insistent, and the highly compressed stories of the people involved told in a carefully cadenced style lived on their own merits. They were unified

CREATING THE MODERN AMERICAN NOVEL

into an artistic whole by the mechanical device of the bridge, and by Brother Juniper's investigation not into the laws of stress and strain in grapevine bridges, but into the lives and souls of those who perished. The resulting stories are beautifully told. They are short, the whole book being less than a third the length of an ordinary novel, yet it gives the effect of a longer work because of the clean economy of the art and the evocative power of its poetic compression. And the short form makes possible a sustained mood. Most of the qualities which distinguished the book were those which the realistic writers had neglected or ignored.

For the setting of THE WOMAN OF ANDROS (1930) Thornton Wilder chose the romantic isles of ancient Greece. The novel was somewhat disappointing because it was an academic piece, it was self-conscious, and the reader was seldom permitted to forget that this was fine writing. It is a danger to poetic prose. The interest in "beauty" had become sentimental, and the robust sense of life in THE BRIDGE OF SAN LUIS REY was gone. In the climactic passage, when, after a long day of fasting and silence, Pamphilus is led, through the influence of the memory of Crysis, to affirm the beauty of life in its dark places, a kind of nobility enters. But it is pale and a little bloodless. The distinction of the novel lay in the perfection of certain scattered passages. "You were happy with her once; do not doubt that the conviction at the heart of your happiness was as real as the conviction at the heart of your sorrow."

It was doubtless inevitable that the praise of critics like William Lyon Phelps for novels of this kind should be extravagant and excessive, and that it should in turn provoke irrelevant rebuttals from those who thought a modern artist should criticize the contemporary scene. Neither seemed to have any great effect upon Thornton Wilder. He followed the dictates of his own genius in his own way. He lectured widely. He was interested in the theater. He translated and adapted a drama for the New York stage, and he wrote a number of one-act plays in many moods as literary exercises in compressed expression. Then, after an interval of four years, he returned to the novel, and in January, 1935, published HEAVEN'S MY DESTINATION.

It is a bizarre fantasia showing few traces of the three earlier novels. It is made of the same stuff that went into some of the one-act plays in THE LONG CHRISTMAS DINNER (1931), particularly PULLMAN CAR HIAWATHA and QUEENS OF FRANCE. The grotesque and potentially comic elements that were peripheral in THE CABALA and THE BRIDGE OF SAN LUIS REY are central in HEAVEN'S MY DESTINATION. The style is bald, realistic, outspoken, less studied and not cadenced. Instead of poise and high seriousness there is hilarious farce and a tone of mockery. It is a comic and satirical version of Channing Pollock's THE FOOL, with liberal suggestions of CANDIDE and DON QUIXOTE, and even a nod toward ELMER GANTRY, but it is still Thornton Wilder. It is diverting, it is provocative, it is irritating. For its hero, George Brush, aged twenty-three, is both superlatively wise and dumb beyond credulity. He is a logical man in a contradictory world, and his logic has its ground in a few elementary propositions that are common to the religious disciplines of the world. He believes in salvation and conversion, in a militant gospel of purity, in pacifism, in voluntary poverty, in chastity, and in honesty. He tries to convert his fellow traveling salesmen, he does not smoke, drink, swear, or distinguish the subtle difference between Ma Crofut's house of beautiful girls where the policeman is welcome and the fine American home of which he dreams. He gives away his surplus money, denounces savings banks as enemies to faith, practices *ahimsa* on a robber, and purifies himself by fasting and exercise. And he takes his job as book salesman seriously and does not pad his expense account. Naturally everybody in the story thinks him crazy, is infuriated by him, and denounces him as "the damdest prig I ever saw."

The farcical humor arises from the simple device of placing so naive and well-principled a young man in situations of whose nature he is blunderingly unaware. On one or two occasions the book seems to grow serious, as in the very excellent speech on criminology before the mirthful caricature of a judge, and in the sane moment when the hero says of himself: "I made the mistake all my life of thinking that you could get better and better until you were perfect." But these interludes are quickly broken by ironic spoofing, and by the sudden transitions into fantastic invention from boldly realistic descriptions of a book salesman and his travels in the Southwest towns. It is full of energy and go, it disturbs several hundred thousands of the tender minded readers of THE BRIDGE OF SAN LUIS REY, and it leaves to a later time the answer to the inevitable question: Which of the two opposed elements in his versatile endowment will Thornton Wilder choose to cultivate? For he has, at least temporarily, abandoned the form of poetic realism in which he distinguished himself.

Other and yet younger writers have been attracted to the new mode, and two or three of them have made contributions of sufficient merit to warrant mention as an indication of the strength and variety of the poetic attack and the promise for its future. Glenway Wescott, born in Wisconsin 1901, is an example. There is no question as to the genuineness of his talent, but he has not yet fully defined himself. His first novel, THE APPLE OF THE EYE, was written in his earliest twenties. It appeared serially in the Dial and then in book form in 1924. It pictured in the dour realism of the day the lives of a group of poor Wisconsin folk centering around Hannah Madoc, the "Bad Han" of the serial title. It is very much like the first section of Ruth Suckow's COUNTRY PEOPLE, except that there are more flashes of poetic phrasing. The third sentence of the novel is, "Summer was falling from the thin trees." In the midst of the drunken scene after Hannah's father had smashed the lamp, "The trembling twilight entered the room." And in after years when Hannah thought of his tragic death, "She went past the memory on tiptoe." In the perspective of a decade, these touches are significant. They promised the more sensitive realism and the care for beauty of detail which distinguished his THE GRANDMOTHERS (1927).

THE GRANDMOTHERS is a fair synthesis of Glenway Wescott's varied gifts. He has so many that they always threaten to get in the way of one another. He writes excellent short stories, and the effect of his labors in that medium appears in the panel technique of the novels. He is also an essayist, finding that form most congenial for what he has to say. He turned aside from the novel he went to France to write, and produced instead FEAR AND TREMBLING (1932), a book of essays on contemporary matters that troubled him. And the prefatory essay to the collection of short stories, GOOD-BYE WISCONSIN (1928), has enjoyed greater fame than the stories themselves. By a happy choice of technique, THE GRANDMOTHERS, although compounded of essays and short stories, achieved a satisfactory unity of effect.

The unity exists in and through the mind of Alwyn Tower, from whose point of view the story is told. By endowing him with a poignant interest in the past history of his family, and by conceiving him in the symbolic act of turning the pages of a picture album containing his grandfathers, great-aunts and uncles and other kinsmen, as well as the grandmothers, Glenway Wescott was able to write speculative essays on the life and history of his people, and piece together fragments of family lore into sketches and short stories. The weakness as well as the strength of such a novel is evident. Nor is the inherent weakness mitigated by a sharp imagination or a bold pen. Like many others among the younger writers, he gives the impression of being preoccupied with beauty of expression as a substitute for the satisfaction denied to actual life because of the absence of beauty. The writing does not come vividly to life nor register in the attention of the reader. That is another way of saying that this talented writer still has much work to do.

The point of view from which he has worked shows the effect of a complex, uncertain age upon a precocious and sensitive spirit. Though not of the "lost generation," he was infected with "the village virus," he wrote with bitterness in the vein of Sinclair Lewis against Wisconsin and the Middle West, and he fled from its borders and its state of mind to the Paris of the exiles. In THE GRANDMOTHERS he was disturbed by the dreary, unsatisfactory results of the life, labors, and sacrifices of the generations preceding his own. And in FEAR AND TREMBLING he was no nearer to a personal adjustment to the dilemma of a poetic nature in a chaotic business civilization. We must leave him there while he works out his vision. It is impossible to foretell whether he may adjust his art to the immediate scene or find refuge in a distant past where the values he would like to live with are less resisting to the creative longing.

Among the youngest writers who are cultivating this mode of expression, the most interesting is Kay Boyle. Her work is uneven, and she has been writing too much and too hurriedly to develop the power that would make her great. But she has done one fine novel that can stand among its contemporaries on its own merit, and she has brilliant facility and a vivid poetic prose that stings and delights the mind with its sharp clarity and its cadenced vehemence.

Minnesota born in 1903, she has spent much of her time in Europe and has lived in France since 1922. She is a poet and a musician as well as a novelist. Some of the distinctive qualities in her novels would seem to derive from these related talents. She is at her best in the intense realization of her subjects through images and word associations of uncommon vibrancy. Her first novel was PLAGUED BY THE NIGHTINGALE (1931). It told the story of an American girl making her acquaintance with and adjustment to the family of her French husband. The general outlines of the narrative and the strong sense of conflict between the culture and vision of life of the young American girl and that of her French family-in-law which gave the novel its theme were familiar to the author from personal experience. PLAGUED BY THE NIGHTINGALE was new and individual; it was pleasing not only as an accomplishment but as a pledge for future performance. And it was bright with sentences like these: "Downstairs there were voices, and the copper odour of tea drifting up the stairs. She came gradually to be awake, lying soft and rested in the plumed bed, deep in the protective palm of his family."

Kay Boyle wrote next GENTLEMEN, I ADDRESS YOU PRIVATELY, but it was not published until 1933 after she had issued her third novel in order of composition, YEAR BEFORE LAST (1932). GENTLEMEN, I ADDRESS YOU PRIVATELY more clearly defined her materials and proved the difficulty they present to the artist who attempts them. Her people are gifted, some of them are geniuses in the arts; they are singular, unconforming, emotional and overwrought, and a few are physically ill. A portion of the comparative unsuccess of the novel is inherent in the characters themselves and in the demand laid upon the powers of the artist to make plausible the exiled musician Munday, his physical and emotional involvement with the irresponsible and effeminate Ayton, and their strange life as refugees under Leonie's protection. The author relied heavily upon the poetic style, and while it is successful in its effort to catch the feel of Brittany, it seems precious when it tries to probe the distorted emotions of her strange men.

YEAR BEFORE LAST was the final union of style with command over characters and their story. She created the illusive and erratic Martin and made him appear the genius she found him to be. She got into the story the emotional conflict between suppressed Eve and the eternally feminine Hannah in their love for the febrile and dying Martin. Without haste and without interruption, she drove the story forward over the rich undercurrent of fear and suffering and tragedy to the grim restraint of its ending.

The book is enriched by its understanding and its sincerity and its style is under such complete control that it is no longer obtrusive. It can describe southern France in sentences like these: "When it was day again they all saw what had happened to the country. It had begun to go smooth with idleness, so unlike the north, with no crops prepared, but with warm currents of tufted grass and deep islands of shrubs, and even a few little olive trees. There were many fancy little trees, twisted as if they had been taken out of glass jars with a fork, and everywhere the soft flowing country broken, tossed-up, dammed and bursting over rocks, rushing up in high peeling waves." But what is more important in this novel than description of the external world is the perception revealed in so rare a passage as this: "Only the matter of love could not be explained. Hannah walked a long way under the palms, with the sea as blue as heaven murmuring on her right hand. It was not rightful, nor was it wrong; she had no name to give it. What can you do with love? she said. On which side does it lie? If love is an element, like weather or wind, then it must go unchallenged. The virtuous can go to shelter, for their strength is in themselves. It's only the frail and the weak who need it; the strong have something else to do."

The publication of MY NEXT BRIDE (1934), dealing with an art colony in Paris fallen upon hard days, raised questions not about the effectiveness of poetic realism as an adequate means of expression but about the desirability of Paris as a dwelling place for American artists. Something about the life there seems to heighten one small element in their nature at the expense of others equally necessary to a healthy literature. That is where we now find and must leave Kay Boyle. Her fine craftsmanship, expended upon too specialized and unimportant materials, protrudes as craftsmanship. All the possibilities of her matter seem to have been realized in YEAR BEFORE LAST, and although she has written four novels she still remains a woman of promise in a mode that offers unlimited possibilities.

Poetic realism continues to attract young American writers. The season of 1934-1935 saw considerable accomplishment in this manner by newcomers in books like Josephine

Johnson's NOW IN NOVEMBER, and the Atlantic prize was awarded to Samuel Rogers's DUSK AT THE GROVE written in poetic style. It is a form capable of wide variations according to the individuality of the writer, its limits are not so rigid as those of objective realism, and it seems to be firmly established in the present-day American novel.

Chapter Twenty

THE PROLETARIAN NOVEL

*T*HE long depression gave a swift impetus to the development of what is loosely called the proletarian novel in America. Throughout the twenties it was a poor thing. It could hardly be said that it existed at all. It was subordinate to the novel of satire and social protest as written by Upton Sinclair, Sinclair Lewis, and the giants of the post-War days. It had a restricted audience, and its material was largely theoretical and derivative. Industry was booming, wages were high, nearly everyone had some illusion of prosperity and owned a motor car, America was never more confident or optimistic. The sickness at the heart of life was permitted to flourish without diagnosis or attention. Even to hint that all was not well behind the glittering façade was Red perfidy. In a time of national prosperity, the proletariat is not passionate for the well-being of its foreign brethren, and so long as suffering is not flagrantly acute, the proletarian novelists have little opportunity to take hold of the minds of any large numbers of the population.

Until the tightening grip of the depression startled the complacent into some knowledge of the misery into which millions had been helplessly plunged, slight attention was paid to the radical thought that had been developing in a few centers in anticipation of the inevitable collapse. The Masses, the Liberator, the New Masses, and to a lesser degree the Nation and the New Republic, had often pointed out the truth according to Marx that capitalism moved toward monopoly and expropriation, that this usurpation of advantage produced the degradation, enslavement, and exploitation of the working class, that the working class was forced into organization for self-preservation, and that the two contradictory forces must meet in conflict and capitalistic private property be expropriated. The events through which the country passed after 1929 seemed to bear out the truth of some of these predictions. Masses of men, eager to work, starved without goods because the instruments of production were held in idleness by the private owners who could no longer sell at a profit. And since machines were run and goods produced for profit and not for use, those who could not buy must do without and subsist on charity. Such an economic paradox in the midst of unprecedented human misery in a rich nation produced a bewildering variety of writing from the point of view of economics, political organization, sociology, and finance, and a large and growing body of fiction picturing the tragic conditions of life into which multitudes of our people have been thrust in the industrial communities.

This fiction is proletarian by implication rather than by direct statement of an ideology. A few novels, notably those by John Dos Passos and THE DEATH AND BIRTH OF DAVID MARKAND by Waldo Frank, are in spirit and frequently in direct expression proletarian in that they portray life in a state of potential revolution or indicate the imaginative understanding necessary for effective action. Most of the real proletarian writing has gone into the radical magazines, and it is there that the canonical articles of faith upon which many of the novels tacitly draw are set forth. They assert the necessity of the class struggle between the capitalists who privately own the means of production and the proletariat upon whose exploitation the existence of capitalistic profits depends. Production for use and for the common good of all cannot be managed so long as the capitalistic system maintains. The system can only be abolished by revolution and the dictatorship of the proletariat. Most of the evils which torment the modern state are the inevitable products of the maladjustment inherent in capitalism. Unemployment, insecurity, general poverty for the masses, and their attendant miseries of ill health, malnutrition, insanitation, moral degradation, and the mass slaughter of peace-loving workers in the wars: all these social monstrosities have their direct origin in the competitive, private-property, capitalistic society where a few thrive and the many suffer, and those who produce do not share justly in the rewards.

These propositions furnish the substance of the speech made by John Byrne before the pitiful miners in THE DEATH AND BIRTH OF DAVID MARKAND. "This land was once yours," he said, "you got a living from it. Now the operators in Howton and Pittsburgh and New York own your land, and they get a living from it, a living of luxury. And all you get, working it for them, is a slow starving. Do you want a living from it again? Then you must make it yours again. . . . The land and the coal that's in the land must belong again to you, who work it. . . . I tell you, friends: it is everything or nothing." This is the point of view John Dos Passos gives to Tim O'Hara in THE 42ND PARALLEL when he comforts his brother who had to run away from the overwhelming debts he incurred during the sickness and death of his wife. "It's the fault of the system that don't give a man the fruit of his labor. . . . The only man that gets anything out of capitalism is a crook an he gets to be a millionaire in short order. . . . But an honest workin man like John or muself we can work a hundred years and not leave enough to bury us decent with."

This ideology with its attendant implications is, however, seldom so plainly stated in the novels. Particularly since the dark days of October, 1929, they have dealt with the plight of the workers in a period of industrial collapse and in a backward state that made no provision for security or unemployment insurance against the evil day. But it has been a descriptive fiction, almost uniformly in the tradition of objective realism, and devoid of an ideology that transcends the inference behind pictures of human misery. It is a record of conditions through the medium of narration and not a considered program of reform. For the workers are stunned and bewildered; they have no understanding of the real cause of their plight, and they are helpless to formulate a way out. Novels that reproduce them as they are, must necessarily be limited in their scope, even were the authors expert economists and sociologists—as usually they are not. And since the magazines and even the newspapers have described the same conditions, often with superior vividness, and since brilliant analyses of the causes and possible cures of the basic world sickness have appeared in books of the strength and popularity of Stuart Chase's A NEW DEAL (1932) and Henry A. Wallace's NEW FRONTIERS (1934) (to mention only two) it is not to be wondered at that the depression novels, excellent and important as many of them are, have not had wider reading or compelled more serious attention.

The substance of many of these novels is, however, so forceful in its appeal to the sense of justice and pity in the human heart that they are able to survive despite the lack of artistic finish or distinction as literature which leaves them less than great. Most of them gain an effect of power from the passionate sincerity and conviction of truth that sustained their authors in their creation. Indeed the condition of literature in America would be tragically grave if men and women of talent were not so moved to attempt to transmute through the medium of an art form the suffering and the despair in the chaos about them. And the conditions through which men have been passing have provoked into creative expression in the novel many people who are not "literary" but who have lived their story and now set down their experiences.

Inevitably there is a sameness about this group of novels. And since there is no single figure of dominating stature among the writers, we may speak of them to better economy in terms of their materials and their purpose. For they have continued the realistic mode, and vestigial traces of the old thesis novels are upon their work.

One of the most insistent themes has been the fate of poor white workers, especially in the mill towns of the South.

All through the twenties the mills moved south, concentrating in Georgia and the Carolinas. They drew in from the impoverished hill country thousands of men, women, and children to hand the new industries—and they got them cheap. The workers were ignorant, their hill cabins were wretched, their crops inadequate for subsistence. To be given a company house with a bathroom, to live in a town, to work for a money income, to be offered employment for all the members of the family: the golden age so long promised by Republican orators had arrived. Potential workers swarmed into the mill towns. But there, alas, new-found miseries proved worse than the old. There were not enough houses. Several families were herded together. The bathrooms had no water. They were used as sleeping quarters, the tubs as beds. The wages did not meet minimum expenses. Mothers saw their babies sicken for lack of milk. The company doctor recommended orange juice! The babies died. The machines, the stretch-out, the increased quotas forced many from their jobs. Pellagra smote them. They brooded in hopelessness. Their incomprehending desperation was the opportunity for the labor organizers. The way out was a strike. The workers strike. They are answered by the state militia and the hired and deputized thugs imported to beat down the workers. They are denied the elementary rights of free citizens. They are clubbed, gassed, shot, imprisoned, starved and evicted. They are caught in the trap of ignorance and of poverty, and what can they do? They can suffer and then they can die. For nothing is cheaper in American industry than human workers.

That is the story told by the proletarian novelists. It varies according to the locality and the type of employment. It is modified by the character of the workers and by the degree of stress placed upon them by the depression. It is documented by the experience of millions of men, and it is authenticated by the daily news when the conditions finally breed a general textile strike or civil war in the coal fields. These novels are all written solely from the workers' point of view. Fundamentally they deal with the system of which all industrial units are a part. Their story is of poverty and the appalling human misery produced by the system, and poverty knows no geography. It is the same whether in a worker's hovel in Georgia, or on the lower East Side of New York where Michael Gold has condensed it in a symbol: "Bedbugs are what people mean when they say: Poverty. . . . It wasn't a lack of cleanliness in our home. My mother was as clean as any German housewife; she slaved, she worked herself to the bone keeping us fresh and neat. The bedbugs were a torment to her. She doused the beds with kerosene, changed the sheets, sprayed the mattresses in an endless frantic war with the bedbugs. What was the use; nothing could help: it was Poverty; it was the Tenement."

The story is told with variations by Fielding Burke (Olive Tilford Dargan) in CALL HOME THE HEART (1932), one of the best proletarian novels in America from a literary point of view. It employs the older biographical narrative method instead of the newer, stylized technique to enlist for these unfortunate and exploited people the deep sympathy of the reader. The story is told by Grace Lumpkin in TO MAKE MY BREAD (1932); by Mary Heaton Vorse in STRIKE! (1930); and by Jack Conroy in THE DISINHERITED (1933), a novel that attains great power and carries conviction by its pictures of the workers in depressed America, centering around young Donovan, orphaned son of a coal miner whose father and older brothers had been killed in the mines, and told by one who obviously knows what he is talking about. It is told by Catherine Brody in NOBODY STARVES (1932), showing how the depression gripped and drove to utter despair the better paid Detroit workers who were trying to buy a home and a motor car. And lest we forget that this was only a more violent enlargement of the distress already abounding before 1929, we should keep handy the case book of the tragedy of unemployment compiled by Clinch Calkins and ironically titled SOME FOLKS WON'T WORK (1930).

The story is told by William Rollins, Jr., in THE SHADOW BEFORE (1934), a novel that follows the prescribed pattern up to and including the inevitable strike in the mill town, here called Fullerton. It is compressed in time and filled with a variety of characters. It is a fine specimen of the way some of the proletarians, like Robert Cantwell and Albert Halper, are attempting to utilize modern experimental techniques to realize the confusion of a mill, the fragmentary experiences of the workers, the mass movements of men and machines, the nerve destroying *"thump* throb: *thump* throb" that leaps from the machines into the workers' blood, and the general plight of the proletariat, who are not news but only "the dark gloomy props that hold up an unaware society."

The story is told of a group of miners by Lauren Gilfillan in I WENT TO PIT COLLEGE (1934), a good piece of reporting by a college-girl onlooker who sees the conditions but does not attain the passionate emotional undertow of Jack Conroy who grew up in them. It is varied by Edward Newhouse in YOU CAN'T SLEEP HERE (1934), a novel that follows an unemployed young newspaper man from his prosperity down through nauseating flop houses in New York to a Hooverville that the police burn over the heads of the victims because the shanties depress real-estate values and do not look well in a beautiful city. And it is told of a different New York group by Edwin Seaver in THE COMPANY (1930), wherein are presented the banal, fruitless lives of representative men and women from different departments of the mechanical organization into which each fits with inconspicuous coglike regimentation and efficiency. And over the gateway to this book where everyone is pressed flat and dry is painted the slogan from the Christian Business Man's Magazine: "Omnipresent Christ, substance, quicken, and prosper me."

In none of these novels is there the slightest indication that men ever feel joy or pride in their labor. Their jobs have been robbed of all personal expression or compensation. Instead, there is ill adjustment and rebellion against wages and hours of work, and employers are the villains. It is well to set over against them William Wister Haines's SLIM (1934) as one of the few books in which men derive any satisfaction from the performance of their job. This novel is aware of the disastrous effect of unemployment not only because of the lost wages, but because, as in THE HAIRY APE, it robs these workers of the sense of "belonging" that was and is theirs when they move carefree, light-hearted, and pleased with their lives, fastening wires to great steel towers about the country.

And we might add for the sake of balance (since these novels are naturally solemn) the salty and sparkling malice and the ironic protest against the sentimentality of the proletarians made by Isabel Paterson, who has lately deserted the historical romances of young lovers in Thuringia to study the droll activities of her contemporaries. In THE GOLDEN VANITY (1934) she causes the realistic Mysie, a representative of the villain group in the proletarian novels, to say: "There would be no social unrest if the poor were supplied with champagne and pâté de foie gras. Instead of being investigated and surveyed at great expense by a lot of ghastly sociologists and uplifters, who then inform them that they are poor. They know it. . . . There is that fact which sentimental sociologists do not take into account; some people are useless. It doesn't matter whether they sit in club windows and turn purple over the insolence of workingmen demanding higher wages, or sit in the kitchen grumbling about the injustices of capitalism; they are a dead loss. What are you going to do with them? They are more useless in a job than out of it."

She utters caustic comments on Henry Ford, J. P. Morgan, and the intellectuals who have adopted the proletarian point of view because it is at the moment fashionable. And she pokes some legitimate fun at the great gap fixed between the workers and the Joycean books written for them when she causes Jake Van Buren to say that the secretary recommended "the method of our literary editor to my attention; she thinks I should acquire the proletarian point of view. I don't know where *he* picked it up; maybe Harvard; and besides, the only proletarians I know read Zane Grey."

A few of the novelists who have worked with the proletarian and the submerging "white-collar" class have made for themselves distinctive reputations and deserve more emphatic mention on the strength of their accomplishments and their promise. Josephine Herbst (Mrs. John Herrmann), born in Iowa in 1897, is another of that generation of American women who could experience a degree of economic emancipation and wander at will through the twenties from college to San Francisco to Detroit, to New York, to Europe. She has been concerned with the break-up of the great middle-class in America who once were prosperous in their share of the nation's wealth, but who have now been forced down among the proletariat.

In two parts of a projected trilogy, PITY IS NOT ENOUGH (1933) and THE EXECUTIONER WAITS (1934), Josephine Herbst has shown through the ramified Trexler family the rise and fall of a class since the Civil War. She is an accomplished technician and a master of her subject. She disdains expository material after the manner of James Joyce, depending upon a series of brief panels accurately drawn and bound together by the blood relationship of the Trexlers. She catches contemporary speech as realistically as Ruth Suckow; nor does she shy away from it when it indulges in obscenity and profanity. The novels are proletarian by reference. There are flashes of an I.W.W. convention in an Iowa town, of the desperation of the farmers in the early thirties, the march on Ford in 1932, and the strikes of 1934. In PITY IS NOT ENOUGH she does not make clear just what more is required. But at the conclusion of THE EXECUTIONER WAITS, David Trexler, once proud druggist and small-time capitalist of the boom days, stands as spectator before an ominous scene during a strike in Pennsylvania. And he hears a speaker say across the coffin of a murdered worker: "Now friends. One thing to remember. They can shoot some of us down, they can't shoot all of us. Everytime they make us dig a grave for one of ours, they are digging the pit from under their own feet. Every time they fire us and cheat us and drive us from our homes, they only increase the forest of hands that will rise up against them. Comrades. One word to remember. The word of Joe Hill, himself shot down in cold blood. . . . *Don't mourn. Organize.*"

And the same general pattern is followed by the late Thomas Boyd's IN TIME OF PEACE (1935) showing the return of William Hicks from the War (THROUGH THE WHEAT), how he rose to upper-middle-class, country-club prosperity in the twenties, how he collapsed with the depression, and how he was shot in a line of job-seekers before Victory Motors when they shouted, "Work or Relief." "If it was war again, he was glad to know it. He at least had something to fight for now."

Michael Gold would have a place in the novel of any nation for his JEWS WITHOUT MONEY (1930). He was born in 1896 in the East Side, a Roumanian Jew, in the poverty of the tenement. He came up through the most miserable conditions in the desperate struggle for existence. He has worked at all kinds of jobs in all parts of the country. He has been in strikes and demonstrations against injustice, he is a Communist, and he was for a time the editor of the New Masses. His autobiographical novel is a vivid picture and indictment of tenement life which traps, holds, and defeats its victims. To read this novel is an experience. It is simple, it is stark, it is poised and yet aflame, it is tender, and it is merciless. The wretched city block comes to life before our eyes in all its pitiful tragedy: the mother, the father slowly reduced to a banana cart from which few will buy, the maimed souls who never had a chance, the degradation of the girls, the searing experiences of the boy about whom the story unfolds. And after the accumulation of misfortunes and the slavery of endless job-hunting and impossible jobs we are ready for the sharp compression of the conclusion:

And my father and mother grew sadder and older. It went on for years. I don't want to remember it all; the years of my adolescence. Yet I was only one among a million others.

A man on an East Side soap-box, one night, proclaimed that out of the despair, melancholy and helpless rage of millions, a world movement had been born to abolish poverty.

I listened to him.

O workers' Revolution, you brought hope to me, a lonely suicidal boy. You are the true Messiah. You will destroy the East Side when you come, and build there a garden for the human spirit.

O Revolution, that forced me to think, to struggle and to live.

O great Beginning!

Robert Cantwell for his novels LAUGH AND LIE DOWN (1931) and THE LAND OF PLENTY (1934) must be placed well to the front among those who have technical facility and latent power. THE LAND OF PLENTY has great merit. It attempts some of the more modern experimental methods of expression which are not fully integrated with the materials supplied by a strike in a lumber mill on the West Coast, much of the action is confused, and some of the characters (especially those who are not workers) are too distorted to be effective as villains of the piece. Its greatest virtues are its sense of narrative in several of the episodes, its pictures of the physical conditions under which men work and sleep, and the despair and bewilderment of jobless men and workers whose incomes will not meet subsistence demands, who have no weapon but the strike, and it ineffective. He is at his best in those parts of his work, notably in LAUGH AND LIE DOWN, where he shows the impact of industrialism on the young men just coming into maturity under its influences.

Albert Halper seems to be equally if not more gifted than Robert Cantwell. His UNION SQUARE (1933) was an accomplishment, and had the banks not collapsed at the time of its appearance it might have had a wider reading. It handled the complex scene of Union Square with orderliness and control, and it gained emotional impact as it unfolded the way of the police with the masses that gather into the Square for discussion, and the sickening brutalities committed upon helpless and innocent men as they are clubbed and ridden down by armed and mounted officers in uniform under the pretense of preserving peace. THE FOUNDRY (1934) was equally good as a picture of a group of men working in a type foundry, realizing them as living characters, and orchestrating them and the conditions of their labor into the cacophony of the foundry.

And there are also the turbulent creations of Erskine Caldwell. He is hardly a proletarian novelist. He is, in fact, an embarrassment to any neat classification. He has certain qualities that he does not share with other American writers. His novels, TOBACCO ROAD (1932) and GOD'S LITTLE ACRE (1933), have a modicum of sardonic humor grimly mortised into their texture that is unusual in American fiction. The novels are much alike, as though the second were a rewriting of the first (which did not sell) with greater emphasis on sex and perversion and a provocative but confused symbolism. They purport to represent the American peasantry on its lowest level of stupidity, poverty, and moral degradation. They approach Faulknerian revulsions in certain episodes like that wherein the starving old grandmother in TOBACCO ROAD is crushed by the new Ford, dies slowly like an abandoned sheep in the yard where she fell, and, when thoroughly dead, is flung indifferently into a shallow ditch by her son Jeeter. In statement and in diction they are blunt and vulgar as depraved life. They relate to the proletarian novels in that the debased conditions in TOBACCO ROAD are the result of economic change that leaves the shiftless and unadaptable people to decay, and in that the important section of GOD'S LITTLE ACRE is a splendid portrayal of unemployment and the tragedy of defenseless workers in a strike. JOURNEYMAN (1935), a short novel about the lecherous preacher Semon Dye, was in the accustomed Caldwellian manner, and gave little comfort to those who had hoped much for his development.

This general mode, conveniently called proletarian, is one of three or four fairly distinct forms in which our novelists are now working. Into it has gone and is going much of the creative energy in the America of the long depression. This energy has also expressed itself in poetry, in painting, in direct action, and in the vigorous dramas of playwrights like Elmer Rice and plays like Peters and Sklar's STEVEDORE at the Theatre Union. And out of the ferment which is still confused by propaganda and indignation one may surely expect a few novels of sufficient scope and power and understanding to establish this form in the expanding body of American fiction.

Chapter Twenty-one

TOWARDS A NEW ROMANCE

*T*HE prolonged depression of the thirties also directed the novelists toward a new mode of expression so different in tone from that of the age of objective realism that it may well be designated a return to romance. The word requires accurate restrictions, but it will suffice here and now to remind ourselves that the boundary between realism and romance is always nebulous, and that the terms are only conveniences by which one distinguishes between the rigid, resisting world of immediate commonsense outside of one's personal control, and the more supple realm of the past or of the fancy where one can by asserting his imagination exercise authority and soften or rearrange details at will.

It seems apparent from the facts we have examined in earlier chapters that several American novelists were already striving for a less rigid form of expression before the depression settled in. The romanticism inherent in the hearts of men had been imperfectly released in the twenties by direct action, or by such creations of the will-to-faith as the stuffed shirt and the myth of the superman of business. A reaction of some sort was inevitable. It is instructive to bear in mind that the period of the realistic novel coincided with the rise of a proud and arrogant industrialism, that it reached its climax during the boom days when the public was marching without conscience or indignation over the Harding scandals into Utopian prosperity, and that it began to waver when the direction of affairs suddenly got beyond our wishes and command and dived into the world depression which left everyone stunned and bewildered. It was easy to take realism and

satire with a high spirit so long as the nation was confident
in its ways. In a time of confusion, strongly realistic novels
describing our plight were neglected in favor of those which,
in one form or another, offered escape from a too-insistent
present and thoughts of insecurity.

If we may isolate from the numerous novels a representative one for each of the last few seasons, then the book of
1931, just a decade after MAIN STREET, was Pearl Buck's THE
GOOD EARTH, on the other side of the globe from our sorrows.
It was romantic in mood, although each page was fully ballasted with carefully observed detail. It dealt in Biblical
phraseology with the primary and timeless emotions: the age-
old struggle of man with the earth and its elements, and with
the lusts of his own flesh. The life was so firmly planted in
the soil, and ennobled by custom and religious ceremony of
long standing, that it maintained at all times a core of dignity.
This feeling of dignity and poise gave to American readers a
sense of escape from the all too vivid pictures in NOBODY
STARVES from which both qualities were painfully absent. In
1932, the book was THE FOUNTAIN, English made and set in a
Dutch castle where a harassed modern sought peace and isolation in the midst of the War in order to ask his soul the questions modern men had refused to confront. And in 1933 and
the following years of its acclaim, ANTHONY ADVERSE has given
its fortnight or more of solace to weary and troubled thousands.

The shift in emphasis of the creative mood of the thirties,
of which these books and their great public favor are typical,
is one of the notable developments in the modern American
novel. The satirical spirit that was so hilariously cultivated
when the nation was prosperous and a little proud of its
crudity has temporarily passed. The Freudian vogue has
waned, leaving some of the dramas of Eugene O'Neill and
many of our modern novels isolated into a period. The War
generation appears static as a result of its excessive self-dramati-
zation in a rapidly changing era. And there was something

symbolic and a little sad about Henry Mencken's retirement from the barricades of the American Mercury to the mists of Baltimore, and the homecoming of Gertrude Stein in the wake of her autobiography.

The altered mood is clearly to be observed in the novels dealing with rural scenes and life on the farm. Dour realism and satire reached their height in treating of life on American farms and in their village centers. In fact, during the period examined in this book, our novelists have gone full circle from romance through realism and back again to romance in their attitude toward the farm. The sentimentalized farmers of the Golden West period, when the land sharks and railroad profiteers were luring settlers into their speculative waste-lands, are familiar to all readers. They were homespun types who whittled or churned and made life seem roseate in commonsense maxims spoken in dialect proving that placidity of temperament, hard work, and frugality were the basis of the good life. The no less sentimentalized types of the red-blooded era, glorifying the adventure of winning the West and exalting the valor of heroes into the legend of sun-hardened, rough-riding supermen, are equally familiar. They extended well into the realistic period in novels like Owen Wister's THE VIRGINIAN (1902).

A realistic age could hardly be expected to resist the challenge of such falsifications. For as a matter of cold reality, the country was a wilderness, and life on the lonely prairies was hard and stark and brutalizing. The most rudimentary amenities were denied to a family of seven in a fourteen by sixteen sod hut under the specter of the mortgage, taxes, and likely crop failure. It was Hamlin Garland's mission to write of these conditions as they were and as he had experienced them on the frontier in Wisconsin and Iowa. His best reports are in MAIN-TRAVELLED ROADS (1891), a group of stories, and in his autobiographies that read like documented realistic novels, A SON OF THE MIDDLE BORDER (1917) and A DAUGHTER OF THE MIDDLE BORDER (1921).

The exploitation came slowly at first, because the population was restless and moved about striking roots slowly, and the novelists were occupied with city and small-town life and the exposure of the evils of the day. But when the pioneers got settled, they began to educate their children for success in urban life. And from its superior height of university culture and a job in the metropolis, the generation represented by Sinclair Lewis and Willa Cather was able, as we have seen, to look back to the dreary life of the farm and present it from the point of view of one who had already escaped. The moods were various, but the dominant one was that of protest and superiority. In those novels richer in emotion and understanding, the protest was veiled and the interest fell upon the heroic quality of the folk who struggled against great odds for a meager reward. Many of these we have seen in our study of the separate authors who created them. A few others are noteworthy. There was Dell H. Munger's THE WIND BEFORE THE DAWN (1912) that got into a novel about Kansas the struggle with adversity in the form of windstorms, droughts, and the plague of grasshoppers. There was Mr. and Mrs. Haldeman-Julius's novel of rural Kansas significantly titled DUST (1921), in the same year with the American translation of GROWTH OF THE SOIL, Knut Hamsun's powerful and simply written epic of man at favorable grips with the crude elements of life on the frontier of Norway. There was young Martha Ostenso's WILD GEESE (1925), differing but little from Ruth Suckow's COUNTRY PEOPLE in its pictures of life farther into the Northwest among the Scandinavian immigrants in the lake district of Manitoba. The life is bleak. It is barren of tenderness, heavy with unspoken tyrannies, and marches toward catastrophe and retribution on dramatic events growing out of primitive character traits.

And there were the powerfully handled novels of Ole Rölvaag, no less native because the author lived a little longer in Norway before he came among us, and wrote them in his native tongue, because it offered him greater freedom in expression. GIANTS IN THE EARTH (1927), and to a lesser degree its sequel, PEDER VICTORIOUS (1929), bring to a climax the saga of immigrant life on the soil of the great Northwest. They are so big that other novels on the same theme seem to be only a preparation for them. For Ole Rölvaag enlarged the vision, and rounded and humanized the people of whom he wrote. By avoiding the exclusions so characteristic of modern authors, he succeeded in creating a group of people fully alive and equipped with a normal set of human emotions, idealized but not distorted. Their lives are interesting for themselves as well as for their place in the epic sweep greater than the individual men who comprise it. They come out of this tremendous contest against overwhelming natural forces with a lift of dignity and of triumph even in defeat.

The author had spent the first twenty years of his life in Norway in a fishing village, six of them on the ships, before he came to the Dakota farms and finally to St. Olaf College, where he remained throughout his literary career. The quality of the emotion in his novels, the psychological analyses of his characters, the communal spirit of the people, are all more Norwegian than native American. But the settlement of the West by these Norsemen is as much a part of the life and growth of the Union as any other of the paradoxical phenomena that comprise America. There is no good reason for not claiming the honor of Ole Rölvaag's work, and recognizing its high place in the creation of the American novel.

Its two most significant contributions were its humanity and its epic sweep. The people are intensely alive. They are giants from a land inured to hardship and they face with valor the barren and unfriendly prairie land. Their spirits are high. " 'Just wait, my girl, just wait. It's going to be wonderful: you'll see how wonderful I can make it for you, this kingdom of ours!' He laughed until his eyes were drawn out in two narrow slits. 'And no old, worn-out, thin-shanked, potbellied king is going to come around and tell me what I have to do about it, either!' " That spirit survives the poverty, the loneliness, the pestilence of grasshoppers, and the long desperate attack of the arctic blizzards.

Amid all the hardships, the house of Per Hansa is sustained by the assertion of qualities inconspicuous in our modern native literature: humor, enthusiasm for living, warm human affections, a code of moral values, a pride in workmanship, endurance, and accomplishment, and boisterous, confiding, good-hearted neighborliness; the mixture of the old and solid human virtues by which men defeat the cold, malicious or indifferent elements against which they struggle.

The hostile forces destroy many of the individual men, but the conquest and the humanity go on. Beret, sensitive to the savagery of the land, lonely for the familiar fiords, tormented by the endless monotony of wind-driven, snow-piled days and nights, breaks under the strain. Hans Olsa is destroyed by a blizzard while protecting his cattle. Per Hansa goes consciously to his own death in the same blizzard, perishing for an ideal of neighborliness and the welfare of Hans and of Beret. But the spirit survives, and Peder, first-born on the prairie, carries on into the struggle between the old and the new—the process by which a native culture is subtly Americanized on the plains of the Dakotas.

The great American success of these novels was portentous. They appeared in 1927 and 1929, the dates that already are emerging with uncommon sharpness as landmarks in American economic and literary history. Added through translation to the growing body of American fiction, they brought to a fruition one distinct phase of the realistic approach to farm and rural life. They used the best that was in the preceding modes and, along with some of the other novels we have examined, pointed to a new one laying some stress on the heroism of the past and the possible dignity of life on the farm.

That change in attitude was reinforced by the conditions of life in the thirties. The abundant jobs, the generous salaries, the gayety of existence that had made the cities irresistible in earlier years were suddenly cut off, and in their stead were faces pinched by want and despair, and frightened men torn from security and tossed into the public park and the bread line. And against the new backdrop, the age-old peace and solidity of life on the farm became romantically attractive. By another curious paradox, this romantic retreat to the farm was coincident with the years during which the actual plight of the farmer was in its most desperate state and was producing riots and mob violence.

The literary group scattered to the rocks and the abandoned farm houses of New England. The exiles returned from Paris and entered upon the life suggested by Robert Coates in YESTERDAY'S BURDENS (1933) and Malcolm Cowley in EXILE'S RETURN (1934). People began to talk about and to project subsistence homesteads. Arty folk tried building cabins or reclaiming houses from Connecticut to California and finding independence in nine bean rows and a hive of bees, and inspiration for work in a return to the cult of Thoreau. The mood of revolt had temporarily passed.

This phase of the spirit of the thirties may be seen in any one of several scores of novels. It will suffice to suggest a representative few, and any reader may easily extend them at will.

The change in mood was shown in the highly popular books of Bess Streeter Aldrich of Iowa and Nebraska, especially her A LANTERN IN HER HAND (1928) glorifying the pioneer mother. These novels were sentimental in mood, but that did not mean that they falsified life. Bess Streeter Aldrich had lived intimately with the kind of people she described, and when she introduced sentiment she was as realistic with her chosen subject matter as her hard-boiled contemporaries were with theirs. The shifting attitude was also evident in the farm novels of Phil Stong of Iowa. STATE FAIR (1932) was a sensation because it discovered an American farm where a family had a very good time with its life. Nobody tortured anyone, no one was twisted with suppressions, and no one worked like a dumb ox or was overwhelmed by disaster. And the novel even had for its hero a fine, blue, prize-winning hog at the moment when the hysteria of the nation had decided that Iowa hogs were to lift it from the depression. The book was not great in any sense, and it is mentioned only because it was an excellent indication of the temperament of the times. But it should be contrasted with the violence and the fury of Anonymous THIS BRIGHT SUMMER (1933) and Josephine Johnson's NOW IN NOVEMBER (1934), and the gratuitous horrors of Vardis Fisher's novels.

In a calmer tone was LeRoy MacLeod's THE YEARS OF PEACE (1932) and THE CROWDED HILL (1934) presenting a supportable way of life in rural Indiana, and Gladys H. Carroll's successful novel of farm life in New England, AS THE EARTH TURNS (1933). And the subject was so interesting that Louis Bromfield, the amazingly fertile author of the tetralogy grouped under the general title ESCAPE (1924-1927) and of at least one novel a year since that time, published in 1933 a book with its setting in Ohio and its title THE FARM. The novel came with a little surprise from the author of THE STRANGE CASE OF MISS ANNIE SPRAGG (1928) and TWENTY-FOUR HOURS (1930). Although its best parts were satirical of corruption and vanity and the forces of destruction, it was, he said, written as an escape, and it dwelt in a spirit of regret on the compensations in the old way of life on the farm.

And as if to add weight to the accumulating evidence of this new attitude toward rural America and specifically the Middle West, there appeared in the summer of 1934 young Paul Engle's AMERICAN SONG, lustily and romantically admiring the cornfields of Iowa without troubling about the mortgages; and young Jesse Stuart's MAN WITH A BULL-TONGUE PLOW, seeking peace and contentment on his hilly acres among the bluffs of the Ohio river. The great and well-deserved success of these books of poems indicated how keenly the loss of their point of view had been felt since the early days of Vachel Lindsay, Carl Sandburg, and Robert Frost, and how welcome its return might be.

The suppressed romanticism of the times has also taken the form of an escape from contemporaneity into the past. The abrupt collapse of the prosperity of the twenties that sent some creative spirits to reporting the misery of jobless or underpaid men, and some to the rediscovery of the simple life in rural settings, inspired others to look back a little way into the manner of living in periods less harassed and less complicated in retrospect than our own. It has not been an unfettered escape into undisciplined imagination after the fashion of the feeble efforts at romance following the war with Spain in novels like MONSIEUR BEAUCAIRE and JANICE MEREDITH. It has usually deferred to the restraint of realism. It is an interesting antithesis to the method of THE STORY OF A COUNTRY TOWN. For that novel, and others like it, was starkly realistic in mood, but the frame of its narrative was romantic and even melodramatic. In the 1930's the structure and detail are realistic but the belligerent mood has tended to soften toward romance, and the materials and the creative passion are derived from the past. For it is not easy to impose order and peace upon the turmoil and the contradictions of the immediate scene. This may be done either with the future or with the past, and novelists have usually preferred the past.

In the perspective of a past distant enough to disengage itself from the confusion of the present it is possible to arrange life into a satisfactory pattern and give it meaning. Sometimes the purpose is to heighten its reality and its resemblance to the fundamental values of good living in all ages, sometimes to render more graphic the older values that have perished. In either case, the remoteness of the settings in time and the imaginative mood in which the author is working tend to relieve the art product of the sharp thrusts common to materials of the active and demanding present.

We have seen in other connections how this new mood began to make itself felt in 1928, and how it affected the work of Willa Cather and Elizabeth Madox Roberts. In the years that have followed it has established itself firmly as one of the modes of expression of the thirties. It has produced in poetry two modern classics in Stephen Vincent Benét's epic of the Civil War, JOHN BROWN'S BODY, which appeared in 1928 as another sign of the times; and in Archibald MacLeish's beautiful and moving recreation of the conquest of Mexico in CONQUISTADOR in 1932. Both were awarded Pulitzer prizes. It has produced in drama such sensitive and poetically expressed plays as Maxwell Anderson's ELIZABETH THE QUEEN (1930), MARY OF SCOTLAND (1933) and VALLEY FORGE (1934), all of which were Theatre Guild successes. And it has been expressed in a score or more of meritorious novels from which a few may be singled out for special mention as representative of this phase of the contemporary novel.

Hervey Allen's ANTHONY ADVERSE (1933), with its two years of overwhelming success in America and abroad, is simply one of those solid facts in the world which make comment superfluous. The author, Pennsylvania born in 1889, was one of the older men of the War generation. Although he was seriously wounded a few months before the Armistice, he accepted the War as one of the facts of life and did not become neurotic about it. He expressed himself in poetry, wrote an account of the War, TOWARD THE FLAME (1926), and a thorough biography of Poe, ISRAFEL (1926), and then turned to the extensive labors of reading for and composing the novel that brought to a focus all the unexpressed romance in a troubled day. It was astonishing in its assumption that a fast-paced and nervous population were ready to forget the insistent worries of the moment and bury themselves in Anthony Adverse's world with its mixture of adventure, travel, geography, history, and psychological and physiological analyses of men and society. Its phenomenal appeal to all sorts and conditions of men is in itself convincing evidence of the shifting mood of the thirties.

Dozens of other novels have turned to the past, particularly to the period of the Civil War, for their materials. James Boyd, a North Carolinian born in Pennsylvania, used it for his novel, MARCHING ON (1927). Leonard Ehrlich made an excellent beginning toward a career with the inexhaustible John Brown in GOD'S ANGRY MAN (1932), and MacKinlay Kantor with the imperishable battle of Gettysburg in LONG REMEMBER (1934). The quieter elements in a departed way of life were carried into best-sellerdom by Stark Young's SO RED THE ROSE (1934), a novel that gently recreated the vanished culture of the South of old romance. The success of that novel, though baffling, is not inexplicable. It is another symptom of the mood of the confused thirties that it should find solace in the contemplation of an order of living made beautiful by the values which have perished from modern society. And they were here recreated by a man of poise and inner peace who had already done well by the milieu in HEAVEN TREES (1926) and RIVER HOUSE (1929).

The list might be indefinitely extended to include a score of recent novels, like Robert P. Tristram Coffin's LOST PARADISE (1934), and like Frank Ernest Hill's novel in verse, WESTWARD STAR (1934), recreating the epic of the western migrations. The important point is that a spirit and a mode of expression long absent from our American novel has reentered it and gives promise of distinction. For it is not only and not all of it an escapist fiction; at its best it is trying to understand the nature of the past which has determined the quality of the culture of the present. And it is only natural that, viewed from the disquiet of the thirties, the past should appear to be more desirable than it really was, and that the romance created by imaginations that have been well chastened by realism should be devoid of giants and a little sad with longing and regret.

Chapter Twenty-two

GREAT EXPECTATIONS

*T*HE American novel has every right to expect great things from the generation just approaching maturity and beginning to find expression. It has a public disciplined to take its literature with no *caveat* except that it must be honest of purpose. And this public is more flexible in its taste and less ridden by schools than it was in the twenties. This generation, born since 1900, has before it unlimited resources in materials and technical facilities. In the short space of its beginnings upon the earth it has been treated to the effects of the greatest war, the greatest boom, and the greatest depression yet experienced by modern men. The necessary and inevitable changes in external conditions demand recreation and reassertion of values. That is the secret of a living literature in the day of Job and Chaucer and Spenser and Wordsworth and now. And yet with all the fine accomplishments of the generations whose work has been the subject of this book, only a beginning has been made toward transmuting the complex welter of American life into satisfactory art forms. Everything of real interest is yet to be done.

The oncoming writers inherit the riches created by a full generation of patient labor expended on the task of getting America into an active fiction. The versatility of the novel as a form has been greatly improved, and the possibility of diverse methods demonstrated. Under the demands of new problems confronted by the more ambitious and original novelists there have emerged the powerful, realistic mass effects of Theodore Dreiser; the careful selection and satirical exaggeration of Sinclair Lewis; the stammering overtones of Sherwood Anderson arising from a relaxed structural form and an interest in the vagaries of a mind trying to know *why?;* the pure clarity, the meticulous selectivity, the classical precision of Willa Cather; the fantastic invention, the fluid style, the disillusioned innuendo of James Branch Cabell; the hard little repetitions, the oblique observations, the first-person simplicity, the telegraphic precision of Ernest Hemingway; the extension of the inwardness of the approach and the materials in the stream of consciousness or the unspoken monologue as developed by Waldo Frank, Conrad Aiken, William Faulkner; the low-pitched, flat chronicle method of Ruth Suckow; the high-pitched, nervous imagism of Kay Boyle; the modernistic, news-flash, motion-picture technique of John Dos Passos; the experiments in the unities of Thornton Wilder, Rex Stout, Louis Bromfield; all these and more and various combinations are now a part of the established yet not too rigidly defined methodology of the modern novel.

Who is to use it, remold it, or manipulate it to convey significant matter? It would be idle and probably foolish to attempt specification. Many of those already making their promising appearance will not mature just as others not yet before the public will eventually arrive. But it will be diverting as a conclusion to this study to give hostage to the future and risk a few observations.

There is the possibility of Thomas Wolfe, North Carolina born in 1900, and author of LOOK HOMEWARD, ANGEL (1929). That book was one of those first novels that flow so easily and sometimes powerfully from the pen of young men in their late twenties as their youthful experiences begin to take on meaning for them. It had passages of considerable strength, sometimes of poetic power, and others so washed with sentiment that the reader cried out for a little fine human scorn to clarify the air and introduce proportion. It created or reported a turbulent life in a small town in the South and the struggle of a boy to break out of a sordid environment. It made good use of the realistic technique and at times the stream of consciousness method of exploring the mind. There is no question of the emotional reserves of this author, but only of his ability to impose order upon the chaos of material not immediately autobiographical. Two novels were announced, one in 1931, another in 1932, and both withdrawn. At last the elephantine, half-million-word novel OF TIME AND THE RIVER was issued in March, 1935. Thomas Wolfe had more nearly defined himself The novel carried on another five years (1920-1925) of the story of Eugene Gant, beginning with his departure from the South for Harvard and following him back to the South, to New York, to Europe, and again to his native shores. And throughout these wanderings the young man is furious and bursting with a lust for the unknowable cosmos. Under the blight of this madness, everything grows strained and exaggerated in a quest for profundity. It leads him to tell you again and again, and then again and again that the earth is old and lonely, that time is brief and strange, that young men are often tormented by the Furies, and that man's journey on the earth is lonely and mysterious. And you believed him the first time.

The same madness leads him to declare that he must know about everything on the earth. This indiscriminate curiosity is fatal and insane, and it destroys proportion and relative significance without which confusion is worse confounded. It betrays him into the attempt to make trivial and contemptible matters gigantic by uttering about them a multitudinous stream of large and cosmic words that have more rhetoric than meaning. There is here a tremendous and overwhelming energy; it assaults and describes the welter of chaos and old night, but no spirit moves upon the darkness of the waters to say with the resolution of a mastered art: Let there be light. Perhaps that is demanding too much of one man. And yet Thomas Wolfe is the kind of young man upon whom we must make demand. So much being given, we must ask the little more, the best. The most powerful sense of fury emerges not from a continuous uncontrolled rage, but from an art that is calm.

The novel is so nearly autobiographical that sometimes the author forgets to preserve the fiction of the third person in describing Eugene Gant's experiences, and subconsciously drops into the first person: ". . . and they, too, would blaze there for a moment in *our* vision with an intolerable etc." It has the virtues and the defects of the autobiographical form. Some things the author does gloriously. Three hundred of the nine hundred and twelve compact pages are splendid and exciting. He can handle the Joycean Bacchanalia, the Proustian minutiae of sense impressions remembered from things past, the word-compounding trick of E. E. Cummings, the Whitmanian catalogue of evocative phrases in a chant about America. He can brood in fiery or nostalgic words over man's fate on the earth: exultation and disease, love and death. He has a gift for seizing upon a dominant aspect of a man's frame or an element in his character and driving it into superhuman and grotesque dimensions. He has magically captured at times the secret longings of a sensitive boy emerging from adolescence and his response to the changing seasons. He has major talents, and he has the weakness of his virtues. He often wastes himself and tires his readers with trivialities and sapless people. He plans on a vast, indiscriminate scale, like Spenser and Michelangelo, and like them he leaves his forgotten Arthurs to drift in the land, and his unfinished statues in which a single powerful shoulder is seen struggling into form against the imprisoning chaos of the uncarved stone. Thomas Wolfe has not frightened chaos, but he is first among the men of promise.

James Gould Cozzens still justifies great expectations, even though he has already written five novels and two novelettes without becoming a significant part of American fiction. Chicago born in 1903, a few semesters at Harvard, and a plunge into Cuban life afforded the background for his first work: CONFUSION (1924), MICHAEL SCARLETT (1925), COCKPIT (1928), and THE SON OF PERDITION (1929). S. S. SAN PEDRO, based on the *Vestris* disaster, won the short-novel contest of Scribner's Magazine in 1931. Christopher Morley in a moment of lapse (May the Shade forgive him!) said, "It seems to me to rank with the best of Conrad's work." It was often excellent in a straightforward descriptive manner, but destroyed as a whole by a feeble symbolism. His promise rests upon the character of Dr. Bull in THE LAST ADAM (1933) and on the technical virtuosity of S. S. SAN PEDRO and CASTAWAY (1934). Except for those bright elements, his work so far goes along with the scores of competent novels about which everyone says, "Have you read THE RETURN OF THE HORIZON?" "No. Is it good?" "Yes. It is very good. And have you read . . ."

George Davis attracted wide attention in 1931 with his novel, THE OPENING OF A DOOR. It was particularly strong in its sense of character and in flashes of style, though weak in form. The fact that he has not rushed in with another book is, on its face, a promising sign, and his name still suggests expectations.

So does that of John O'Hara. His APPOINTMENT IN SAMARRA (1934) was hard, and unsparing in its vigorous realism that was astringently applied to a contemporary country-club set. It was fast moving, cynical, unreserved in diction, and more brittle than its progenitors of the 1920's. The young man can write.

So can Tess Slesinger. She has an astonishing facility in the manner that is being so extensively cultivated in the youth of the land by Story. It is a nervous, highly wrought type of writing, narrow in scope but intensely concentrated on its subject which is ostentatiously up to the minute and minces no words. The subject matter of this young group is not always on the same plane with the technical treatment accorded it. And they are still essentially short-story writers who are trying to extend into the novel, as Josephine Johnson in NOW IN NOVEMBER (1934) and Bessie Breuer in MEMORY OF LOVE (1934). Tess Slesinger's THE UNPOSSESSED expanded backwards a brilliant short story. The novel was excessively regional and New Yorkish, and dealt with a group of people more specialized and less important than those in the novels that certain metropolitan reviewers love to call "regional" because they deal with North Carolina or Alabama. But there was enough talent expended upon these wastrels, misnamed Intellectuals, to cause any reader to feel excited over the prospects of a matured Tess Slesinger.

Victoria Lincoln must be mentioned in the same breath for her accomplishment in FEBRUARY HILL (1934). It is full of spirit, but it is calm at its center, and it reports with conviction the unusual and lusty doings among the Harris family dwelling in a shanty on February Hill in New England. The crisp style, the realization of character—especially that of Jenny—the gentle humor, the moments of pathos, and the sense of form promise much for the future.

Leane Zugsmith is still more at home in the short story of the hard, concise realism in vogue among the little magazines. She has indicated a promising talent in NEVER ENOUGH (1932), in which she gives vivid flashes of American life from 1918 to 1928; and in THE RECKONING (1934), where her genius for significant detail is employed to indict a society that warps kids like her Costie Petrella and then uses its ponderous legal system to send them to Welfare Island.

Nancy Hale arouses interest with her NEVER ANY MORE (1934) because of the character portraits of the three girls of diverse natures who are spending a month on an island away from their established circles. It is clever, flashing, and, as might be expected, not profound. Something must be left to time.

There is George Anthony Weller, who gave an unusually fine picture of the newest "lost generation" in NOT TO EAT, NOT FOR LOVE (1933). The theme is sounded by the quotation from Emerson which supplies the title: ". . . . four snakes gliding up and down a hollow for no purpose that I could see —not to eat, not for love, but only gliding." And there are possible dark horses among an extensive group that would include Howard Baker for his ORANGE VALLEY (1931), Edwin Granberry for his STRANGERS AND LOVERS (1928) and THE ERL KING (1930), Kenneth Horan for his IT'S LATER THAN YOU THINK (1934).

We must wait for more and better things before hoping too much from Caroline Miller, author of LAMB IN HIS BOSOM (1933). On the strength of her two delicately understanding novels dealing with North Carolina hill folk, somewhat preempted by the Mariston Chapmans, THURSDAY APRIL (1931) and THE HILLS STEP LIGHTLY (1934), Alberta Pierson Hannum offers..expectations. And Caroline Gordon's PENHALLY (1931) and ALECK MAURY, SPORTSMAN (1934), done in the best manner of the new literature of the South; and Alexander Laing's END OF ROAMING (1930), dealing with the college years of a young man and his first adjustments to the world, and THE SEA WITCH (1933), recreating the days of the clipper ships, are full of promise.

These authors and their contemporaries already mentioned in other connections are among those who will carry on toward the forties. An equally hopeful but somewhat different list might be compiled. This one is representative at least of the many developments now promising to unfold. Everything that the novel can do, it is either doing or attempting. And, given men of genius, there is nothing that it cannot do.

PULITZER PRIZES IN LETTERS—THE NOVEL

1918. Ernest Poole, HIS FAMILY.
1919. Booth Tarkington, THE MAGNIFICENT AMBERSONS.
1920. No award.
1921. Edith Wharton, THE AGE OF INNOCENCE.
1922. Booth Tarkington, ALICE ADAMS.
1923. Willa Cather, ONE OF OURS.
1924. Margaret Wilson, THE ABLE MC LAUGHLINS.
1925. Edna Ferber, SO BIG.
1926. Sinclair Lewis, ARROWSMITH. (Rejected by author.)
1927. Louis Bromfield, EARLY AUTUMN.
1928. Thornton Wilder, THE BRIDGE OF SAN LUIS REY.
1929. Julia Peterkin, SCARLET SISTER MARY.
1930. Oliver La Farge, LAUGHING BOY.
1931. Margaret Ayer Barnes, YEARS OF GRACE.
1932. Pearl S. Buck, THE GOOD EARTH.
1933. T. S. Stribling, THE STORE.
1934. Caroline Miller, LAMB IN HIS BOSOM.

Bibliographical Note

In addition to those books mentioned in the text, the most helpful and important general books on the novel of this period are:

Beach, Joseph Warren, THE TWENTIETH CENTURY NOVEL (STUDIES IN TECHNIQUE). New York: The Century Company, 1932.

Chamberlain, John, FAREWELL TO REFORM. New York: The John Day Company, 1932. (Especially for the thesis novels of the muckrake period and the beginnings of realism in America.)

Hartwick, Harry, THE FOREGROUND OF AMERICAN FICTION. New York: American Book Company, 1934.

Kunitz, Stanley J., AUTHORS TODAY AND YESTERDAY. New York: The H. W. Wilson Company, 1934.

Lewisohn, Ludwig, EXPRESSION IN AMERICA. New York: Harper & Brothers, 1932.

LIVING AUTHORS, A BOOK OF BIOGRAPHIES. New York: The H. W. Wilson Company, 1931.

Parrington, Vernon Louis, MAIN CURRENTS IN AMERICAN THOUGHT, Vol. III. New York: Harcourt, Brace & Company, 1930.

Pattee, Fred Lewis, THE NEW AMERICAN LITERATURE. New York: The Century Company, 1930.

Van Doren, Carl, CONTEMPORARY AMERICAN NOVELISTS. New York: The Macmillan Company, 1931.

Ward, A. C., AMERICAN LITERATURE, 1880-1930. London: Methuen & Company, 1932.

INDEX

297